A Plot of Her Own

THE FEMALE PROTAGONIST
IN RUSSIAN LITERATURE

Edited by Sona Stephan Hoisington

NORTHWESTERN UNIVERSITY PRESS / EVANSTON, ILLINOIS

Northwestern University Press
Evanston, Illinois 60208-4210

"Mother as Mothra: Totalizing Narrative and Nurture in Petrushevskaia" copyright ©
1995 by Helena Goscilo.

ISBN 0-8101-1224-8 (cloth)
      0-8101-1298-1 (paper)

Library of Congress Cataloging-in-Publication Data

A plot of her own : the female protagonist in Russian literature /
    edited by Sona Stephan Hoisington.
            p.   cm. — (Studies in Russian literature and theory)
        Includes bibliographical references.
        ISBN 0-8101-1224-8 (alk. paper). — ISBN 0-8101-1298-1 (pbk. :
    alk. paper)
        1. Russian fiction—19th century—History and criticism.
    2. Russian fiction—20th century—History and criticism. 3. Women
    in literature. I. Hoisington, Sona Stephan, 1941–   . II. Series.
    PG3096.W6P57   1995
    891.709'352042—dc20   95-1989
                                                                 CIP

The paper used in this publication meets the minimum requirements of the American National Standard for Information Sciences—Permanence of Paper for Printed Library Materials, ANSI Z39.48-1984.

A Plot of Her Own

Contents

Acknowledgments

I thank all the contributors to this volume for their enthusiasm, cooperation in meeting deadlines, and sense of humor—all of which lightened my task and made the job of editor a rewarding one. Caryl Emerson provided further support and encouragement in her capacity as general editor of Studies in Russian Literature and Theory. To Susan Harris, Managing Editor of Northwestern University Press, I owe a deep debt of gratitude for the deft way in which she steered this collection toward completion. Susan always found time to answer my calls (or faxes), and provide encouraging words and sound advice at the moment needed. Finally, I feel obliged to render thanks to computer technology for facilitating the preparation of this manuscript.

The following essays were previously published in somewhat different form and appear here by permission. Amy Mandelker's "The Judgment of *Anna Karenina*" appears in slightly different form in the author's *Framing "Anna Karenina": Tolstoy, The Woman Question, and the Victorian Novel*. Copyright © 1993 by Ohio State University Press. Reprinted here by permission. Gary Saul Morson's "Sonya's Wisdom" originally appeared as part of "Prosaic Chekhov: Metadrama, the Intelligentsia, and *Uncle Vanya*" in *TriQuarterly* magazine, a publication of Northwestern University. Elizabeth Klosty Beaujour's "The Uses of Witches in Fedin and Bulgakov" was originally published in *Slavic Review* (1974) and is reprinted here by permission of the American Association for the Advancement of Slavic Studies.

Contributors

Elizabeth Klosty Beaujour is Professor of Russian and Comparative Literature at Hunter College and the Graduate Center of the City University of New York. She is the author of *The Invisible Land: A Study of the Artistic Imagination of Iurii Olesha* (New York: Columbia University Press, 1970) and *Alien Tongues: Bilingual Russian Writers of the "First" Emigration* (Ithaca: Cornell University Press, 1989), as well as of a number of articles on Ilya Zdanevich and on the interaction of literature and architecture.

Jane T. Costlow is Associate Professor of Russian at Bates College. She is the author of *Worlds Within Worlds: The Novels of Ivan Turgenev* (Princeton: Princeton University Press, 1990) and co-editor, with Stephanie Sandler and Judith Vowles, of *Sexuality and the Body in Russian Culture* (Stanford: Stanford University Press, 1993).

Thea Margaret Durfee is a doctoral student in Russian Studies at the University of Southern California. She is currently working on her dissertation, tentatively titled "Between Salon and Gallery: Nadezhda Evseevna Dobychina and the Dobychina Art Bureau, 1900–1920."

Caryl Emerson is Professor of Slavic Languages and Literatures and Comparative Literature at Princeton University. She has translated and commented upon the works of Mikhail Bakhtin, and has written on nineteenth-century Russian literature, Musorgsky and Russian music, and most recently on Bakhtin's reception, or "reclamation," in Russia as he approaches his centennial year.

Helena Goscilo teaches at the University of Pittsburgh. She has published collections of translations, including *Balancing Acts: Contemporary Stories by Russian Women* (Bloomington: Indiana University Press, 1989; New York: Dell, 1991) and *Lives in Transit: A Collection of Recent Russian Women's Writings* (Ann Arbor: Ardis, 1994). Most recently she has edited *Skirted Issues: The Discreteness and Indiscretions of Russian Women's Prose*

(Armonk, N.Y.: M. E. Sharpe, 1992); *Fruits of Her Plume: Essays on Contemporary Women's Culture* (Armonk, N.Y.: M. E. Sharpe, 1993); and *From Bathhouse to Ballroom: Russian Women's Culture* (with Beth Holmgren; Bloomington: Indiana University Press, 1995). She is currently completing a monograph on Tatiana Tolstaia and a volume of essays on the construction of womanhood in Soviet and post-perestroika Russia (to be published by the University of Michigan Press).

Sona Stephan Hoisington is Associate Professor of Russian at the University of Illinois at Chicago. She has published articles on nineteenth- and twentieth-century Russian literature and is editor and translator of the collection *Russian Views of Pushkin's "Eugene Onegin"* (Bloomington: Indiana University Press, 1988).

Amy Mandelker is Associate Professor of Comparative Literature at the Graduate Center of the City University of New York. She is author of *Framing Anna Karenina: Tolstoy, the Woman Question, and the Victorian Novel* (Columbus: Ohio State University Press, 1993) and articles on Russian and European literature and literary theory. She is currently working on a book, *Icons of Theory and Theories of Iconicity in Russian and Western Aesthetics*.

Gary Saul Morson is Frances Hooper Professor of the Arts and Humanities at Northwestern University. He is the author of *The Boundaries of Genre: Dostoevsky's "Diary of a Writer" and the Traditions of Literary Utopia* (Austin: University of Texas Press, 1981; reprint, Evanston, Ill.: Northwestern University Press, 1987), *Hidden in Plain View: Narrative and Creative Potentials in "War and Peace"* (Stanford: Stanford University Press, 1987), *Mikhail Bakhtin: Creation of a Prosaics* (co-authored with Caryl Emerson; Stanford: Stanford University Press, 1990), and, most recently, *Narrative and Freedom: The Shadows of Time* (New Haven: Yale University Press, 1994). He is at present working on a study of Russian writers and the intelligentsia, from which the essay in the present volume is drawn.

Harriet Murav is Associate Professor of Russian and Comparative Literature at the University of California at Davis. She is the author of *Holy Foolishness: Dostoevsky's Novels and the Poetics of Cultural Critique* (Stanford: Stanford University Press, 1992).

Gary Rosenshield is Professor of Slavic Languages and Literatures at the University of Wisconsin–Madison. He is the author of *Crime and Punishment: The Techniques of the Omniscient Author* (Lisse: Peter de Ridder Press, 1978) and numerous essays on nineteenth- and twentieth-century Russian prose. He is currently writing monographs on the theme of madness in the works of Alexander Pushkin and on Dostoevsky and the law.

Sona Stephan Hoisington

Introduction

ENTITIES CAN BE characterized by absences as well as presences. Such is the case with the present volume: it does not deal primarily with literary works authored by women nor does it concern itself with neglected texts by women writers. Pioneering studies in these areas have been done recently by a number of talented and dedicated Slavists, some of whom are contributors to this collection.[1] On the other hand, this anthology is not merely a survey of images of women in male-authored texts that attempts to measure how true (or untrue) these images are to real-life experience.[2]

In several senses, this volume can be said to be a "revisionist" work. First of all, it takes issue with the old, "unconscious" assumption of critics, male and female alike, that women characters in fiction (even if idealized) are marginal, mere appendages to male protagonists, not worthy of investigation in their own right. It demonstrates how when we transform these old habits of thought and old ways of seeing and enter texts from a new and fresh perspective that foregrounds women—in particular, the *female* protagonist— the results can be fruitful. Contained herein are compelling new readings of major texts in the Russian literary canon, all of which are readily available in translation. The interpretations offered strive not to be reductive or doctrinaire, not to be imposed from the outside but to arise from the texts themselves and the historical circumstances in which these texts were written. The result? (Re)visions that expand our understanding of the major works they address and liberate new significance from them.

Old habits of thought affect even the translation of novel titles, as Jane Costlow points out in her essay on women in Turgenev's most influential novel. The accepted title of that novel in English is *Fathers and Sons*, when, in fact, Turgenev named his work *Fathers and Children*. Costlow's faithful translation of Turgenev's title leads her to focus on the rich cast of female characters in the novel and to show how their typicality stands in marked contrast with the anomalous position of its enigmatic female protagonist, the

1

motherless Odintsova, whom she aptly characterizes as "woman alone." In her essay, "The Judgment of *Anna Karenina*," Amy Mandelker makes a forceful case for Tolstoy's Anna Karenina as tragic heroine, a status frequently denied her not only by traditional critics but by recent feminist readings as well. Gary Saul Morson in his "Sonya's Wisdom" reminds us that, even when correctly translated, titles may be deceptive and that we must learn to reverse our perceptions and spot their "decoy technique." Such, he argues, is the case with Chekhov's play *Uncle Vanya*; the title suggests that the real hero is Ivan Voinitsky, when, in fact, it is the unsung and undervalued Sonya, who is by far the most admirable and wisest character in the play. Sonya is silently evoked by the title: "Uncle Vanya" is her term of endearment for Voinitsky. Thea Durfee demonstrates that the new Soviet woman, Dasha Chumalova, plays the pivotal role in Gladkov's novel *Cement* and shows that Dasha, in fact, is mentor to her spouse, Gleb, the prototypical positive hero of socialist realism. I myself argue that I-330, the female protagonist of Zamyatin's anti-utopian fantasy *We*, is "woman as hero"—both in the sense of prime mover and as the character who best exemplifies the novel's governing values—despite the fact that critical attention has focused almost exclusively on the male protagonist, D-503, and his "rebellion." Caryl Emerson's essay on Pushkin's Tatiana is likewise a "revisionist" piece. Emerson argues for a new understanding of Tatiana's appeal; it is not her moral purity (as Dostoevsky insisted) or her typicality as an embodiment of the Russian woman (as Belinsky claimed) that draws Pushkin, the narrator, the reader, and Evgeny himself to her but rather an aesthetic quality: Tatiana represents the energy caught in synaesthetic poetry.

The assumption that female characters are predictable and fit certain stereotypes—that they are either angels or monsters—is also challenged by this anthology.[3] In her essay, "Mother as Mothra," Helena Goscilo shows how the Mother figure, idealized in literature and art and venerated in both Russian and Soviet culture, is demythologized in Petrushevskaia's novella "Night Time," where she is revealed to be a creature of the night, a destroyer rather than a nurturer. Elizabeth Klosty Beaujour establishes that in Russian modernist texts, such as Fedin's *Cities and Years* and Bulgakov's *Master and Margarita*, there is a marriage of heaven and hell; paradoxically the witch becomes a source of good and a healer. My related essay argues that in Zamyatin's *We*, also a modernist text, I-330 is an energizer rather than an enslaver; not the Eve figure some critics have identified her as, but rather an incarnation of both Satan *and* the crucified Christ. Taken together, these two essays suggest that there is a special type of Russian modernist heroine that is, in fact, demonic in a sacral way. Harriet Murav in her essay on women in Dostoevsky argues that, while much of Dostoevsky's fiction may seem to depend on female victims who are silenced, there are actually other markers of agency and subjectivity in his works besides "discourse" and that *A Writer's Diary* reveals Dostoevsky's special skill in "reading women."

Questions raised by Amy Mandelker in her essay on *Anna Karenina* resonate through the entire volume. What is it that sets apart female protagonists? Or, to put it differently, what is it we look for in women characters that, in turn, affects the way in which we perceive them? Do we search out positive role models? Do we want women who measure up to men? Is it maternity we seek? Even the terminology is problematic. What do we call the central female figure in a literary text? Some have argued that the term "heroine" is pejorative and implies a lesser.[4] Others have countered that by using the term "hero," we expect women to emulate men. Mandelker staunchly defends the use of "heroine," and it is used by many of the other contributors to this volume as well. By subtitling the collection "The Female *Protagonist* in Russian Literature," I circumvent the issue, but in my own essay I opt for "woman as hero," a term used by Carolyn Heilbrun and Lee R. Edwards.[5]

Most of the contributions to this volume deal with female protagonists in texts written by men. Proponents of "feminist critique" contend that male authors ipso facto victimize their female characters—whether consciously or unconsciously—and that their ineluctable misogyny must be exposed. This critical position is vigorously disputed by the revisionist readings offered here. The anthology also rejects any kind of "group thinking"; that is to say, that it is gender or class that defines one and determines one's critical approach or what one should write about. "Gynocritics,"[6] to the extent that it *expects* women to research women-centered topics or engage in supportive criticism of female-authored texts, is not the answer to the problem but rather part of it. For how can we do away with the confines of sexual categorization if we eliminate one of the categories altogether?[7] The limitations of gynocriticism—as well as the misguidedness of "feminist critique"—are addressed by Rosenshield in the collection's Afterword. The only piece in the volume that deals with a female-authored text is Helena Goscilo's essay on Petrushevskaia's "Night Time." Its inclusion, however, is deliberate: it demonstrates how the Russian literary canon keeps changing and attests to the central role now played by women writers in Russian culture.

It is the assumption of the critics contributing to this collection that the female protagonists in the works examined are inextricably linked with the fundamental issues raised by the novels they inform. Thus Emerson insists that the final image of Tatiana, heroine of Pushkin's "novel in verse," embodies Pushkin's understanding of poetry: neither an ecstatic outpouring of feeling nor a fixed accomplishment but a "poetics of tension," a "pattern of resolved stresses," analogous to a standing wave. Morson contends that the quiet, practical wisdom exemplified in Chekhov's Sonya is emblematic of a whole tradition in Russian prose that he terms "prosaics." Costlow maintains that the challenges of passion with which Odintsova and Bazarov grapple are as central to Turgenev's *Fathers and Children* as the critiques of ideology. Murav argues that the role of woman as skilled interpreter and receiver of the word, coded in Dostoevsky's fiction, was subsequently assumed by the author himself in order to "read" not only women but the life of Russia in general. Beaujour contends that the reinterpretation of the witch in Fedin and Bulgakov's works is indicative of the Change of Signs that informs them. Durfee's essay, which contrasts the bold and resolute Dasha in Gladkov's *Cement* (1925) with shy and submissive Taia in Ostrovsky's *How the Steel Was Tempered* (1934), shows how changes in policies, values, and expectations about women in the early Soviet period were clearly reflected in its fiction, and how, as the gains in equality made in the 1920s eroded, women once again were relegated to a subordinate position.

Evident in these essays is the belief that gender is not an absolute. Repeatedly the contributors show how the authors under consideration challenge and subvert gender assumptions. Thus women are shown to be active as well as passive, possessing moral and intellectual authority as well as having powers of intuition, living for themselves as well as for others, childless as well as maternal figures. And men are shown to be victims as well as victimizers, skilled readers as well as oppressive silencers. Murav, in particular, addresses the matter of the blurring of gender boundaries with reference to Dostoevsky's *Writer's Diary*. In showing how lines of gender difference are redrawn in new and energizing ways in Zamyatin's *We*, I do the same. In the Afterword, Rosenshield calls into question the validity of *any* rigid gender-based criticism, using Dostoevsky's works as a test case.

While sharing certain assumptions, no two essays in this anthology are alike. The articles utilize different approaches, bring to the fore different concerns, and reach different kinds of conclusions. Thus the collection can be said to be dialogical rather than monological. In some instances the critics take issue with one another. Morson, for example, argues that the real hero of *Anna Karenina*—in the sense of the character who embodies the novel's deepest-held values—is Dolly, while Mandelker insists that it is Anna herself. The intent of the collection is to engage readers in dialogue as well, to embark with them on a shared journey of critical inquiry rather than providing final, or facile, answers.

A word should be said about the order of these essays. Those articles dealing with female protagonists in nineteenth-century Russian literature are arranged chronologically, while the four focusing on female protagonists in twentieth-century Russian literature are grouped to show similarities and differences: the two pieces dealing with modernist texts are placed side by side, while Durfee's essay on variations in the new Soviet woman is followed by Goscilo's article, which demonstrates the demythologization of "Soviet" values. Finally, since the volume is intended for both non-specialists and specialists, all the material quoted from Russian sources is given in English translation. Russian names in the text reflect the most common English spelling. Russian quotations in the text as well as all Russian bibliographical information follow the Library of Congress system of transliteration.

Caryl Emerson

Tatiana

[Tatiana], as is well known, besides being Onegin's ill-starred partner and the coldblooded wife of the general, was Pushkin's personal Muse. . . . I even think that's the reason she didn't start anything up with Onegin and remained true to her unloved husband, so she'd have more free time to read and reread Pushkin and to languish over him.
—Abram Tertz [Andrei Sinyavsky], *Strolls with Pushkin*

"Prostite mne: ia tak liubliu Tat'ianu miluiu moiu." (Forgive me: I so love my precious Tatiana.)
—The narrator, *Eugene Onegin*, chap. 4, XXIV

THE HEROINE OF Pushkin's *Evgenii Onegin* (*Eugene Onegin*) bears the most famous, deceptively complex female name in Russian literature. Paradoxes abound in her image, which is in varying degrees derivative, abject, impulsive, renunciatory, passive, majestically disciplined and inexplicably faithful. Starting with the narrator who tells her story and ending with many generations of critics, almost everyone who touches this image falls in love with it—or with its unrealized potential. It could be argued that Tatiana and her exquisitely "withheld" personal fate functioned as the single, most richly inspirational source for Russian literary heroines well into the present century.

This essay grew out of my bewilderment over the Tatiana cult. What has made this sentimental collage of female attributes—naive, stubborn, largely silent—so resilient and irresistible? Tatiana's energies and virtues have been enormously inflated, by detractors as well as devotees. In one of the earliest portraits, Belinsky, smitten by Tatiana but resisting the fate that Pushkin provided for her, lamented that she could not break free into her own autonomous life; Dostoevsky, pursuing the other extreme in his Pushkin Speech of 1880, elevated that fate to the level of hagiography by crediting Tatiana with every possible civic and metaphysical virtue, eventually investing her marital fidelity with the cosmic dimensions of Ivan Karamazov's challenge to an unjust universe.[1] And then there is the troublesome denigration of Evgeny that usually attends the exaltation of Tatiana. He is made "super-fluous" not only to his own life and times but also to the novel that bears his name; his honest and honorable actions vis-á-vis the rural maiden who thrust herself inopportunely upon him are read as mental cruelty, frivolity, even depravity.[2] (Here, Tchaikovsky's wonderfully nuanced 1879 reworking of the novel into opera—"lyrical scenes" that probably should have been titled *Tatiana*—must figure as a crucial stage in the maturation of the cult.) To be sure, there are eminent Pushkin scholars (Gukovsky, Bondi, Slonimsky, and Makogonenko in the Soviet period) who have attempted a rehabilitation of Evgeny. This move is too often linked, however, with an extratextual, politically motivated fantasy cobbled together from the fragmentary chapter 10: Evgeny was "becoming a Decembrist," and thus he deserved Tatiana's (and the reader's) sympathy.[3]

Perhaps more serious than these facts of reception and transposition is the disjointed and confounding image of Tatiana within the text itself. There are the obvious incompatibilities: for example, that Tatiana is assembled from imported sentimentalist scraps and yet, on the strength of one folklore-laden nightmare and a love of winter, represents the "Russian soul"; or that the moments of Tatiana's most profound transformation are concealed from us by the garrulous and possessive narrator. But there are also more radical discontinuities. Foremost among them is the hectoring, sententious and holier-than-thou tone that Tatiana adopts in her final rebuke to Evgeny in chapter 8: a lecture, as I shall argue below, that Tatiana in all likelihood could never have delivered to Onegin in the form Pushkin transcribes it.[4] In this essay I suggest an alternative reading of Tatiana's role in the novel, one that acknowledges her extraordinary vigor and potency but makes it more aesthetic than moral, and—here's the blasphemous, countercultic rub—that sees this potency as largely Evgeny's achievement.

FALLING IN LOVE WITH TATIANA: FOUR HYPOTHESES

All three creators in the novel (Pushkin, the narrator, and Evgeny in his capacity as title role) sooner or later come to love Tatiana, each for his own reasons. Although the courtships of these respective suitors are carried out on different planes and often overlap, the following motivations for eros can be distinguished. First there is the "forbidden fruit" argument, largely associated, I would argue, with Evgeny's sphere. The narrator does not doubt its power, over the hero and over people in general, as he tells us in the famous lines from chapter 8, XXVII:

Chto vam dano, to ne vlechet,
Vas neprestanno zmii zovet

K sebe, k tainstvennomu drevu;
Zapretnyi plod vam podavai,
A bez togo vam rai ne rai.

(What's given to you does not entice,
The serpent calls you incessantly
To himself, to the mysterious tree;
The forbidden fruit must be offered you,
Without it, paradise does not seem paradise.)

We must remember who is offering this wisdom. Being deeply in love with Tatiana himself, the narrator has his own reasons for discounting the possibility of anything like genuine growth or spiritual commitment on the part of his rival Onegin—whose sudden passion for Tatiana he would prefer to fob off as a perverse psychological universal. But even so, we must admit that the forbiddenness of the Tatiana–Onegin bond always lent it enormous erotic energy. He likes her now because she is off limits; in the provinces she had been in the palm of his hand, and so, in Byronic fashion, he had yawned and turned away. The portrait of Onegin back from his travels (8, XII–XIII) suggests that right up until the end of the novel, the pattern of his life—transitory stimulation and restlessness followed by renewed anesthetization—has not altered. Only illicit love will effect that change. Interestingly, both parties share this economy: Onegin's unavailability had earlier fueled Tatiana's passion as well. As she put it in her fateful letter, she might have been satisfied with casual social contact but Onegin, being "neliudim" (unsociable), could be reached only in this covert, confessional, maximally risk-laden, epistolary way. The letter prematurely formalizes the terms, celebrates her helplessness and heats up the terrain.

The dynamics of Tatiana's life, it could be argued, remain in this covert zone. Richard Gregg has done a persuasive reading of Tatiana's dream along these lines, interpreting its "phallic shapes," "priapic creatures" and shuddering, violent denouement as punishment self-imposed by Tatiana for her illicit desire: "It becomes clear," he writes, "why Ol'ga first breaks in on the would-be lovers; for her shallow, conventional, and well-advertised love differs from Tat'yana's deep, clandestine passion for the 'demonic' . . . Onegin."[5] Both nanny and mother had been married off without love and the sister was en route to being married off without obstacle: neither of these options are, for the likes of Onegin or Tatiana, "paradise." "Pogibnesh', milaia," the narrator intones, "no prezhde / Ty v oslepitel'noi nadezhde / Blazhenstvo temnoe zovesh' . . ." (You shall perish, my dear, but first in blinding hope you summon forth dark bliss) (3, XV). The prophecy is only a half-truth. That Tatiana does not perish, as do the ill-fated sentimental heroines Julie, Clarissa, and Delphine upon whom she modeled her life, is an issue to which we will return. For now, suffice it to note that throughout the novel, eros between Tatiana and Evgeny is propelled forward by the clandestine and forbidden.

There is a second argument for falling in love with Tatiana, this time associated with Pushkin as author. The 1820s, the decade of *Evgenii Onegin*, inclined Pushkin increasingly toward prose, toward national history, toward genealogy and family—and aggravated his anxieties over social status and rank. Compulsively attractive here for the mature Pushkin is the image of the married Tatiana as *kniaginia* (princess), and the host of chilling and elevating epithets she gains in this context: Pokoina. Vol'na. Ravnodushna. Smela. Nepristupnaia boginia roskoshnoi, tsarstvennoi Nevy (Calm. Unconstrained. Indifferent. Bold. The inaccessible goddess of the luxuriant, regal Neva) (8, XXII-XXVII). It has been argued that placing Tatiana in *very* high society— so high that coquetry, a primary medium for the bachelor Pushkin, had no place at all ("ego ne terpit vysshii svet" [highest society does not tolerate it] 8, XXXI)—was an act of wish fulfillment on Pushkin's part. Negotiating in 1829 to become a bridegroom himself, Pushkin desired to believe what was certainly contrary to his own high success at seducing other men's wives: that female constancy in marriage was possible.[6] And then there was the poet's own social ambition. Douglas Clayton, one of Pushkin's best close readers, has suggested that the married Tatiana's graceful persona and accomplished hostessing skills were a surrogate for her creator's personal fantasies. "Pushkin, the marginalized, the invalidated, the heretic . . . was metamorphosed into the heroine—not the hero—of his poem," he writes. "Her acceptance at court, her brilliance, her tenderness, passion, and conviction—all these were the qualities Pushkin sought for himself."[7]

Even without the poet's envy of his own heroine's fate, however, Tatiana as princess is a powerful external success. By the novel's end she has mastered what salon society of the early nineteenth century valued most of all: the ability to adapt oneself effortlessly to any appropriate role in the interest of social harmony. It is in this sense that William Mills Todd considers Tatiana's "cultural maturation" complete once she has become the hostess of a Petersburg salon—which was, he reminds us, "the highest form of creativity open to a woman at this time," and one that enabled her to impose "what her age considered an aesthetic order upon reality."[8]

Aesthetic considerations lead us to a third argument for falling in love with Tatiana, perhaps the most profound, this time identified with the narrator's persona. Unlike his friend Onegin, the narrator is a poet. But unlike the poet Pushkin, whose stylized image he represents, the narrator can be garrulous, inefficient, sentimental. As befits a "novelist" (even a novelist writing in verse), the narrator might be understood as embodying some aspects of Pushkin at the turn of the decade, a poet on the brink of turning to prose, since the novel, as we know from Pushkin's famous quip to Bestuzhev, requires above all *boltovnia* (chatter). The unity of this narrator's voice throughout the nine years of *Onegin*'s genesis is problematic.[9] On one point, however, the narrator is unflaggingly constant, and that is his love of Tatiana. From her initial introduction onward, she is revered as something untranslatable, as a quality that cannot be completely transmitted, as that which inspires us but that eludes precise description. The narrator refers to this elusive presence as his Muse. (We first hear of this Muse—who grants a voice to the poet only after the storm of love has passed—at the end of chapter 1. At the beginning of chapter 8 she is personified, identified with a chronological sequence of Pushkin's literary heroines, and finally is "presented" to Petersburg society in a gesture coterminous with Tatiana's coming-of-age in the salon.) How does the narrator present Tatiana as both beloved subject and Muse?

We first meet Tatiana in chapter 2. One of the more remarkable aspects of her opening portrait, surely, is how little of it there is. In her initial description, negatives abound: "Ni krasotoi sestroi svoei, / Ni svezhest'iu ee rumianoi / Ne privlekla b ona ochei" (She would not attract anyone's eye with her sister's beauty or rosy freshness) (2, XXV). Unlike the heroines of the sentimental novels upon whom she models herself, and unlike Olga, Lensky, and Onegin in Pushkin's novel, Tatiana is endowed by the narrator with no precise physical attributes: no colors, clothes, supporting equipment, musical or domestic activities (we *assume* she is dark because her sister is blonde). From early childhood on, Tatiana's primary characteristic has been a detachment from her surroundings. She had not snuggled up to father or mother; she had not frolicked with the other children; she had not played with dolls or shown interest in news or fashion. She has deep feelings; but in contrast to the heroines of her favorite books, she is not in the habit of using these feelings to manipulate the behavior of others. She does not swoon or faint, weep in public, pray noisily, or interact commodiously with the world.[10] Tatiana, we might say, attaches to the inside and not to the outside of things.

This "insideness" and inaccessability continue to characterize Tatiana even at her most exposed moments, and for this we must thank her jealous mentor and most passionate protector: the narrator. He filters out large parts of her life, keeps them for himself, and gives them to us only in translation. Tatiana's love letter to Onegin is originally in French but we only see its cooled-down Russian version (whereas Onegin's letter, by contrast, is immediately in the public domain—for who cares, here it is, "toch'-v-toch'" [word for word]). After Tatiana moves from country to city and becomes a princess, we sense she is a marvel. But somehow the narrator cannot find Russian words to describe her: she is "comme il faut," "not *vulgar*" (8, XIV, XV), and these foreign words convey not so much a physical image as a mode of behavior, a sense of everpresent appropriateness, of not doing anything awkwardly or wrong. Like the veil draped over the face of a harem favorite, they conceal from casual passers-by the essential positive thing. For this the narrator disingenuously apologizes: "Ne znaiu, kak perevesti . . . Ne mogu" (I don't how how to translate it . . . I can't).

Indeed, he must not translate her. Tatiana sits by the window, waits, watches, and perceives; the narrator only rarely makes us privy to her thoughts. I would argue that he cannot do so, for Tatiana is poetic inspiration—which, according to Pushkin's own inspired definition, is neither an ecstatic outpouring of feeling nor a fixed accomplishment but something more intimate, private, disciplined, and creative: a cognitive receptivity of the mind to potentials. Or as the poet drily put it: inspiration is a "disposition of the soul to the most lively reception of impressions and thus to a rapid grasp of concepts that facilitate explaining them."[11] Tatiana takes in, understands, and orders impressions, but (except for the single very large instance of her passionate letter) *does not spend*. And thus the fourth hypothesis: that as readers we love Tatiana because she represents the energy (and knowledge) captured in a certain sort of poetry.

TATIANA AS SYNAESTHESIS

"It is the essential privilege of beauty," Santayana writes, "to so synthesize and bring to a focus the various impulses of the self, so to suspend them to a single image, that a great peace falls upon that perturbed kingdom."[12] The Tatiana of chapter 8 has just such an effect on the boisterous tempo and restless variety of *Evgenii Onegin*—if not on its aroused and bewildered hero— and it is her unexpectedly abrupt departure that brings the novel to an end. How might we understand Tatiana's spiritual economy? Admittedly the heroine of a novel, she is also and crucially a heroine *in verse*; and as such she is more, I suggest, than the mere sum of her personality and plot. She is also an aesthetics.

The Romantic period knew various Dionysian theories of poetry: as emotive release, as madness, as divine spontaneity. But there were countervailing views as well, which understood poetry either as that residuum following the moment of rapture (Wordsworth's celebrated formula, a "spontaneous overflow of feelings recollected in tranquillity," shared by Pushkin's narrator in *Onegin*) or, more conservatively, as something akin to passion under constraint, to a "pattern of resolved stresses." With his strong neoclassical inclinations, Pushkin certainly would have been attracted to such a "poetics of tension." In more recent times, the thinker who has given most elegant expression to this aesthetic is the English analytical critic and poet I. A. Richards.

In Richards's view there are two fundamentally different types of poems, based on the two ways in which impulses may be organized: by inclusion (synaesthesis) or by exclusion.[13] The most powerful and stable poems—the ones least vulnerable to disruption though irony—belong to the former, "synaesthetic" category; that is, they sustain a maximally large number of opposed, heterogeneous impulses in meticulous balance. Associations then form between "stable poises," which enable and constitute memory.[14] Such verbal art is profoundly arousing, but in a special, aesthetically "disinterested," almost architectural way. We begin to see "all around" things, in larger and wiser context, for "the less any one particular interest is indispensable, the more detached our attitude becomes. . . . One thing only perhaps is certain; what happens is the exact opposite to a deadlock, for compared to the experience of great poetry every other state of mind is one of bafflement" (Richards, *Principles*, 252).

It could be argued that Tatiana functions at the end of the novel as a tension-filled, exquisitely balanced, stable, harrowingly lucid synaesthetic poem. Can such an analogy help us understand her ultimately dazzling effect on Onegin, the inveterate prosaicist who comes to read her most passionately? Several obvious factors mark her as a synaesthetic Muse: her autonomy and detachment from her immediate surroundings, her literariness, the tenacity of her memory, and the vivid inwardness of her imagination. (In an intriguing supplementary analogy from acoustics, Tatiana and the type of poetic tension she represents might be seen as a "standing wave," a complex resolution of internal antagonisms occurring within a closed air column or along a plucked or vibrating string that only incidentally, and as part of its own inner task, radiates energy in the form of music to the outside world.)[15] After the initial "pluck" or impact of Evgeny, Tatiana's tensions in matters of love are essentially self-generated, independent of further outside event. This self-absorption and stasis is crucial to her image. Much work has been done, for example, on the specific textual links between Tatiana and the sentimental heroines she adores: Rousseau's Julie, Richardson's Clarissa.[16] But we should note that Pushkin's love-smitten heroine employs these borrowed motifs in her letter quite without cause. As one chronicler of Tatiana's fate has sensibly remarked, Rousseau's Julie appeals to St. Preux's honor in trying to fend off his amorous advances, but "Tat'jana is not in need of defense from Onegin's passions."[17] Onegin has hardly given her any real-life grounds for considering him, even potentially, a "kovarnyi iskusitel'" (treacherous tempter).[18] If anyone tempts in this novel, it is Tatiana herself: as she well knows, she is the one who oversteps the bounds and presents premature options (guardian angel, seducer) to this near stranger.[19] Such an understanding of Tatiana's self-generated, already wholly formed love, for which she takes full and anguished responsibility, lends support to John Garrard's thesis that in the famous triad of Tatiana's literary prototypes—"Clarissa, Julia, Delphine" (3, X)—the "Yuliia" in question is not Rousseau's sentimental and lachrymose Julie but rather the "Donna Julia" of canto 1 of Byron's *Don Juan*.[20] Donna Julia is an emotionally experienced woman, deeply marked by her passionate and ill-fated love for the immature Juan, who, after the scandal is discovered and she has been immured in a convent, writes him a stunning letter of love and renunciation that the poor adolescent can hardly comprehend.

Let us pursue this Byronic subtext. "Man's love is of his life a thing apart, / 'Tis woman's whole existence . . . / And so farewell—forgive me, love me— no, / That word is idle now, but let it go" (canto 1, 194–95)—these famous lines from Donna Julia's letter to Don Juan do indeed suggest the same intoxicating mix of active passion, resignation, surrender, memory of the past and reconciliation with the present that so resonates in Tatiana's final noble scene with Onegin.[21] But viewed from within the economy of a synaesthetic poem, one that balances opposing tensions but that does not spend, this is renunciation only in a special sense. It must not be understood wholly as sacrifice or loss. Tatiana herself does not indulge in explanation, as Byron does for his Donna Julia and as Tatiana's sentimentalist predecessors most assuredly would have done. She does not motivate or justify her action beyond her one efficient statement to Evgeny, and the frame surrounding her final monologue is stripped of almost all narrative commentary. She simply departs. And just as we must not read Tatiana backward to those overdetermined eighteenth-century heroines, so must we resist reading her forward. It is a mistake, I submit, to see in Tatiana a realistic heroine out of Turgenev or Tolstoy, a woman with a strictly biographical fate and fully psychologized significance.

Some highly unorthodox implications will be eased out of this idea at the end of this essay; but now to return to the mature Tatiana as Muse. I suggest that she be appreciated not as tragic heroine or renunciatory object but as a special sort of dynamic poetic principle, authoritative because of its lucidity, its ability to maintain all its parts intact under pressure, and its willingness not to spend impulsively merely to resolve the external, overtly manifest plot. This reading shares some terrain with the intriguing hypothesis put forth by the great Soviet developmental psychologist Lev Vygotsky, whose chapter 10 of his youthful treatise *The Psychology of Art* contains a reading of *Evgenii Onegin*.[22] Because we are predisposed to assume static protagonists in this tightly spinning verse tale, Vygotsky argues, Pushkin easily confounds us with his misleading symmetries. All the loves, love letters, and parallel confrontations that so neatly mirror one another distract us from the possibility that both hero and heroine have genuinely matured by the end of the novel. Vygotsky takes seriously the dozen or so questions that crowd into stanzas VII and VIII of chapter 8: "Is it really Onegin? Could it be him? Is he the same or has he changed? What's he like now? Do you recognize him? Yes and no . . . " (ellipsis in original). These questions matter, Vygotsky intimates, because real inner change is never perfectly transcribable on the outside. In the first half of the novel, so taken up with descriptions of Onegin's cluttered,

13

thing-packed life, the narrator does indeed give the illusion of biographical transcribability—but that is because on both sides, love begins as an artificed construct. Onegin is defined as "the sort of person who cannot be the victim of a tragic love," Tatiana as the maiden who falls in love with a fabrication of her own devising and thus must perish. But then, Vygotsky argues, "Pushkin develops the story against the grain of the material." He introduces real drama—which, unlike the expected, fixed outcomes of sentimentalism or tragedy, is always open. According to Vygotsky, the greatest art always prepares us for this sort of catharsis. What we see in great dramatic art is only one provisional resolution; and the more lucid and lighthearted this resolution is, the more it bespeaks a plurality of other possible resolutions swarming underneath. Vygotsky claims that Pushkin's poetry always contains at least two contradictory feelings; when these opposing impulses collide, we experience aesthetic delight.[23]

THE ENDING: PERHAPS IT DIDN'T HAPPEN?

The final portion of this essay is undertaken in Vygotsky's developmental spirit. Throughout *Evgenii Onegin*, the narrator sings the praises of the perfectly calibrated and predictable life: "Blazhen, kto smolodu byl molod / Blazhen, kto vovremia sozrel" (Blessed is he who is young in his youth / Blessed is he who matures at the right time) (8, X). The advice is apt, for the plot of the novel is one massive demonstration of the unblissful effects of ill-timed growth and missed opportunity. But juxtaposed to this value is a corollary that celebrates open, uncertain process: the magic crystal and the "free novel" only dimly discerned in it. These two values are best focused in the conflict between Onegin's letter to Tatiana and her excruciatingly delayed response, which brings him to her feet.

Tatiana in that final encounter is perfect control and passionate constraint. Whatever she means, she will not spend that meaning in the present tense of the novel; when she leaves, she carries that energy poised within her. In contrast, surely one of the more discrediting aspects of Onegin's lovesick letter is that he now spends extravagantly. He has collapsed entirely into the present, which must hold the promise of her presence: "Ia utrom dolzhen byt' uveren / Chto s vami dnem uvizhus' ia" (In the morning I must be assured that I will see you in the afternoon). Evgeny now imagines his life desperately closed down. As if recalling the narrator's warning—"No zhalok tot, kto vse predvidit" (Pitiable is he who foresees everything) (4, LI)—Onegin opens his letter to Tatiana on a hopeless note: "Predvizhu vse" (I foresee everything) (8, XXXII). We recall how he had facilely predicted disaster for marriage in his initial remonstration with Tatiana over her letter; now he sees the grim side of just such an approach to life, so unavailable for surprise or renewal. It is not that Onegin is dishonest. Quite the contrary: as several scholars have noted and as I remarked above, in his own letter to Tatiana, Onegin is more conscientious at recalling their shared past than is Tatiana in her reconstruction of events during their final accounting. Onegin is honest enough; his problem is that he has lost all control over time, all sense of time's richness and unpredictability, and he is thus unable to displace or contain himself. At just this point the narrator pulls out abruptly, without having sealed the plot with a marriage or a death (as Pushkin's friends complained), with Tatiana fully contained and Onegin wholly vulnerable. Such elegant reversals and symmetries have encouraged some astute Pushkinists to see in *Onegin* a variant of the Echo and Narcissus myth.[24] But if process narratives and Pushkin's own capriciously parodic practice urge us to anything, it would be to distrust the absolute illusion of the mirror. Is there any way that this poetically symmetrical ending might be opened up into the hopeful, linear type of narrative, kaleidoscopically complicated and strewn with potentials, that the "magic crystal" of this novel appears to value so highly?

In response to that question, let us pursue an alternative reading of chapter 8. Taking our cue from its opening digression (also billed as a belated introduction), this final chapter will be about the Muse: how the poet-narrator has glimpsed her image—radiant, volatile, caressing, *sauvage*—at crucial moments in his life. Apprehensively, the narrator now brings his Muse for the first time "na svetskii raut" (into high society) (8, VI). In her ultimate embodiment, however, she is no cause for apprehension: respectful of hierarchy and order, she has mastered the chill decorum of the salon and works flawlessly within it.[25] The Muse is Tatiana, and this is her final enabling transfiguration.

And Onegin? He has always been more aggressively stubborn and contrary, yawning where he should applaud, foreseeing everything, opposing himself to poets. Having suffered this extraordinary, inexplicable onset of love, he is at first totally without mechanisms for processing its effects. But the sequence of his reawakening is worth noting. Whereas before he had reflected his exquisite image in various mirrors, reacted trivially to events, attended little or not at all to memory, and distracted himself at life's various feasts, now his past begins to align itself in answerable patterns and haunt him. His attempts to confess this inner shift to Tatiana are rebuffed. As a man who had always preferred the fashionable closed forms of disillusionment and despair, how convenient it would be to act out the romantic hero who can spend recklessly, throw himself at his beloved's mercy and be done with it; then he might return to that familiar state where, once again, events begin boisterously, end tediously, and life holds no secrets because always "khandra zhdala ego na strazhe" (spleen lay in wait for him) (2, LIV). But if Tatiana as provincial maiden was vulnerable to such Byronic posturing, Tatiana as mature, creative Muse is absolutely indifferent to this temperament. She now contains her energy like a standing wave, composed and resonant, and is no longer needful of outside provocation. Onegin seeks signs of confusion, compassion, some trace of tears on her face, but detects nothing: "Ikh net, ikh net!" (There aren't any, aren't any!) (8, XXXIII). Eerily, Onegin begins to "tune himself" to Tatiana, to duplicate her trajectory in the novel. He withdraws, grows pale, begins to read obsessively. But he cannot keep her at bay; in her realm—a realm that absorbs and reworks rather than reflects—memory is born; Evgeny's past begins to intrude, he is forced to come to terms with the trivial and violent acts of his youth; and as backdrop to this birth of a responsible biography, between the lines of his reading, he sees a country house, "I u okna / Sidit *ona* . . . i vse ona!" (And at the window she sits . . . always she!) (8, XXXVII).

Against the grain of most readings of the final chapter, I suggest that at this point in the novel all real interaction between the hero and heroine ends. To be sure, Evgeny "ne sdelalsia poetom, / Ne umer, ne soshel s uma" (did not become a poet, did not die, did not go out of his mind) (8, XXXIX). But the winter was not an easy one. Unable to settle accounts with the past or project a future because of the unforgiving needs of his present, driven to despair by Tatiana's nonresponsiveness and stimulated by a season of indiscriminate reading, Onegin commits the only act that can bring about a permanent present tense in his life: he *fantasizes* his final visit. The strangeness of that sudden visitation has long been noted by critics.[26] The speed with which Evgeny moves through the city toward his beloved, the uncanny absence of any domestics at the door or in the halls of the Prince's house, the extraordinary ease with which Evgeny gains access to Tatiana's boudoir—all this has been interpreted variously as dreamlike activity, fairy-tale logic, or the narrator's irony. Indeed, hints of dream space prefigure Evgeny's infatuation in chapter 8, immediately after his reacquaintance with Tatiana: "That girl . . . or is it a dream?" (XX; ellipsis in original); and later, Evgeny's "sleep [*son*] is disturbed by fantasies [*mechtoi*] now melancholy, now charming" (XXI).[27] But as we approach the final decisive tête-à-tête, we come upon many more fantastical and fantasizing details that signify a more substantial phase change, not only in the hero but in the larger narration as well.

The first three dozen stanzas in chapter 8, and especially the elegiac, quasi-autobiographical digression on the Muse that opens the final chapter, is almost entirely free of the narrator's ironic and undercutting banter. Now that tone is back, jostling Onegin, "moi neispravlennyi chudak" (my unreformed eccentric) and making asides to the reader at his expense: "Kuda . . . / Stremit Onegin? Vy zarane / Uzh ugadali" (You've already guessed / where Onegin is rushing) (8, XXXIX–XL). At an ominously rapid pace, the narrative begins to resemble *erlebte Rede* or inner speech: "He was hurrying to her, to his own Tatiana" (k svoei Tat'iane)—since when is she "his own"? Only in the reality of his own deep longing. Unseen by anyone, he slips into her private rooms; it is, after all, a mental journey he has now been rehearsing for months. But two conditions must obtain before the creative inner fantasy can begin to unfold in earnest. First, Onegin must reassure himself that Tatiana cares for him, that she spends the same obsessive time over his image that he has spent over hers, that she weeps (albeit in private) and that there are traces of "confusion, compassion and tears" on her face. Second, he must be persuaded that time is reversible.

The second condition is held in suspension: Is she in fact the "prezhnia-ia Tania" (former Tania) of earlier years, and can that image be recovered? Until the very end of the scene, the reader is not allowed to know. The first condition, however, is easy to imagine and is immediately supplied. It is the stock-in-trade device of the beloved woman accidentally discovered, alone, "neubrana, bledna" (not yet made up, pale), shedding tears over passionate letters sent her by her repentant lover. (Pushkin will use this scene to healthy comic effect in "Baryshnia-krest'ianka" [The Lady-Peasant], the last of the *Belkin* Tales.) Tatiana does not cast him away but neither does she urge him on; she is as impassive as a shade. In this intense and static scene, what does Evgeny seek? He is still no poet; he is not being endowed with a poetic Muse. But Tatiana *is* available to him, I suggest, as inner conscience, and it is this voice that is internalized in him and matures in her presence.

Interpretations of Tatiana as Onegin's "fatum," as "the tangible expression of the weight of his conscience," are not new in the literature on this final scene.[28] But such readings assume that the Tatiana of this scene is real; it is only Evgeny's conscience and the quality of his love that might be fraudulent. I argue the opposite case here: that precisely because Evgeny's love and suffering are real, because there has been this genuine, inexplicable change in him brought about by—who knows?—the passage of time, or love, Tatiana does not need to be physically present; she can be conjured up, which is, after all, the proper ontological state for an ethical Muse. Nowhere in his drafts or variants for chapter 8 does Pushkin suggest that such was his intention. But we do know that Pushkin worried over the ending of his novel and experimented with various means for deepening the reader's knowledge of the hero, including a travel diary and a salon album, both ultimately abandoned. As Leslie O'Bell chronicles the novel's composition: "It was the *razvjazka* or resolution that came hard. . . . The Journey and the Album, like the sequence in Onegin's Library, were both devices for the self-revelation of the hero."[29] I argue here that Tatiana's crowning lecture to Onegin can be read in precisely this way, as a "self-revelation of the hero."

Astute readers have long expressed dissatisfaction with this final encounter. Vladimir Nabokov, arguing against the mass of "passionately patriotic eulogies of Tatiana's virtue," insists that her altruistic rejection of Onegin is simply a cliché of French, English, and German romantic novels and, what is more, that "her answer to Onegin does not at all ring with such

17

dignified finality as commentators have supposed it to do."[30] More radically, T. E. Little urges us to take the entire love relation between Tatiana and Onegin as ironic from the start: Tatiana's silence might well be due neither to moral strength nor clandestine pining but simply to indifference or disgust, and the ending scenario, where "sentimental heroine meets a reconstructed Byronic hero," is simply "a typical Pushkinian jest" in which Tatiana mercilessly teases her victim.[31] Richard Gregg, turning to the form and content of Tatiana's final monologue, finds in it a dozen inaccuracies, or, more kindly, subjectively emotional opinions on Tatiana's part that unfairly slander Evgeny.[32] Such verdicts are justly motivated by a sense that something is awry in this final scene. But to my mind they unjustly trivialize both parties— and especially the hero.

Gregg is certainly correct that Tatiana's memory is faulty and her tone with Evgeny gratingly abrupt. I would go further: her tone is almost male, as if this painful but necessary denouement had to begin with Evgeny addressing a portion of his own self. In my scenario, of course, he is. (Tatiana refers to him throughout as "Onegin," the way men do to one another, the way Evgeny did with Lensky). In fact, much of what she says to him makes better sense if understood self-referentially, as confession. Tatiana rejects Onegin—just as his inner self, now more sensitively attuned and responsible to its own past, knows that she must. If Tatiana now remembers "only severity" (*odnu surovost'*) in Onegin's reaction to her letter and reproaches him for his "cold glance" and "sermon," we know that this misrepresents his actual tone and tenderness on that day. Under present conditions, however, Onegin quite forgivably desires to punish himself for having let something pass him by that is now so utterly indispensable to him. Onegin also knows in his heart (and thus Tatiana makes the point to him explicitly and repeatedly) that at crucial moments in their unsynchronized courtship he had indeed acted honorably, given what he was and what he knew about himself at the time.

Tatiana's final speech is peculiar in other ways. Measured against the one anguished and hopelessly loving letter of Evgeny's that we are shown in the text, Tatiana's response is capricious, harsh, and explicit in ways unseemly for a woman of her tact and station. Although Evgeny does indeed have erotic designs on her person, Tatiana gives him very little quarter (that is, for a woman in love, as she claims she is); she insinuates that he loves her now primarily because she is rich, noble, close to the court, married to a battle-scarred older man of princely rank, and that this love could only serve to bring shame upon her and "scandalously alluring fame" (*soblaznitel'naia chest'*) to him. Again, where such aggressive candor might seem inappropriate from the tactful, superbly disciplined Tatiana (even if temporarily reverted to her more innocent and untrained rural self), Evgeny, freshly burdened with a conscience about his past, could easily have had such shameful suspicions about *himself*, and might wish to exacerbate them in a punitive reflex of self-castigation. One of the final monologue's most often-quoted lines—"i schast'e bylo tak vozmozhno, tak blizko" (and happiness was so possible, so close) (8, XLVII)—is, logically speaking, only something that Evgeny could say; in that now-distant time, lest we forget, it was only for him, who held all the male rights to initiative in these matters, that "happiness was close and possible." From the very first line of her desperate love letter, Tatiana had been always in a terrible state of risk and premature intimacy. In Tatiana's final speech, however, love is not the primary value. The recurring themes are those male virtues so precious to Pushkin himself: *upriamstvo* (stubbornness), *gordost'* (pride), *chest'* (honor).

When Tatiana abruptly rises and leaves the room, Evgeny is "kak budto gromom porazhen" (as if struck by thunder). Usual readings of this denouement admit of irony, or (in more earnest interpretations) of Evgeny's simple shock at her moral excellence, her self-control, and the concomitant painful ridiculousness of his own position. In the present fantasized context, however, the thunderbolt is one of realization and inner growth. No wonder Evgeny is impressed at her speech. It belongs to him, to his own better self, to his conscience (which is the Muse now speaking from within, available for inspiration and inner moral orientation). Evgeny is still no poet, in the sense that Lensky and the narrator are poets. But the ideal inner companion that Tatiana had become for him could in fact serve many purposes.

And here we might speculate on the end of *Onegin* in the context of Pushkin's own creative biography. By 1829 Pushkin himself was beginning to investigate other, more prosaically grounded muses. These included the muse of prose, of history, perhaps of his own imminent marriage. What all these new conditions have in common—and here we should recall the second condition that Onegin longed for in his fantasy with Tatiana, the one that was not granted him—is the realization that time is irreversible. The hero of reversible time had been the chameleonlike "salon pretender" of the mid-1820s, epitomized by the flexible, carefree Dmitry *Samozvanets*, a man whose many masks were all equally authentic and for whom a search for a "real self" would have been utterly inappropriate. By the turn of the decade this "reversible" pretender is about to be replaced in Pushkin's creative imagination by the somber, infinitely more serious one-way pretendership of Pugachev, for whom risks are high and historical responsibility is real.

Evgenii Onegin presages this shift. When Tatiana walks out, Evgeny is left with an irreversibly needful self that feels the weight of events in time. When the General's clanking spurs are heard, both Onegin and the reader look up with that sinking, anguished feeling that comes upon us when we are caught "in the act"; that is, in the middle of a terribly necessary, deeply private, still partly illicit conversation with a beloved and loving voice whose intimations of truth about ourselves we have only begun to summon the courage to confront.

19

Caryl Emerson

Whither Tatiana? Contrary to the teachings of Belinsky (with whom the critical history of *Evgenii Onegin* began, and under whose brooding person much of it remains), and contrary to the childhood passion of the precocious Marina Tsvetaeva, so taken with that "unlove scene on the bench,"[33] we cannot worry about Tatiana's fate. Muses do not have fates in that sense. Even to put that question to the text is a modal impropriety. *Evgenii Onegin* is neither a sentimental eighteenth-century novel nor a realistic novel of the Tolstoyan or Dostoevskian sort.[34] Rather it belongs, as one critic aptly placed it, in a group of two together with *Dead Souls*: a one-time-only novelistic experiment in form and genre by a genius in a transitional period.[35] For as the Formalist critics repeatedly remind us, this is a novel in verse, and the verse component constantly deforms both the shape of the work and the personalities that mature within the work.[36]

Here we might heed the advice of one of America's most seasoned Pushkin scholars, Thomas Shaw, who warns: Do not overemphasize the prosiness of Pushkin's novel. Although the hero does not become an actual producer of poems, "actually, the entire novel suggests the importance of being poetic. Perhaps the basic underlying question of the novel is not simply the stages of development, but how a poet (or the poetic in man) can develop to maturity and remain, or once more become, poetic."[37] With these priorities, the eponymous hero still remains the hero. Tatiana is best appreciated as a *verse presence* in the work. She is there to enable what Shaw calls Evgeny's "mature re-enchantment," an inner process that, once having begun, releases him from the need to be narrated from without. In this reading, *Evgenii Onegin* is a finished work, over when it is over and complete as it stands. With its mixed sense of gratitude, nostalgia, and absolute irreversibility, the final leave-taking of the poet-narrator resembles Tatiana's abrupt departure several stanzas earlier, which had brought Evgeny to his senses. The truncated end is thus another well-constructed illusion, designed to launch the now matured and newly sobered hero across an unimagined threshold where we cannot follow him. In the final stanzas, Pushkin dismisses his readers with the same congenial, leisurely open-endedness that he invests in Onegin's unknown future. And it is Tatiana's very poeticity, I have argued, that enabled this emergence of a genuinely *novelistic* hero. May we all part on such self-respecting terms with our creations.

20

Jane T. Costlow

"Oh-là-là" and "No-no-no": Odintsova as Woman Alone in *Fathers and Children*

> Turgenev Women discuss events,
> know about actors,
> look for oil,
> talk about medicine,
> perform on the stage . . .
> Turgenev Women in the morning mist,
> Turgenev Women right beside you . . .[1]

"TURGENEV WOMEN," the contemporary song suggests, look for oil and go to sea, descend into subways and peel potatoes—asking us to believe that the superachieving, inexhaustible (and exhausted) women of late- and post-Soviet Russia are the spiritual and literal daughters of Ivan Turgenev's heroines. Can there truly be a connection? Surely ironic, rather than direct, to imagine Natalya, Liza, and Elena, among others, as Heroines of Labor (or Heroines of Love)? To pose the question as Vasily Shumov does is to ask, in a slightly offbeat way, what the legacy of Turgenev is for Russia; what connection there is between classical Russian culture and contemporary daily life (*byt*); and for our own purposes—as American and not Russian readers—how we can "read" these novels of more than a century ago, from a culture not our own. For in reading nineteenth-century novels we ourselves head out to sea a bit, or set off in search of black gold: compelled (or repelled) by figures who are both familiar and distant to us, convinced that there are ways in which their lives and identities, despite historical distance and difference, nonetheless reflect for us some of our own dilemmas. Who are these Turgenev women, and how can we read them? How can we let them read us?

The central heroines in each of Turgenev's first three novels—Natalya in *Rudin*, Liza in *A Nest of Gentle Folk*, and Elena in *On the Eve*—are young women of great conviction and courage, qualities that at the novels' beginnings seem to exist only *in potentio*, but are elicited and actualized by the

21

appearance of the novels' central heroes: Rudin, Lavretsky, and Insarov. To some extent the heroines' convictions are negative, at least initially: they are convinced that the world into which they have been born (the affluent and refined world of Russia's Europeanized, landowning gentry) is lacking; they are endowed with a kind of negative clairvoyance that allows them to discern, despite their relative innocence, the hypocrisy and emptiness of those around them. Their positive convictions—religious, political, and moral—emerge in and through their experience of love. These heroines become touchstones of virtue and valor, helping the reader to perceive the inadequacies of the microcosm of Russian society we enter when we move into Turgenev's drawing rooms. The heroines' courage—their willingness to act rashly, in defiance of convention, risking parental and societal approprium—saves them from being the frail and too-often victimized embodiments of virtue we encounter in the Victorian tradition.[2] These are no pale and withering lilies; they are passionate, defiant rebels constrained by conventional roles for women, and ultimately, by the lack of worthy heroic partners.

Turgenev's heroines are also typically women "on the threshold" of adulthood; in their encounters with leading figures of Russian (and Bulgarian) thought and politics, they step across that threshold into a world of more momentous ("adult") sensual, moral, and political life. In a prose poem written at the end of his life Turgenev presented this heroinic figure for one final time: the young woman is challenged by a "ponderous, muffled voice" that depicts for her the sufferings that await her, once she steps across the threshold. She responds to that litany resolutely; when she steps across, she is proclaimed a fool by some, a saint by others.[3] The figure of the woman on the threshold is articulated here as a kind of secular icon, a figure toward whom Turgenev directs enduring reverence and expectation. As more than one critic has pointed out, Turgenev invested great hope in these impassioned and relatively innocent women, as though an "Amazonian" spirit of rectitude and courage could take Russia by storm and turn her toward a more promising future. The "heroines" of the Shumov song would, alas, have despaired long ago of any such expectation.[4]

Having sketched some of the features of this Turgenevan "iconic" womanhood, however, we must acknowledge that it is harder to find her—or it—in the novel generally viewed as Turgenev's greatest, *Fathers and Sons*. There is a rich cast of female characters in this novel, one that occasioned stormy disagreement in Russian society. It is a novel in which encounters with women serve as fulcrums to the plot, and in which the challenges of passion are at least as unsettling as the critiques of ideology.[5] It is also a novel in which the "woman question"—the extensive public discussion of women's role in society, their rights to education and work—is explicitly if parodically addressed.[6] It is, in short, a novel in which the emblematic hero Bazarov (and the society whose tensions he may seem to embody and evoke) passes through the worlds and minds of women, on his way to an encounter with stark destiny. Surely, then, it is legitimate to wonder who these women are, what we can know and say of their lives and worlds and minds.

We begin with the odd but perhaps illuminating fact that the canonic English translation of the title errs: Turgenev's title refers to fathers (*ottsy*) and *children* (*deti*), thus at least allowing for the possible importance of female offspring to the ideational intentions of the novel.[7] The English title urges our concentration on the relationships of male generations: Kirsanov father and son, Bazarov father and son, the men of the sixties and the men of the forties, the father within the son (Nikolai within Arkady) who will unravel the momentary idolatrous bond to Bazarov the ideologue. If we consider the novel's women, however, other familial relationships will emerge as significant: the bonds of mothers and sons (Bazarov's mother's passionate, unrequited affection; Fenichka's maternal, "Marian" beauty, bespeaking a renewal of the sacred mother Mariia Kirsanova, a departed but vivifying presence at the Kirsanov estate); the nurturing labor of peasant nannies; the cycles of birth and death that women preside over in their wedding and laboring and mourning (Fenichka and Katya join the company of such women in the novel's epilogue). But we will also become attentive to what is perhaps the most important feminine familial relationship, one that informs in its divergence from the maternal: the novel's most significant female character is Anna Sergeevna Odintsova, a woman of "oh-là-là!"(150) and "no-no-no" (144);[8] a solitary, regimented woman who both discovers and retreats from her kinship with Bazarov; a nihilist of passion; a motherless child; a daughter—like the goddess Athena—of men, of her father and of a husband old enough to claim paternity; a woman who is *odin* (one, alone; masculine form), not *odna* (one, alone; feminine form). Surely it is Odintsova whom Turgenev had in mind in calling the novel *Fathers and Children*, not *Fathers and Sons*: there are mothers aplenty and mothers important in Turgenev's fourth novel, but it is the motherless daughter who most compels and confounds our attention, whose mind and body and denials rivet the narrator and Bazarov—and us. Who are these women? Who is Odintsova? Who are we, reading and responding to these women?

Odintsova is, in a profound sense, a woman *alone*, as her name suggests; we as readers must grapple with the question of what her solitude means, and why she chooses to perpetuate it. Her solitude stands in contrast, however, to all the other women in the novel, who are drawn as creatures of context, of relationship, of imitation; women who are representative or emblematic of larger social and symbolic groups. This is most obviously true of the mothers in the novel (Mariia Kirsanova, Fenichka, Arina Bazarova, Katya at novel's end), but it is also true of Kukshina (who is presented as emblematic of "emancipated women") and of the enigmatic Princess R. (who is perhaps trapped in her identity as a "society woman" [*svetskaia dama*]). Bazarov, ever the rigorous natural scientist, suggests in conversation with Odintsova that individuality is illusory; that humans, like trees, are essentially alike (277). While Turgenev no doubt takes issue with his naturalist hero on this matter, it is nonetheless true that all of the women characters *except* for Odintsova are presented as "typical," a typicality that grounds their identity and suggests how they are placed in Russian and more broadly human society. Bazarov makes repeated attempts to "classify" Odintsova: when he meets her at the provincial ball he wonders what species of mammals she belongs to (151), but he also notes that she is unlike the other "dames" (*baby*) there (148). Turgenev's novel presents its own classification of women, a psychic and symbolic taxonomy that contextualizes Odintsova's ambivalently "odd" position.

In thinking of the novel's mothers, one automatically thinks of Arina Bazarova, chin in hand, weeping at the sight of her long-absent, now returned son; or of Fenichka's tender concern for the infant Mitya. These two women present us with the novel's most powerful images of maternity, invoking a semantics of mothering that is grounded in intense and unwavering attention, and in forms of labor that nurture and protect—quite literally—the body. We first see Fenichka as she herself keeps watch over her baby; Nikolai hasn't yet introduced her to his son, but we glimpse her as "now listening, now dozing," framed by the open door through which she watches her son. She is lovely, "with a white kerchief thrown over her dark hair" (89), and we will come to know in ever greater detail the beauty and awkward grace of this young mother, who waddles and blushes (95). "Is there anything in the world," asks the narrator—wholly rhetorically—"more captivating than a beautiful young mother with a healthy child in her arms?" (109). This is Turgenev's narrator as Raphael, portraitist/iconographer of blooming, abundant maternity.

Fenichka (and later Katya) are both *young* mothers, women in their early twenties who charm and beguile with their intense and innocent attentions to the very young. Bazarov's mother, on the other hand, is maternity in its aged aspect, verging on the ridiculous when she directs at her grown son the same adoring gaze we imagine in Fenichka's eyes. "[Bazarov's mother] paid no attention to Arkady, . . . propping her round face on her little fist— her full cherry-coloured lips and the moles on her cheeks and over her eyebrows gave her a most benign expression—she never took her eyes off her son and kept sighing" (200). Whether we are to imagine that Fenichka could *become* someone like Arina Vlasyevna is debatable; the narrator suggests, ruefully, that "nowadays such women as she have ceased to exist" (203). Fenichka enchants, not just Nikolai but his brother Pavel and ultimately Bazarov himself; she is a blooming rose (as Bazarov suggests in the tête-à-tête that provokes the duel), a "small wild animal" half-hidden in a field of rye when Nikolai calls out to her (112); a maker of gooseberry jam (her husband's favorite); and a seamstress whose pincushion eclipses the fierce General Yermolov, whose picture hangs in her room (108–9). Arina Vlasyevna, on the other hand, is a "true Russian gentlewoman of the old school" (202), preoccupied with signs and portents, devout and superstitious, kindhearted and unquestioning of the world around her. Maternity has lost its charms in her; its limited concerns with fleshly sustenance come nearer to engulfing the spirit—as Bazarov will be "engulfed" by disease, by Russia, by the earth itself. For all her charms and all the narrator's efforts at approval, Arina Vlasyevna is part of a domestic world that encloses and stultifies, and serves as Bazarov's last stop en route to death. This is the obverse of the sentimentalized maternity of the Kirsanov homestead.

Fenichka and Arina Vlasyevna are both associated with highly articulated domestic spaces; Fenichka's room in particular stands as a wonderful emblematic rendering of the woman, seen through the eyes of Pavel, a man who, we come to find out, loves Fenichka and surely laments his own solitude. Fenichka's room is "clean and snug," with smells of a freshly painted floor, "of camomile and lemon balm." There is an icon of St. Nikolas the Miracle-Worker (appropriately enough, since Nikolai has worked a kind of "miracle" in Fenichka's life), hung with an easter egg; it nicely figures the comfortable mixture of Christian and pagan, Orthodox and popular religiosity, that the narrator will suggest is characteristic of Arina Vlasyevna as well. There are jars of her own jam; a cage with a goldfinch; bad photographs and the picture of Yermolov—objects that convey labors of love, gentle enclosure, and the domestication of the political. They are also a series of objects that *enclose*, just as the room itself does; but Turgenev's implication, surely, is that such enclosure is benign, creative, productive, and capable of beauty. Fenichka has come from the rye into a domestic world; she is a kind of "caged bird," but she bears her taming freely and lightly. This is a room that articulates all the novel's fondest virtues, the values it most longs to embrace and perpetuate.[9] And it is a woman's world, a room that bears the marks of her affectionate labors and many connections: affectional, religious, national. Loving labor has created this room and these objects (those jam jars), and it is that evocation of love bodied forth in fingers as well as eyes that touches most deeply here. When Arkady returns to his father's house he sleeps under a quilt that his peasant nanny made: these quilts and jam are emblems of the real labors and loves of maternal women in the novel.

Fenichka's room is, however, only one place in the world of *Fathers and Children*, and we pause there quite briefly. If we look beyond the novel's mothers we will acknowledge two other female figures who provide important context for Odintsova: Avdotya (Yevdoxia) Kukshina[10] and the mysterious Princess R. Both women are associated with other kinds of rooms and enclosures, much less benign: Kukshina with a disorderly, ash-strewn study; Princess R. with the drawing rooms and ballrooms of high society; Kukshina with the "excesses" of emancipated women, the Princess with the excesses of passion. Both women are associated with destruction, rather than with the creation and nurturing of life: Kukshina with the destructive fires that periodically burn down sections of provincial Russian towns,[11] and the Princess with the immolations of the Cross. If the novel's mothers define a spectrum of maternal affection, Kukshina and the Princess establish realms of excess; *both* groups of women seem to establish a range of alternatives for women in Russian society—none of which Odintsova herself will adopt. It is Kukshina and the Princess, however, who represent the most potent "dangers" for a solitary woman.

The Princess R.'s story is told by Arkady to Bazarov, as a way of explaining Pavel to the radical newcomer. The Princess is an "enigma" (Pavel himself called her a "sphinx" [101]), whose life is represented as an increasingly tormented alternation between the coquetry of drawing rooms and the "wringing anguish" of solitary prayer. The Princess might in fact seem to be a pale version of one of Dostoevsky's "infernal woman," or an unlikely combination of women from Turgenev's second novel, *A Nest of Gentlefolk*: the seductress of that novel, Varvara, plays out her manipulative melodramatic scenes in a country drawing room; its heroine, Liza Kalitina, ultimately leaves the world for the solace and solitude of monastic prayer.[12] The main function of the Princess R. story in *Fathers and Children* seems to be to "explain" Arkady's uncle; but in a larger sense it is a cautionary tale of the perils of passion: perils lived out to the death in the case of the Princess herself, and lived out to near madness in Pavel Kirsanov. The Princess is a woman who has in some profound sense *lost control of herself*: "She seemed to be in the grip of mysterious forces, unknown even to herself, which played with her at will, her limited intelligence being unable to cope with their caprices" (101). The Princess is the woman in the novel who seems most nearly to accede to certain codes of convention; she is to all appearances "a lady of fashion" (100). But the constraints of such convention-bound existence are seen to be powerless against the darker forces that take her as their prey.

Kukshina, on the other hand, is the victim less of dark and impassioned forces than of her own silliness, and of an ideology that Turgenev ridicules quite ruthlessly in his depiction of the "femme émancipée" (139). We meet her in a room that is as emblematic of the woman as was Fenichka's: it is, significantly, "more like a working study than a drawing-room" (and certainly not the repository of any homemade gooseberry jam). The study is filled with dust, cigarette butts, and uncut journals; the lady of the house reclines on a leather couch, "her blonde hair was rather dishevelled and she was wearing a crumpled silk dress, with heavy bracelets on her short arms and a lace kerchief on her head" (140). This room provides a symbolic and literal counterpoint to Fenichka's tidy domesticity and the elaborately constrained drawing rooms of polite society. It is also, however, a "study" in loose sexuality and intellectual pretensions: since the journal pages are uncut and the woman's pose readily suggests "loose" behavior. Turgenev reiterates *and* perpetuates in his portrait of Kukshina some of the charges that were leveled against women of the 1860s who challenged convention: such women's efforts at obtaining an education or entering traditionally male professional domains were repeatedly smeared with insinuations of flightiness and sexual misconduct.[13] If the Princess R. represents the excesses of passion, Kukshina is made to embody the purported excesses of emancipation; she is a woman who celebrates her independence (143), but "freedom" in Kukshina is represented as disintegrative and physically repulsive. One senses Turgenev the aristocrat in the narrator's aversion to a woman rolling a cigarette: "[Kukshina] rolled a cigarette between her fingers which were brown with tobacco stains, put it to her tongue, licked it up and started to smoke" (143). The energy of Turgenev's prose works to induce a moral repulsion in the reader that is grounded in visceral disdain; we have left Raphael far behind, and come closer to the debauched intimacies of Toulouse-Lautrec's brothels.

What is striking about both Princess R. and Kukshina is the extent to which their stories provide foils for Odintsova's; we are meant in part, I believe, to read the accounts of their lives as roads that a woman like Odintsova might take but doesn't. It defies the reader's imagination to imagine Odintsova a mother (she is eight years older than her sister, but very much a sororal, and not a maternal, figure to Katya). Princess R., on the other hand, and Kukshina represent quite credible options for, or versions of, Odintsova. Odintsova is certainly a woman of the drawing room or study, not a woman of the nursery or kitchen; she is a woman with intellectual pretensions, articulate and well-read (her journal pages are cut); she is intensely desirable, even erotic (as both the "oh-là-là" of Bazarov's first account and the narrator's repeated admiration of her body remind us); she is independent, without children, a woman slandered by many of her neighbors as a (sexually) "emancipated woman" (153–54). She is, finally, a woman who flirts with passion, who seems to glimpse within herself some of the forces that prey on the Princess R. But she is also a woman of negation, introduced with a string of negatives, insisting that Bazarov misunderstood her and that she misunderstood herself, a woman who says no to Bazarov and to whatever it is within herself that she glimpses in the course of her encounters with him. She is sister to both Kukshina and Princess R. (Kukshina claims she's a friend and in fact "introduces" her to the reader [144]), and her story can be read as a refusal of their excesses. But that refusal is, I believe, one of the most compelling enigmas of this novel, at least as compelling and problematic as Bazarov's "succumbing" to love and death—the narrative turn whose explanation has formed the focus of virtually all critical discussion of the novel. But who is Odintsova, and why does she refuse Bazarov? How can we read such refusal: as cause for celebration or lament? What, finally, does this solitary woman in a world of mothers and excess have to say to us?

The question is, on one level, not difficult to answer: Odintsova is an affluent and accomplished landowner, orphaned early, married to a "hypochondriac" much older than she, widowed after six years. She lives on her estate in the company of her sister Katya and her maternal aunt; she is a woman who has with care and calculation constructed a world of order and routine; she is a woman of "independent and determined" character (154). She is characterized from the first as a woman of great beauty and sensuality (Bazarov's first comment is "I say, what a splendid body!" [155]), but as a woman of quite chill demeanor: images of coldness follow Odintsova from Arkady and Bazarov's first conversation about her through to the epilogue. She is, in Arkady's words, "charming . . . but so cold and reserved"; Bazarov counters, "You say she is cold; that just adds to the flavour. You like icecream, don't you?" (150). We are told in the last chapter of the novel that she ultimately remarries, a man "kind-hearted and cold as ice" (292).

The effect of such imagery is to suggest that beneath Odintsova's calm, chill demeanor there lie some sort of subterranean forces, a strength of passion that is generally repressed: this is implied in Bazarov's initial proverbial comment ("Still waters . . . you know" [150; ellipsis in original]) and in the plot itself, in which Odintsova draws Bazarov into increasing intimacy, playing a kind of risky and flirtatious game that she herself ultimately disclaims responsibility for. "I did not understand you—you did not understand me, . . . I did not understand myself either" (183).

On a warm, almost sultry summer evening Odintsova invites Bazarov into her private chambers, alone. These chapters are among the most compelling of the novel; they begin on the ideological terrain of Bazarov's discussions with Pavel Kirsanov (Odintsova asks about a chemistry text, and challenges Bazarov's taxonomic disrespect for individuality), but they move into the realm of charged eroticism and a complicated dance (both verbal and physical) of desire and repression. Their conversation moves from chemistry to the possibilities of "being carried away" (175); from the rejection of individual difference to a game of confession: Odintsova volunteers that she is "unhappy because . . . I have no desire"; Bazarov suggests she's "longing to fall in love" but can't; Odintsova asks if he thinks it would be "easy to surrender oneself completely" (176–77; ellipsis in original).

Bazarov accuses Odintsova of "playing the coquette" (177), but it is clear that they have moved from the "objective" world of classification and rationality into a much murkier realm. And part of its murkiness is the difficulty of attribution of will: it is not clear what Bazarov himself wants, just as it is unclear what Odintsova herself desires to happen. In this languid evening encounter, however, they *both* move beyond the strictly ordered existences they have set themselves, and *both* are challenged—perhaps by those "unknown forces" that victimized the Princess R. The effect of Turgenev's prose in these chapters is, moreover, to submit the reader to some of the same experiences of sensuality and confusion as Bazarov and Odintsova themselves feel: we follow the currents and undercurrents of their words and gestures (the sudden, crashing opening of the window as Bazarov trembles with emotion [174]; the swaying blind and the "pungent freshness of the night"; Odintsova's "agitation," which communicates itself to Bazarov [175]; the mantilla Odintsova draws across her bare arms; her flush at meeting Bazarov's eyes [176]). Turgenev presents this encounter with a cinematographer's attention to gestural detail; he evokes a desire in the reader that echoes that of his characters.

Our desire, however, like Odintsova's and like Bazarov's, is frustrated: not just by her rejection of his embrace, but by the closure of their first discussion, when warm sensuality gives way to Odintsova's more accustomed chill: "A maid came into the room with a decanter on a silver tray, Madame Odintsova stopped short, told the maid she could go, and sat down again, deep in thought. Her hair slipped loose and fell in a dark coil over her shoulders. The lamp went on burning for a long while in her room while she still sat there motionless, only from time to time chafing her hands which were now beginning to feel the chill of the night air" (178). The moment is emblematic of much of what we know about Odintsova: the elegance and comfort of her well-appurtenanced life; the lovely body, with the implication of sensuality in her loosened hair; the juxtaposition of heat and chill—the burning lamp and the chilling body—and through it all the enigma of the thoughts that roil within the woman herself. Odintsova, too, is a sphinx: but her enigmatic presence will not be resolved for us by a single word, as was that of Pavel's beloved Princess.

Why does Odintsova refuse Bazarov? And, in refusing him, does she not refuse a part of herself? The novel offers some answers: Odintsova herself justifies the rejection (immediately after the fact) by suggesting that "various vague emotions—the sense of life passing by, a longing for novelty—had forced her to a certain limit, forced her to look behind her—and there she had seen not even an abyss but only a void . . . chaos without shape" (184; ellipsis in original). Bazarov himself implies that she is a woman who might flirt out of boredom or curiosity, but that she is incapable of falling in love (176–77). The narrator faults her wealth: "If she had not been rich and independent she might perhaps have thrown herself into the struggle and experienced passion . . ." (165; ellipsis in original). Do such explanations suffice? May we not still want to interrogate what is at work here, precisely in an *independent* woman's rejection of a passion she obviously experiences? (This is, after all, a woman created by an author whose women are shown repeatedly to take risks, and to act on their passionate impulses.) Might we not want to interrogate the ways in which Odintsova is emblematic of larger forms of refusal—both in the Russian literary tradition and in our own world? Let us recontextualize her "enigma" and ask why (and to what) women say no.

In purely legal terms, it would be considerably easier for Odintsova to say yes to Bazarov than it was for some of her literary sisters: the most famous refusal in Russian literature, Tatiana's refusal of Onegin, is enunciated by a married woman; Pushkin makes sure that we know the depth of Tatiana's feeling for Onegin, an emotion that makes her refusal that much harder, but that much more programmatic: the strength of passion will *not* overcome the bonds of matrimony.[14] The most famous counterexample in Russian literature is, of course, Anna Karenina's: she reverses Tatiana's submissive but deeply painful refusal, with disastrous results. One notes two things about Odintsova in such company: (1) that she is not bound, as are her sisters, by marriage bonds; and (2) that Tolstoy's novel—contra his own intentions—is an argument for the absolute necessity of honoring the desires of a passionate heart. Anna's dilemma is tragic precisely because to have honored her marital vows would have accomplished a different kind of suicide: slower, more hidden, but still suicide.[15] Turgenev's novel is positioned chronologically between the Pushkin and Tolstoy texts; it may also occupy a quite different ideological terrain, acknowledging the primacy of the heart, but playing out suicide in a different fashion. Bazarov is the novel's most obvious "suicide": his death is a bitter acknowledgment of the inability of science to encompass the enigmas and conflicts of human hearts and human souls. But Turgenev implies that there are two other metaphoric corpses in the novel: Pavel Kirsanov ("In the glaring daylight his handsome emaciated head lay on the white pillow like the head of a dead man . . . And, indeed, to all intents and purposes, so he was" [253; ellipsis in original]) and Odintsova herself. I would submit, then, that the *refusal* of passion (of bodies "carried away" erotically and emotionally) marks for Turgenev the inverse of what it does for Pushkin and Tolstoy: to refuse love is to refuse life—which both Odintsova and Bazarov, for different reasons and in different ways, do.

It is significant, I believe, that Odintsova is drawn as a "motherless" child, a woman whose life and order and place are legacies of her father and of a husband who was nearly the age of her father. The estate she rules is a world constructed (in more ways than one) at the wishes of her late husband; his portrait presides iconically over that world (156–57). Odintsova's name, as noted earlier, derives from the Russian word for "one": *odin*. But it is the masculine form of that word, a root I take as suggestive of something essential to her character. She is, as I proposed at the beginning of this essay, an Athena figure: woman *odin*, alone, for herself—in the masculine sense. Athena is the great goddess born not of woman but of man, burst from the head of Zeus—suggesting that Odintsova, like Bazarov, is a creature of the head, and not of the heart. The opposing figure in the Greek pantheon was Artemis: a virginal goddess who is also a woman alone, but *odna*, for herself—in the feminine sense.[16] Where lies the difference? In the imbalance of intellect and eroticism; in the advocacy of authoritarian order at the expense of a wilder, impassioned existence; in the allegiance to men rather than to women; in the denial of the relationship to the body and its cycles—Artemis (or Diana, to the Romans) was the goddess of childbirth and death, as well as of the hunt.

In an earlier essay on *Fathers and Children* I argued that Bazarov, as he is dying, alludes to the myth of Actaeon and Artemis: he has a vision of himself consumed by hunting dogs. Artemis, in that story, is bathing with nymphs in the forest, when Actaeon the hunter happens upon them.[17] He sees Artemis in her nakedness, her beauty, at her most revealing; and for that he is punished. His "transgression" elicits Artemis's anger; she turns him into a stag, and his own hounds turn on him, devouring him in their frenzy. This tale suggests the wildly destructive energies that ensue from a kind of "transgressive" intimacy, from the aggressive hunter's vision and knowledge of the sacred goddess. And what does the story suggest in the context of Turgenev's novel? Surely Odintsova is no Artemis. Both she and Bazarov, the narrator tells us, are "indifferent" to nature (169); she, unlike her sister Katya, fears garden snakes (265); she is a creature of the manor—of rules, order, regularity—not of the wilder *loci* of creation. But that is perhaps the point. The plot of Turgenev's novel brings Odintsova to a glimpse of herself as an impassioned, "animalistic" being:[18] no longer as the chill, intellectual Athena, but as Artemis, whose virginity is wild. The agent of that transformation is Bazarov: the twist on Ovid's story is that it is not just Actaeon/Bazarov who "sees" Artemis/Odintsova; it is Odintsova herself who transgresses the boundaries she has so carefully constructed. "She had seen not even an abyss but only a void . . . chaos without shape" (184; ellipsis in original). That is Odintsova's ex post facto rationalization of her action; it is "Athena" speaking. We can only speculate on whether the energies within her that a liaison with Bazarov would have unleashed could have been creative (rather than destructive).

It is worth noting, though, that there is a long tradition in Western culture of depicting female sexual energy as inherently dangerous, and Russian literature generally follows that tradition.[19] Russian literary texts that narrate the refusal of passion might be read in company with cautionary tales (such as Leskov's "Lady MacBeth of the Mtsensk District," Turgenev's *Smoke*, Ostrovsky's *The Storm*): both kinds of narrative imply the danger of giving "free rein" to women's sexuality; they also suggest that women themselves would prove unable or unwilling to restrain it. Maternity is traditionally the only "safe" form of female sexuality, an institution and practice that has confined women and directed their erotic energies toward nurturance. In this sense one might read the "mothers" of Turgenev's novel as bearers of such convention; Fenichka's sexuality is innocent and directed toward children. But we also remember the more threatening, ambivalent figure of the archaic mother who devours the spirit: the superstitious, aging, slightly pathetic mother of Bazarov, who stands at his grave as a final reminder of the devouring "maternal" earth.

One might still find allies for opposing voices in unexpected places: Does not Tolstoy, in his crazed and murderous Pozdnyshev, suggest that the brilliant *dialogue* of creativity and eroticism, of masculine and feminine, that we find in Beethoven's "Kreutzer" Sonata will be possible only when men no longer fear women and their sexuality; that is, when men take responsibility for their own hostilities, their own "fall"? Odintsova, however, will never play the piano with the passion and brilliance of Pozdnyshev's wife; she will never break with her routines and journey to Venice and Bulgaria in service of revolutionary change (as does Elena in *On the Eve*); she will never experience the emotion that consumes Anna Karenina and drives her, tragically, to extinguish the very fire of life that had made her a passionate being; she will never follow Artemis into places of wildness and risk. We might imagine quite "sensible" reasons for not doing any of these things, but Turgenev's heroines have been creatures of passion, not sensibility; they have been defiant and exultant, not carefully resigned. Odintsova avoids the excesses of Kukshina and Princess R., but she does so at great cost. Bazarov is "consumed" at the end by the great maternal earth, which brings regeneration at the price of anonymity. One can only wonder what other ending there might have been, had Artemis and Actaeon been able to forge a new vision and order, grounded not in repression but in passionate acceptance of the hearts and souls and bodies they and we all are.

Amy Mandelker

The Judgment of *Anna Karenina*

FEMINIST IDEOLOGICAL criticism seems a particularly appropriate tool with which to critique *Anna Karenina*, a novel that strenuously interrogates the gender implications of marital relations and romantic love. The critical issues that yield to the probe of gender-oriented criticism adhere to the central thematic concerns of the novel, and most important, to the ways in which its eponymous heroine is judged in both moral and aesthetic terms. Curiously, Anna's status as a heroine and the tragic tenor of her narrative is frequently denied, not only by traditionalist, masculinist critics, but by more recent feminist readings as well. Thus, both masculinist and feminist readings of the novel have tended to diminish the potential heroism of Anna's transgression and to mute the mythological tones of her quest and fall.

Both feminist and masculinist readings concur in finding Anna guilty and in labeling her a bad, even an evil woman. Her failure according to these interpretations is both proximate and ultimate since she transgresses against the values of a patriarchal society, yet fails to liberate herself and thus remains a compliant prisoner of the patriarchy. Even if the profundity of Anna's conflict is recognized, her emotional reaction is condemned: "A whole society, perhaps the species itself, is at stake, and here a wretched woman temporizes about it, numbs herself with opium, whimpers over her own precious individuality, and finally jeopardizes everything by suicide."[1] Alternately, Anna is castigated because she fails to assume responsibility for healing her own psychic conflicts and repressions:

> Anna's story is not a tale of social oppression or a drama of failed liberation. Tolstoy, it should be recalled, insisted that people have no rights, only responsibilities. . . . Anna abandons her flawed human relatedness to which she is responsible. . . . But Anna is not destroyed by others, and self-indulgence is not her fundamental flaw. Anna is not punished by Tolstoy for her sexual fulfillment. In a fuller sense, Anna's story is a moral tragedy of self-enclosure.[2]

33

Sexual stereotyping is common to both traditionalist male-dominated criticism and to the more recent feminist criticism. The following view expressed by a nineteenth-century reader of the novel still seems to underlie contemporary judgments:

> All the meaning of the family, all its potential and all its morality depend, do they not, on the wife and mother, and if she destroys the family will not the woman perish along with the purpose of her life and any meaning she might have as a person? . . . If only [women] could understand that in the self-denial and self-sacrifice of a wife and mother there is more value and more moral satisfaction than in the pursuit of their own appetites and fantasies.[3]

Even Mary Evans, in her recent avowedly feminist reading of *Anna Karenina*, relies on the perpetuation of these attitudes in contemporary society when she subscribes to the notion that mothering is natural while fathering must be learned: "After all, the mother, a married woman, who deliberately chooses an adulterous relationship rather than her maternal responsibilities, would still today be labelled as a deviant and 'unnatural' woman."[4]

ANNA KARENINA AGAINST ANNA KARENINA

The case against Anna, the "strategy of the novel" that "is directed against [her]" so that "Anna must be destroyed,"[5] is based on readers' perceptions of the inevitability of her suicide, which is construed as a death sentence, a form of divine or social retribution, prefigured in the novel's epigraph, "Vengeance is mine, I will repay." So common is the death of the transgressing heroine in nineteenth-century fiction that it has come to be seen as an obligatory sop thrown to conventional morality that gives the author the latitude to portray his or her heroine sympathetically or, alternately, reveals the author's discomfort in affirming deviance. According to one feminist critic: "The overall message is to all intents unequivocal; in *Anna Karenina* Levin makes the right choices and so lives and flourishes beyond the back cover of the book; Anna chooses wrongly, and therefore must die even before the last chapter. Nothing could be clearer."[6]

However, most critics have found this aspect of the novel extremely problematic and far from clear. To begin with, Tolstoy's use of the biblical epigraph, especially in its incomplete form (omitting "saith the Lord"), creates a disconcerting uncertainty in the reader as to who is speaking: Does Tolstoy quote God or speak for God or as its surrogate? Or is Tolstoy God? Is authority equivalent or superior to divine nemesis? As Boris Eikhenbaum complains: "The point is not, of course, that Tolstoy makes the solution of guilt and criminality subject to the will of God, but that this God [is] now undoubtedly subject to the will of Tolstoy as the author of the novel."[7] According to an alternate critical tradition, Anna's death is not the result of God's vengeance on her, but is instead the culmination of the cruel and unforgiving treatment she received at the hands of her fellow man: "Society is the villain of the piece,"[8] or, as Viktor Shklovsky proclaimed, "Genuine human morality contradicts the Biblical quotation, and it was not God, but people . . . who pushed Anna under the wheels of the train."[9]

These two readings reflect the distinction that needs to be made between the Old and New Testament judgments on sexual transgression and punishment. In Deuteronomy 32:35, God reserves vengeance to himself and promises that punishment shall ensue without mercy whereas in Romans 12:19–21, Paul exhorts his listeners to leave vengeance and punishment to God: "My dear friends, do not seek revenge, but leave a place for divine retribution." Since Tolstoy does not cite chapter and verse for his epigraph, it remains unclear whether he intended to refer to either Old or New Testament, or to establish tension between the two. Interpretations of the epigraph, therefore, have tended either to assume that it reflects an Old Testament morality and the punitive action of a wrathful God through worldly events or to follow the Christian precept that it is not for humanity to judge, but for God; and not on earth, but in heaven.[10] The latter view is expressed by Dostoevsky: "There are not, and cannot be any healers or *final* judges of human problems other than He who says, 'Vengeance is mine; I will repay.' He alone knows the *whole* enigma of the world and the final destiny of man."[11] What we know about the origination of the epigraph in Tolstoy's novel argues for this latter interpretation. Eikhenbaum demonstrates that Tolstoy originally borrowed the biblical quotation from a passage in Arthur Schopenhauer (*The World as Will*, book 4, chap. 62) in which the philosopher demands the suspension of human judgment: "No person has the authority to set himself up as a moral judge and avenger, to punish the misdeeds of another with pain which he inflicts on him. . . . This would be, rather, presumption of the highest degree; hence the Biblical 'Vengeance is mine; I will repay.'"[12]

The biblical quotation may also be found in other novels of the period dealing with adultery, specifically in two works Tolstoy was known to have read and admired: Trollope's *Phineas Redux* (1876) and Mrs. Henry Wood's *East Lynne* (1861). In *Phineas Redux* the eponymous hero attempts to soften the wrath of the abandoned husband by quoting this passage from Scripture. Similarly, in *East Lynne* the cuckolded husband restrains himself from acting against his rival by quoting the same biblical passage. Within this literary tradition of adulterers and adulteresses spared punishment by the avenging husband, the scriptural passage becomes more obviously associated with that other biblical text so frequently repeated throughout *Anna Karenina*: Let he who is without sin cast the first stone.[13]

Critics like Robert L. Jackson[14] and Martin Price have noticed the coloration of fatality in the details that overdetermine Anna's suicide and regard Anna as a tragic heroine, "because, for reasons that are admirable [she] cannot live [a] divided life or survive through repression."[15] "The tragic situation is a situation from which there is no escape," observes E. B. Greenwood. "[Anna's] fate has a contingency and yet a pattern that bears the marks, not of the author's vindictiveness, but of the poetic inevitability we associate with tragedy."[16]

If the novel has the tenor of tragic form, such that "destiny is the plot,"[17] and "character is revealed as a determined shape, as an embodiment of an already existing fate,"[18] it is curious that most critics nonetheless deny Anna the status of a tragic heroine. Is this because they are reluctant to read an apparently ultrarealist novel as a tragedy or because there is something problematic in Anna's characterization that causes them to resist designating her fall as tragic? Or is it because the conventional image of Tolstoy as misogynist and ultraconservative has blocked their critical judgment? Even leaving aside the notion of tragic form, the very concept of Anna as a heroine of any kind has recently been challenged and reread so that she is either denied the status of eponymous heroine,[19] or castigated as a self-styled heroine, willfully and wrongfully scripting her overwritten narrative of fatal romance.[20]

WHO IS A HEROINE?

The notion of heroinism[21] is problematized most obviously by gender concerns, to the extent that one feminist critic feels it necessary to elevate Anna to the level of "hero, while leaving it to Kitty, Masha and Natasha to remain mere heroines. In other words, Anna transcends the constraints of her gender."[22] Although this statement is meant to "mount a feminist defense" of the novel, it is itself antifeminist. Anna must cross over gender boundaries and cross-dress as a masculine hero since Armstrong denies the heroic quality of the kinds of deeds that a heroine may be called upon to perform. Armstrong's statement implies that masculine heroism is superior to feminine heroinism and denies us a female model for heroinic activity that we would recognize as morally and spiritually equivalent to masculine heroism. Her claims for Anna's heroism invoke her "masculinization"; she observes that Anna, as a writer, wields the pen, notorious emblem of the male member, and engages in the study of architecture, economics, and physics, traditionally male areas of knowledge. Armstrong further argues that Anna acts like a male hero in the sense developed by Vladimir Propp and defined by Lotman as the transgressor of boundaries. Thus, Armstrong overlooks the path taken by many feminist critics of searching for female-based alternatives to male-defined patterns and paradigms; for example, maternal versus paternal models of "anxious influences" or, in this case, a narrative model for female heroinism.

36

In considering the ways in which a paradigm of heroinism has emerged in modern literature in tandem with heroism, Rachel Brownstein comments: "The paradigmatic hero is an overreacher; the heroine of the domestic novel . . . is overdetermined. The hero moves toward a goal; the heroine tries to be it."[23] The hero ascends the throne; the heroine marries another's destiny. The static and passive role of the heroine in a hero-centered text was described in Lotman's plot typology and was subsequently criticized for being phallogocentric by Teresa de Lauretis.[24] In the above typologies, the feminine principle constitutes the inert, spatial ground for the masculine heroic action.

However, there are heroine-centered models of narrative that are equally antique, classical, and mythological: for example, the myths of Psyche or Persephone, whose activity, transgressions, and fulfillment of heroic tasks resemble those of classical heroes, yet who must be interpreted differently as heroines because of their gender.

What kinds of heroinic behavior might we discern in the heroine of a novel? Evans argues that Anna cannot be elevated to the status of a heroine, "since we might expect at best some evidence that a heroine attempts to rise above her fate," and Anna "offers no model of how women might resist the strictures of conventional patriarchal authority."[25] It is difficult not to feel that the kinds of feminist criticism that require a heroine to be a satisfactory role model have not evolved much beyond the views of Samuel Richardson, who in his 1759 preface to *Clarissa* demands that a heroine be an "exemplar to her sex." This prerequisite leaves it up to the critic's own moral code to define the exemplary: virtuous and compliant subjection to the patriarchy or militant and potent rebellion. Arguing against a similar judgment brought on Nora in Ibsen's *A Doll's House*, Joan Templeton comments:

> Nora falls short according to unnamed, "self-evident" criteria for a feminist hero-
> ine, among which would seem to be one, some, or all of the following: an ever-
> present serious-mindedness; a calm, unexcitable temperament; . . . perfect sincer-
> ity and honesty; and a thoroughgoing selflessness. For *A Doll House* to be
> feminist, it would, apparently, have to be a kind of fourth-wall morality play with
> a saintly Everyfeminist as heroine, not this . . . excitable, confused and desper-
> ate—in short, human—Nora.[26]

The type of argumentation one would have to pursue to debate this issue further would curiously resemble discussions of socialist realist art, whose proponents demanded that perfectivized men and women of the future be depicted if there were no ideal role models to be found among the men and women of contemporary society.

Were there no candidates in Russian society of the 1870s worthy to be represented as the heroine of a novel? Is there no heroine therefore in *Anna Karenina*? It may be argued that Anna's claim to heroinism is denied because of her gender and the nature of the escape open to her in her attempt to "rise above her condition." Even if she is forgiven her sexual transgression, she is never excused for abandoning her son and ignoring her daughter. But is she judged by the same criteria as a hero who might act similarly? A hero who abandons his impoverished family in Ireland to pursue his muse in Europe, or who leaves his wife and children to paint in Tahiti or study at Oxford, or who even sells his wife and children into bondage with no higher goal in mind, will usually be written and read as having heroically shaken free of the mundane and will not come under the same terms of literary evaluation as a heroine who acts in the same way. Consider Irving Howe's (by now infamous) commentary on the opening of *The Mayor of Casterbridge*:

> To shake loose from one's wife; to discard that drooping rag of a woman, with her mute complaints and maddening passivity; to escape not by slinking abandonment but through the public sale of her body to a stranger, as horses are sold at a fair; and thus to wrest, through sheer amoral wilfulness, a second chance out of life— it is with this stroke, so insidiously attractive to male fantasy, that *The Mayor of Casterbridge* begins.[27]

Not only does Howe elevate the criminal sale into slavery over the more common action of abandonment (which would have left the woman free, eventually even to remarry); he does not even acknowledge the existence of the daughter, whose body is also sold. His indifference is in striking contrast to Anna's agony and refusal to obtain a divorce, in spite of the cost to herself, because it would force her to completely abandon her son. The imbalance in the critical handling of these two lapses in parenting suggests the common prejudice that the power of the paternal instinct, if it exists at all, in no way resembles that of the maternal instinct. In the stereotyped view of parental roles, paternity is primarily seen as a condition of often oppressive responsibility that deprives the male of the freedom to pursue his true path in life, while maternity is considered to be the only fulfilling path in life for a woman, in whom maternal instinct presumably induces a state of self-less-ness and willing sacrifice.

In the Continental tradition of the novel of adultery, motherhood is rarely a significant event in the heroine's life: recall Mme. Bovary's indifference to her children once she realizes she cannot afford the pleasure of purchasing a lavish layette. Most Continental novels separate the passion of the adulterous woman from the passion of the mother; perhaps this represents a fissure in social perceptions of women's potential to fulfill multiple roles. As Tony Tanner comments: "The wife and mother in one set of social circumstances should not, and cannot be, the mistress and lover in another. It is well known how bourgeois society tends to enforce unitary roles on its members. . . . From the point of view of that society, adultery introduces a bad multiplicity within the requisite unities of social roles."[28] Tolstoy's depictions of an adulterous heroine who is both passionately maternal (at least in the first half of the novel[29]) and sexual thus represents that threatening combination of maternity and sexuality that the Western Judeo-Christian ethic has sought to fragment. Within this ideology, a good woman is a good mother; that is, endowed with a proper maternal instinct that supersedes and eclipses all other drives. Evans poses the argument, in keeping with recent feminist theory,[30] that the experience of maternity automatically generates higher moral values, a "woman's way of knowing" and a "different voice of a caring morality."[31] This theorizing runs the risk of essentializing and biologizing the experience of maternity to a degree that many critics have seen as being virtually protofascistic. According to this view, taken to its extreme, it is not that a good woman is a mother, but rather that a mother is and must necessarily be a good woman, one who, by mothering, automatically creates a higher moral sphere for her children by not subverting or threatening the patriarchal system within which she unavoidably exists and on which she is necessarily and often painfully dependent.[32]

According to these criteria, Evans elects Dolly the true heroine of *Anna Karenina*, because she endures her oppression in the patriarchy, because she is maternal to the exclusion of her own interests and needs, and because she holds to a morality that is unconstrained by social mores; for example, she visits Anna in spite of the social stigma attached to such an act. In fact, the reader ought not to place too much emphasis on this visit, since the familial relationship between the two women is sufficient to lift the social taboo against private visits between households. Ultimately, when Anna most needs her, Dolly lets her down; she feels it more important to counsel Kitty about breast-feeding than to respond to Anna's obvious distress.

For different reasons, Gary Saul Morson suggests that "Dolly Oblonskaya is Tolstoy's moral compass,"[33] and appoints her the "hero" of Anna Karenina, "if by the hero of a book, we mean the character who best exemplifies its governing values."[34] For Morson, however, the texture and warp of Dolly's life is as significant as her social and moral status as the embodiment of the Victorian ideal of the angel in the house. Morson reads *Anna Karenina* as a novel that exalts and exemplifies the prosaic and "prosaics," and he finds Dolly's eventless, plotless, and "excessivement terre-à-terre" existence to be the most prosaically effaced testament to the quotidian and minute processes of life celebrated by the novel. In this sense, Morson seems to imply that Dolly shares the features of the saintly Praskovia Mikhailovna of *Father Sergius*.

While Dolly is unquestionably one of the positive characters of the novel, one could certainly argue, contra Evans, that she does not succeed in creating a desirable moral atmosphere for her children. They will grow up in a home that is based on a hypocritical, fictitious marriage; as they mature, they will increasingly recognize that their mother is passively enslaved to a patriarchal society and an abusive husband. In fact, it is very difficult to read Dolly in any other way than as a failed sister of the exalted angels in the house of Victorian fiction. Compared to those warm, rotund, matronly queens, surrounded by a bevy of adoring children who lovingly clasp their mother's neck and thick curls with chubby fingers, Dolly is emaciated and worn, a hack dray horse among sleek thoroughbreds; she is surrounded not by plump cherubs, but by dirty, misbehaving urchins. The neat, tidy, and cozy domestic arrangements of the Dickensian or Trollopian matron—the bubbling teapot, lovingly netted slippers warming before a crackling fire, hearty but simple meals of clotted cream and home-baked scones—are reflected ironically in Dolly's desperate attempts to feed and clothe her children, in their reckless play with milk and jam, and in her moment of humiliation, when her patched bedjacket, the economy "of which she had been so proud at home," puts her to shame in front of the servants at Vronsky's estate.

Tolstoy's description of Dolly anticipates his subsequent journalistic accounts of the burdens of pregnancy, childbirth, and childrearing. Although he does homage to the indomitable spirit of woman, Tolstoy does not idealize or romanticize. He exposes the cult of domesticity for what it often becomes in a bad marriage: an oppression of woman and a denial of her selfhood perpetuated by the myth of the glories of maternity and housekeeping. In this sense, Morson's characterization of Dolly as the embodiment of prosaic virtues is closer to the truth. But does she represent the values that the novel espouses? If we assume, as Morson does, that the novel attacks the notion of romantic passion, a close examination of Dolly's own views on love and marriage, the same views that sustain her, makes this assertion problematic.

The positive perception of domestic life in the novel is presented by Levin, just as Dolly's idealization is achieved through Levin's eyes, for whom she represents "that picture of family life his imagination had painted" (282), an ideal of domesticity in which Levin is himself destined to be disillusioned. Fantasizing about his future family life, a vision clearly derived from Victorian literary models,[35] Levin "actually pictured to himself first the family, and only secondarily the woman who would give him a family" (101). The woman herself and the notion of an intimate relationship are irrelevant, so that any of the three Shcherbatsky sisters would have done for his wife. Thus, Levin's dreams are based not on notions of romantic love but on the romantic idyll of domestic life. And since Levin is disillusioned in his expectations of family happiness, we might expect even greater disillusionment on Dolly's part. Yet, humiliated and impoverished by Stiva's extramarital affairs, she still allows herself to be deluded as to the true nature of their marriage, and thus colludes in the bourgeois myth of marriage, as it is recounted by Anna:

> Such men are unfaithful, but their own home and wife are sacred to them. Somehow or other these women are still looked on with contempt by them, and do not

touch on their feeling for their family. They draw a sort of line that can't be crossed between them and their families. . . .

I saw Stiva when he was in love with you. I remember the time when he came to me and cried, talking of you, and all the poetry and loftiness of his feeling for you, and I know that the longer he has lived with you, the loftier you have been in his eyes. . . . You have always been a divinity for him, and you are that still, and this has not been an infidelity of the heart. (76)

That Dolly still believes in the bourgeois myth of romantic love and marriage, despite her awareness of its failures, is evidenced in her reactions to Kitty's wedding:

[Dolly] was deeply moved. The tears stood in her eyes, and she could not have spoken without crying. She was . . . going back in thought to her own wedding . . . she glanced at the radiant figure of Stepan Arkadevich, forgot the present, and remembered only her own innocent love. She recalled not only herself, but all the women she was intimate with or with whom she was acquainted. She thought of them on the day of their triumph, when they had stood like Kitty under the wedding crown, with love and hope and dread in their hearts, renouncing the past and stepping forward into the mysterious future. Among the brides that came back to her memory, she thought too of her darling Anna, of whose proposed divorce she had just been hearing. And she had stood just as innocent in orange flowers and bridal veil. And now? "It's terribly strange," she thought. (479)

Dolly's description of the transition from maidenhood to married estate curiously echoes the romanticized narrative—complete with reference to the most romantic of topoi, the Alps—that Anna had spun to Kitty's wonder earlier in the novel: "'Oh, how good it is to be your age!' pursued Anna. 'I remember, and I know that blue haze like the mist on the mountains in Switzerland. That mist which covers everything in that blissful time when childhood is just ending, and out of that vast circle, happy and gay, there is a path growing narrower and narrower. . . . Who has not been through it?'" (79). Tolstoy contrasts Dolly's romantic, if disturbed, reverie at the wedding to the conversation of the peasant women who observe the ceremony from the doorway. Speaking as a united community of women, they speculate as to whether the bride is being married against her will or for money, and they flinch at "how the deacon rumbles, 'Fear your husband.'" No one asserts that the marriage is for love (perhaps an unconvincing notion). And the concluding comment, "What a pretty dear the bride is—like a lamb all decked out [for the slaughter]! Well, say what you will, we women feel sorry for our sister" (479), expresses a folkloric wisdom regarding the realities of married life in stark contrast to Dolly's sentimentalizing.

Dolly's seemingly heroic endurance is thus exposed as being sustained by the same dangerous bourgeois delusions of romantic love that drive Anna Karenina's passion. In depicting Dolly, Tolstoy drew yet one more portrait of the oppression of women: in this case, a spiritual rather than a physical death, a life based on self-deception, dissimulation, and ultimately, on cowardice.

In a novel whose author unceasingly interrogates the institutions of marriage and romance, the only genuine feminist heroine might be a woman who rejects the two familiar, fatal choices of marriage or passion to pursue her own autonomous path, who refuses to be the submissive partner in the patriarchal institution of marriage and similarly resists being construed as the object of male desire. Only one character in the novel meets these criteria, and not only is her choice hard and uncomfortable, but she is too minor a character to lay claims on heroine-ship. Nonetheless, Varenka's choice not to enter into marriage with Koznyshev[36] and her constant occupation with social service offer a glimpse of an alternate path for a heroine, one that Tolstoy would increasingly valorize in the coming years. Varenka is a heroine of the Florence Nightingale–type, the Lady with the Lamp, rather than the angel in the house, or the fallen woman out of the house.[37]

Does viewing Varenka as a heroine imply that genuine feminist heroines must resist marriage? Or genuine Tolstoyan heroines? Are there no happy families in *Anna Karenina*? Although Levin and Kitty's marriage is usually seen as successful, some critics suggest that theirs is a relationship of increasing estrangement, that by the end of the novel "lack of communication has become a way of life for Kitty and her husband."[38] The only unadulteratedly happy family in the novel appears to be that of the Sviazhkys, who are childless. It might be argued that their childless state implies the kind of chaste Christian "fictitious" (in the sense of being unconsummated) marriage—a relationship like that of brother and sister—that Tolstoy would later advocate.

If ideological criticism of this novel has foundered on any one problem, it is on the need to take Anna on her own terms, of which her gender is an essential element, but an element that should not be allowed to essentialize her or the meaning of her narrative. Lamentably, feminist readings of *Anna Karenina* all too frequently deny Anna's status as a unique woman: in one case, because Anna does not perform as the kind of maternal, sisterly woman that Evans's code of feminism demands, she is supplanted by Dolly as the heroine of the novel. In Armstrong's reading, Anna is denied any arena for heroinic action because women's actions are considered to be potent only when masquerading in masculine dress. Since the view that Tolstoy is a misogynist is still well entrenched, a feminist critic of the novel who starts from that assumption must either develop a strategy for reconsidering the traditional values of domesticity in keeping with recent feminist theory (the approach taken by Evans), or argue that Tolstoy's unconscious desires granted Anna a force and vitality that survive her textual extinction (the thesis submitted by Armstrong).

We need a feminist reading of Anna that will liberate her from the sex-based roles and stereotypes that generate certain evaluative responses in both feminist and nonfeminist critics, without overlooking the specific differences in her experiences that her gender entails. Feminist criticism of Anna is needed that neither sutures femininity to maternity nor masculinizes it.

Among the first words we hear Anna speak in the novel are that she takes "not the Petersburg view, but a woman's view" (67). We might realize that she means not just "women's views" but "*a* woman's view," a woman who follows her own proximate and imperiled experience of motherhood, marriage, passion, and death. Even though her trajectory through the novel is highly plotted according to the narratives of romance and ruin, her failures and her sufferings are unique.

Harriet Murav

Reading Woman in Dostoevsky

Vy skazhete, chto . . . tut prosto bylo "bab'ie delo." (You
will say . . . that here was simply "women's business.")
—Dostoevsky, *A Writer's Diary*, May 1876

GUBERNANTKA, imeiushchaia diplom, ishchet mesto kom-
pan'onki ili pri detiakh; soglasna i na ot"ezd' (GOVERNESS,
possessing a diploma, seeks the position of companion or
governess for children; willing to travel).
—Advertisement in *Golos*, no. 120 (13 May 1876)

DEAD BODIES TELL NO TALES

The November 1876 issue of Dostoevsky's *Writer's Diary*, his one-man monthly journal, is devoted entirely to a story narrated in the first person by a "husband whose wife lies on the table, a suicide."[1] The piece, called "A Meek
One,"[2] is subtitled "A Fantastic Story," and in the preface Dostoevsky
explains that what is fantastic about the story is not its content, which he considers highly realistic, but its form. Dostoevsky asks his readers to imagine a
stenographer recording everything the husband says:

> The telling of the story, of course, takes a few hours . . . it is disconnected in form,
> for he either argues with himself or addresses some unseen listener, a judge as it
> were. However, it is always like that in real life. If a stenographer could have lis-
> tened to him and taken it all down, it would have sounded rather less smooth and
> finished than my account, but I do believe that the psychological sequence would
> have probably been the same. Now this hypothetical stenographer (whose notes I
> have given shape to) is what I call "fantastic" in my story.[3]

Bakhtin is particularly struck by Dostoevsky's use of this peculiar narrative device and concludes that the fantastical stenographer makes it possible
for Dostoevsky to put the hero's discourse about himself in his own words
without destroying the essential nature of the story. According to Bakhtin,

44

this emphasis on the hero's self-consciousness, expressed in his own discourse about himself, reveals an entirely new relationship between author and hero, which the critic terms "dialogic," as opposed to the traditional "monologic" relationship. The author's dialogic relation to the hero, Bakhtin writes, is "one that affirms the independence, internal freedom, unfinalizability, and indeterminacy of the hero. For the author the hero is not 'he' and not 'I' but a fully valued 'thou,' that is, another and other autonomous 'I.'"[4]

There is both a formal and an ethical dimension to Bakhtin's concept of the dialogic. He switches from one to another, now emphasizing author, character, and discourse, and now emphasizing the person. For example, for true dialogue to take place, the author has to address the character as discourse. But the character cannot be reduced to mere discourse. The discourse is attached to a human being, a person with a point of view. Bakhtin abandons the terms "author" and "character" and speaks of "my discourse" and "someone else's discourse." He writes that only in a dialogic orientation "can my discourse find itself in intimate contact with someone else's discourse and yet at the same time not fuse with it, not swallow it up, not dissolve in itself the other's power to mean" (64). We can say that the dialogic relationship between author and hero has in addition to the formal components of the hero's self-consciousness expressed in confessional self-utterance this apparently ethical concern for the other's status as a human being, which, Bakhtin seems to be suggesting, is given by the "power to mean." "Character" as a category of analysis has been replaced by "consciousness" and "discourse," but the concept of the "person" is nonetheless fundamental to Bakhtin.

The concept of the gendered person does not, however, concern Bakhtin.[5] What is the position of the female character in the dialogic relationship between author and hero? Does the new authorial relation to the hero depend on some particular relation between author and heroine or hero and heroine? To put the question in terms of "A Meek One," the relationship between the "husband whose wife lies on the table" and the construction of the hero's self-utterance has to be examined. The analysis of gender, dialogic discourse, and narrative structure in "A Meek One" will serve as the basis for a more general discussion of the female protagonist in Dostoevsky's work as a whole.[6]

Dostoevsky's hero in "A Meek One," a forty-year-old man, is an "underground" type. Many years earlier he was kicked out of his regiment because of cowardice. He lived on the streets until he received a small inheritance, which he used to open a pawnshop. There he meets a young woman who pawns a few pitiful items in order to pay for an advertisement in the newspaper—a real-life example of which serves as one of the epigraphs for this essay. Upon making inquiries, the pawnbroker learns that she is desperate

for any sort of work. Her abusive relatives plan to marry her off to a shop-
keeper, many years her senior, who is responsible, the narrator suggests, for
the death of his two previous wives. The pawnbroker proposes marriage to
the heroine, who accepts him.

Here the narration of events becomes tangled and what follows is a
series of unreliable explanations from the husband as to why he was cruel to
his wife. We might note that in *Crime and Punishment* Raskolnikov similarly produces a series of shifting explanations for his crime to Sonya Marmeladova. The pawnbroker sets in motion a "system" of silence and strictness
with the meek one, repulsing all her outpourings of love. (We do not know in
what these outpourings consisted.) The hero's "idea," he tells us, is for his
young wife to see for herself, without explanation on his part, that he has
wrongly suffered at the hands of society. He wants her to see him as a proud
and noble sufferer, who needs no one. Later in the narration the husband
confesses that he was indeed a coward, but did not want to admit it, and married his wife in order to torment her. But the "meek one rebels" against his
system. She lends money on her own, leaves the apartment by herself, and
begins to meet the very officer on account of whom her husband was forced
to resign from the military. One morning, the narrator discovers that she is
holding a revolver to his head. The husband pretends to be asleep and the
"meek one" ultimately leaves the room, "defeated." After this episode, the
husband buys her a separate bed. The meek one falls ill. Upon her recovery,
the husband discovers that she periodically sings in his absence. On one
occasion, she forgets his existence entirely and sings while he is still in the
apartment. He falls to her feet, begs her forgiveness, and promises to sell the
pawnshop and start a new life with her. When he leaves the apartment to get
their foreign passports, she jumps out of the window holding an icon of the
mother of God in her arms and kills herself.

The pawnbroker is not only the narrator of the story; he is the cause of
his wife's death. The hero's two roles as tormentor of his wife and as simple
expositor converge. This leads us to ask whether the female character's narrative situation is a function of this particular narrative, in which the narrator
is also her tormentor, or whether Dostoevsky's narratives in general, or
indeed, narrative in general, require a (female) victim. Laura Mulvey puts the
question in terms of the relation between sadism and narrative: "sadism
demands a story."[7] Teresa de Lauretis comments on the "suggestion of
reversibility" implicit in this statement, that is, that stories demand sadism.
She asks: "Is a story, are all stories, to be claimed by sadism?"[8] Does dialogic
discourse, distinguished from "story" on the grounds of its open-endedness,
also demand sadism? This is the question that we shall return to as we
explore the narrative dynamics of "A Meek One."

The convergence of the hero's two roles leads to a very spotty explanation of the events. Because the husband marries the wife in order to torment

her, because she is a means of satisfying his need for revenge, and never a human being, he does not have very much to say about her, aside from what his inquiries reveal. He simply knows very little about her. For example, he is amazed to discover that she sings. After the wife's death, the husband resolves never to part with the servant Lukeria, because "she knows every-thing . . . she will tell me everything" (24:32). Yet in spite of his ignorance about his wife, the hero performs several narrative actions with regard to her that can only be termed "monologic." There is no "confessional self-utterance," to use Bakhtin's term, from the heroine of this work. Indeed, nearly all of Dostoevsky's heroines are denied this—a point to which I shall return

Beyond this absence on the formal level of the story's composition, on the ethical level as well the hero has absorbed within himself the heroine's "power to mean." Even the suicide has no meaning in the hero's eyes. He insists that it happened only because he was absent. If only he had entered the room five minutes earlier, she would not have killed herself: "she would have understood everything" (24:34). Here the husband claims an omni-scient knowledge of his wife's actions in a condition contrary to fact.

The hero is not only a monologic narrator, but a bad monologic narrator. The central event of the story, the wife's suicide, is never explained. Why does she kill herself, and why does she takes the icon with her? There are many other, lesser gaps in the husband's explanation. The husband is far more concerned with an explanation of his own actions than those of his dead wife. He is absorbed in himself and what will happen to him, while the "meek one" enters and leaves the story as a corpse. The first-person narra-tion of the husband begins:

> While she is still here, everything is alright: I come and have a look; but they will take her away tomorrow—how will I remain alone? She is in the hall on a table, two card tables pushed together, and the coffin will come tomorrow, white, white satin, but that's not what I meant . . . I keep walking and want to explain this to myself. (24:6; ellipsis in original)

And the last line of "A Meek One" reads: "no, seriously, when they carry her away tomorrow, what will become of me?" (24:35).

Several observations can be made at this point, beginning with the phys-ical position of the hero as he stands looking down at his prone wife. The rel-ative positions of the husband and his dead wife offer a stark contrast to what Bakhtin says about the relative positions of the author and the hero in Dos-toevsky's dialogic writing. Bakhtin concludes his discussion of "A Meek One" by remarking that "this is no stenographer's report of a *finished* dialogue, from which the author has already withdrawn and *over* which he is now located as if in some higher decision-making position" (63; emphasis in original). The author does not stand over the hero's discourse about himself, not even metaphorically, but exists on the same plane.

While the hero of "A Meek One" remains unfinalized with respect to the author, an initial reading would suggest that the same cannot be said for the heroine, neither with respect to the author, nor with respect to the hero/narrator. She seems "finalized" in all senses of the word. A dead body cannot enter into dialogue, Bakhtinian or otherwise. L. Michael O'Toole sees the body as speech, "the silent comment of the body in the coffin," to which the pawnbroker's discourse is oriented.[9] I would suggest that the body is a referent in and not an addressee of the hero's discourse. At one point, the narrator wonders why the meek one took any time at all in choosing him over the merchant as her husband. He asks: "Who was worse for her at the time?" and concludes, addressing an imaginary audience, "the answer lies on the table" (24:12). An "answer" cannot lie on a table. It has to be spoken by someone who would give it a unique inflection, emphasis, and meaning. Bakhtin himself writes: "It is one thing to be active in relation to a dead thing, to voiceless material that can be molded and formed as one wishes, and another thing to be active *in relation to someone else's living, autonomous consciousness*" (emphasis in original).[10]

Bakhtin captures, without meaning to, the hero's relation to the meek one. She is for the hero, in her life as in her death, inert "voiceless material" which he attempts to mold according to his wishes. The hero tells us that the consciousness of his cowardice tormented him, that he needed a "friend," but one that he "prepared" and "finished" (24:24). Having withstood the revolver, he took revenge on his past. He could no longer be considered a "scoundrel" in her eyes. But he decides to postpone the "denouement," even though he has "enough material." The hero says: "I decided to postpone our future" (24:23). The use of the literary term "denouement," the relation between "I" and "our," and the effort to manipulate time all suggest an image of the hero as an author, who would write not only his life, but that of another. All of this is on the surface. The hero admits it to us. He tells us how he tried to shape the heroine in accordance with his own desires. In molding her, he creates himself anew, not as a coward, but as a noble sufferer. The hero needs the heroine, as he tells us. That need has, as Bakhtin would put it, "form-shaping significance." The death of the "meek one" not only precipitates but is a necessary condition for the construction of the hero's "confessional self-utterance." That accounts, perhaps, for Dostoevsky's peculiar language in the preface to the story: "Imagine a husband, whose wife lies on the table" (24:5). The husband's existence as discourse depends on the body lying on the table.

If, as Bakhtin claims, "A Meek One" reveals Dostoevsky's radically new artistic form and radically new ethical relation to the person, then that new form and that new ethical relation depend on the victimizing of the female.

This relation holds true for much of Dostoevsky's writing, since most of Dostoevsky's heroes commit and confess to if not crimes, then at least transgressions against females. *Notes from Underground, Crime and Punishment*, and *The Possessed* (particularly Stavrogin's confession to Tikhon) provide further examples of confessional self-utterance that demands a female victim. The female protagonist in Dostoevsky provides the occasion for her representation as a victim in the confession of a male hero.[11]

This tentative conclusion leads to several questions. Perhaps examining the female protagonist in Dostoevsky in this way, from the perspective of the masculine confession, provides too narrow a focus. Of course the female is "finalized," rendered and represented as silent and prone, as Barbara Heldt puts it, in the discourse of the one who victimizes her (37). Certainly there are aspects of this matter that require further attention. What about Dostoevsky's female transgressors? What about female characters who appear independently of masculine confession? Are they nonetheless "inscribed . . . in someone else's story," to borrow from de Lauretis? Or do they "author" themselves in any significant way? Finally, are there markers of agency and subjectivity in Dostoevsky besides the production of "discourse," words?

WOMEN AND THE "WORD"

To answer these questions, let us first return to "A Meek One," and in particular, the striking image of the suicide. The heroine leaps from the window with the icon of the mother of God in her arms. Does the suicide have the power to mean taken separately from the hero's self-consciousness? The moral of the tale, perhaps, is that it does. The suicide signals the radical unknowability of another's consciousness. Can we say why the "meek one" kills herself? Dostoevsky juxtaposes the limits of the hero's self-consciousness—the hero thinks he knows everything, both the meaning of the suicide (it was an accident that he could have prevented) and our responses to his interpretation—with the unknown and hence open-ended interpretations of future readers. In terms of the narrative structure of the story, the suicide of the meek one becomes a place-marker for an ultimate open-endedness, even for that which cannot be stated because it cannot be known. The heroine's leap represents, in this reading, the limits of discourse, and paradoxically, the possibility of discourse, in the sense that it represents polyvalence. To be the condition of discourse or the limit of discourse is not, however, to be a participant in discourse.

The reading I have just suggested, however, neglects the remarkable detail of the icon. Dostoevsky created his fictitious suicide from a newspaper account of the suicide of a Maria Borisova, who jumped from the roof of a six-story building with an icon of the mother of God. Dostoevsky, reading the

Harriet Murav

story, wrote: "This icon in the arms is a strange and unheard of feature . . . this is a meek and humble suicide. Here there is no murmur or reproach: simply—it became impossible to live, 'God didn't want it,' and she died, praying" (23:146).

The detail of the icon suggests a view of the person not as a speaking subject, but as a creation in the image and likeness of God, who bears the image of the divine. (I shall address the question of gender in a moment.) The hero-narrator represents and renders the heroine as "silent and prone," as a corpse. He has the body, and does not want to give it up. All he sees are dead bodies: "Everything is dead, and all around are corpses. . . . 'People, love one another'—who said that? Whose testament is that?" (24:35).[12] The narrator has forgotten the figure of Jesus, has forgotten the possibility of resurrection.[13]

In Matthew, Mark, and Luke, the Resurrection is described in the episode of the visit of Mary Magdalene and "the other Mary" to Jesus' tomb. The women expect to find a corpse, which they will anoint with spices. As Louis Marin shows, "the anointing by the women at the tomb *was intended to preserve the body* as a dead body" (emphasis in original).[14] But the women discover the tomb to be empty. It is the absence of the body, its disappearance, and not its preservation, that signifies the Resurrection and thus the possibility of salvation. Marin argues that the burden of the narrative of the Resurrection is carried by this "blank space" in the text of the New Testament. Russian Orthodox iconography similarly uses the episode of the empty tomb to picture this fundamentally unrepresentable event.[15] I shall say more about the significance of the women's role later.

In the pawnbroker's hellish rewriting of the New Testament, Jesus' tomb would not be empty, but would contain a corpse. He can see only the corpse of the meek one, and speaks of corpses everywhere. To borrow an image from *The Idiot*, the pawnbroker's gospel would enshrine the Holbein Christ, which is a medically graphic portrait of a dead body, a portrait that could lead to a loss of faith. The object of the pawnbroker's desire, as I have argued, is, and always has been, the corpse of the meek one. But the reader can desire something else. We can read beyond the limits of the hero-narrator's interpretation. The meek one is not merely a dead body lying on a table. In taking the icon in her arms, and leaping to her death, the "meek one" transcends finalization. The meek one falls to the ground, but she is not ultimately bound by the laws of nature, or blind chance, as the narrator is. In carrying the icon of the mother of God in her arms, we can imagine that she seeks and receives intercession. She carries the icon and is being carried by the mother of God, born aloft. The Christological imagery of the scene resonates with an earlier passage, in which the narrator pokes his finger into the spoonful of blood next to her body, like doubting Thomas who pokes his finger into Jesus. The narrator has the last word, but the meek one is with the Word.

"A Meek One" reveals a pattern that may be found elsewhere in Dosto-evsky's writing. In *Crime and Punishment* Sonia Marmeladova reads John's account of the raising of Lazarus to a skeptical Raskolnikov. In so doing she is associated with the "Word" that resurrects, in opposition to Raskolnikov and his "new word" that kills.[16] In *The Possessed* Maria Lebiadkina exposes Stavrogin as an impostor. As Johanna Hubbs puts it, her "enigmatic pro-nouncements puncture the logic of the talkative . . . intellectuals around her husband." Hubbs shows that Maria is "an expression of Mary, the Mother of Christ, who waits in vain for her savior."[17] Maria defines the mother of God as "the great mother damp earth" (10:116). In *The Brothers Karamazov*, Alyosha remembers his "possessed" mother holding him before an icon of the mother of God. As in "A Meek One," in *The Brothers*, the icon is a dou-ble of the woman. Fyodor Karamazov torments his wife by threatening to desecrate her icon.[18]

In the Dostoevskian universe, as we may observe from these few exam-ples, the heroine's link with the madonna has a certain twist. In *Crime and Punishment* Svidrigailov comments to Raskolnikov that Raphael's Sistine madonna "has a fantastic face, the face of a suffering holy fool" (6:369). Dos-toevsky, according to his wife, made a similar observation. Dostoevsky's madonna is mad, described as either possessed or holy-foolish. Her dis-course consists of silence, sobs, and incoherence.[19]

It would seem significant that *The Idiot*'s Nastasia Filippovna, that rare Dostoevsky heroine who attempts to "author" her own life,[20] invents her own icon, substituting Christ for Mary and thereby feminizing the masculine divinity by putting him in the maternal role. Her icon of Christ, touching the head of a child who plays next to him (8:380), may reflect what Olga Matich has identified as the feminine and maternal features in Prince Myshkin.[21] There is an affinity between the "meek one" and Nastasia Filippovna, but there is also a great difference. The "meek one" enters the narrative as a corpse, but leaves united to a transcendent image. Nastasia Filippovna, in contrast, enters the narrative as an image—her portrait is circulated among various characters before we actually meet her—but she leaves as a corpse.

"A Meek One" simultaneously inscribes its heroine as an occasion for representation in another's "self-utterance" and as that which transcends representation in utterance. Whatever woman is in Dostoevsky—absence, image, memory trace, a blank space, albeit a Christological blank space—she is not a speaking subject. In the Christian context in which she is found, sub-jectivity is not constituted by self-utterance, but by proximity to the divinity. The pawnbroker is correct, in a certain sense, when he says that "in women there is no originality" (24:15).[22] In his reinvention of Christianity for late nineteenth-century Russia (in distinction from his reinvention of the novel as an artistic form), Dostoevsky does not value "originality" (that is, in the sense of self-definition, or, to use Bakhtin's term, "self-utterance") in either the female or the male protagonist.[23] Alyosha Karamazov, for example, who is particularly associated with the icon of the mother of God, and who in the novelistic universe of *The Brothers* plays the role of Mary the intercessor, is not "original," but a "plagiarist."

As noted, "A Meek One" appeared in the November issue of Dostoevsky's *A Writer's Diary* for 1876. In the October issue, in a piece entitled "Two Suicides," Dostoevsky also writes about the "meek one"; that is, about her real-life prototype, Maria Borisova (*WD*, 650–53). We have already mentioned Dostoevsky's comments about this death, how it was, in his view, a humble submission to the will of God. In "Two Suicides" Dostoevsky juxtaposes Borisova's death with that of Liza Herzen, daughter of Alexander Herzen. The narration of this event offers a direct and explicit contrast not only to the journalistic remarks on Borisova but to the fiction created out of her death, namely, "A Meek One."[24] An examination of the *Diary* account of Liza Herzen's suicide offers the opportunity to return to the questions posed earlier: What is the relation between author and heroine? To what extent is the "finalization" of the female a necessary ingredient of Dostoevskian discourse?

A WOMAN'S DYING WORD: LIZA HERZEN

In the Borisova suicide the outstanding detail is the icon of the mother of God. But in the Herzen suicide the details that Dostoevsky finds "curious" are the cotton wadding and chloroform. Dostoevsky tells us that according to the newspapers, Liza Herzen "soaked some cotton wadding in chloroform, tied it around her face, and lay down on a bed" (23:145). Dostoevsky then reproduces what he tells us is the suicide note, both in the original French and in Russian: "I am setting off on a long journey. If the suicide does not succeed, let everyone get together to celebrate my resurrection from the dead with glasses of Cliquot. But if it does succeed, I only ask that I not be buried until it has been made certain that I am dead, because it is very unpleasant to come to in a coffin under the ground. *It is not chic!*" (23:145).

The text Dostoevsky provides his readers does not correspond to the original in several respects, the most outstanding being the line "it is not chic."[25] Dostoevsky finds the interpolated line to be the most offensive feature of the note: "in this vile, coarse 'chic,' in my opinion, can be heard a challenge, perhaps indignation, spite—but at what?" (23:145). He then goes on to answer his own question: "At what could there be indignation? . . . At the simplicity of what manifests itself, at the emptiness of life? Is it what those too well known judges and deniers of life become indignant about: the 'stupidity' of the appearance of man on earth, the senseless accident of that appearance, at the tyranny of the inert cause, with which it is impossible to reconcile oneself?" (23:145, ellipsis in original). According to Dostoevsky, Liza Herzen was taught to believe from childhood on in a universe in which the material phenomena of life in the here and now represent the limit of human existence and human knowledge. He goes on to say that although she accepted this belief, she could not tolerate it—her "soul demanded something more complicated" (23:146).

In his account of Liza Herzen's suicide Dostoevsky emphasizes what he perceives as her existential despair. That Dostoevsky is a good judge of character can be seen from another letter Liza Herzen wrote, one that was not available to him at the time, in which she says that "life . . . is a flat and stupid joke, an unsuccessful pun."[26] Dostoevsky concludes that Liza Herzen killed herself because her materialistic set of beliefs did not satisfy her soul's need. She killed herself because of an idea that failed her. Dostoevsky describes a consciousness that cannot accept the limits it has no choice but to believe in. This consciousness and the language in which it expresses itself strikingly resembles what we see in Dostoevsky's male protagonists. The narrator of "A Meek One" rails against the laws of chance, using the same term "inert" that Dostoevsky ascribes to Herzen. The hero of *Notes from Underground* also protests against the laws of nature. As Bakhtin writes, the hero's "thought is developed and structured as *the thought of someone personally insulted by the world order*, personally humiliated by its blind necessity" (236).

In the emphasis on the ideational causes of the death, Dostoevsky's essay in the *Diary* differs significantly from other accounts of the suicide available at the time. The newspaper *Golos*, for example, blames "the despotism of the stepmother and hopeless love for a certain Italian doctor."[27] Dostoevsky's source for the suicide note, Pobedonostsev, says that Liza Herzen was "of course raised from childhood in complete materialism and atheism." But he devotes most of his attention to what he calls the "hell" of daily life in the Herzen–Ogarev household. Herzen himself, according to Pobedonostsev, said about Ogareva: "c'est une vipère." Pobedonostsev writes: "the daughter . . . is as venomous as the mother, and the daughter and the mother hated one another and squabbled from morning to night."[28] The scene that Pobedonostsev creates of two infernal, snake-like women who seek to destroy one another could come out of one of Dostoevsky's novels: Nastasia Filippovna and Aglaia in *The Idiot*, or later, Grushenka and Katerina Ivanovna in *The Brothers Karamazov*.

In contrast, Dostoevsky constructs Liza Herzen as a heroine with an idea, and as a heroine who produces discourse. In December 1876 (*WD*, 740–42), Dostoevsky returns to the story of Liza Herzen.[29] A correspondent had insisted that the suicide did not merit much attention. Since Liza Herzen wanted to celebrate her "resurrection" with champagne, "she did not suffer much in this life." In response to this complaint Dostoevsky offers a

53

remarkable reading of the suicide note. He gives the correspondent a lesson in how to read what Bakhtin calls "the word with a sidelong glance."

Bakhtin defines this type of speech in his analysis of *Notes from Underground*. He describes the discourse of the hero as follows: "The destruction of one's own image in another's eyes, the sullying of that image in another's eyes as an ultimate desperate effort to free oneself from the power of the other's consciousness and to break through to one's self for the self alone—this, in fact, is the orientation of the Underground Man's entire confession. For this reason he makes his discourse about himself deliberately ugly" (232). Dostoevsky's answer to the correspondent, particularly with regard to the champagne, offers a strikingly similar interpretation. Liza Herzen wrote about champagne, Dostoevsky says, in order to give her suicide a certain "twist" that was "more insolent and dirtier" (24:53). "She picked champagne because she "could not find anything dirtier or more insolent than this picture of drinking it on the occasion of her 'resurrection from the dead'" (24:53). According to Dostoevsky, Liza Herzen felt the need "to offend . . . everything that she left on earth, to curse the earth and her earthly life, to spit at it and display this spit to those close to her" (24:53–54). In this very strong language we see what Bakhtin calls "the destruction of one's own image in another's eyes." As Dostoevsky reads the suicide note, Liza Herzen's words represent a calculated effort to repulse others. Dostoevsky stresses that Liza Herzen's discourse about herself is, as Bakhtin says with respect to the underground hero's, "deliberately ugly."

But underneath the deliberate distortion Dostoevsky finds suffering: "But precisely this note, precisely because she was so *interested* in creating such a dirty and malicious twist at such a moment, precisely this leads to the thought that her life was immeasurably purer than this dirty twist . . . and that the immeasurable malice of this twist bears witness, on the contrary, to her suffering, tormented state of mind, to her despair at the last minute of her life" (24:54). In this reading of the suicide note, we can see Dostoevsky's dialogic address to the woman inside the woman, to paraphrase the much-quoted line from his 1880 notebooks: "with utter realism to find the man in man" (27:65). Bakhtin draws attention to this type of address, which he calls the "penetrative word," a word that finds and activates the "interior dialogue of another person" (242). Dostoevsky's reading of this suicide does not finalize the female protagonist, as does his fictitious narrator in "A Meek One." That narrator uses his eye, his all-knowing silent gaze, to render and represent his wife as a corpse. She has no voice, she is only a body. Even if she were to come back to life, he wants only to be able to look at her. Even if she were to live again, he would make her into an object. Unlike that narrator, Dostoevsky here uses not his eye, but his ear. He hears another voice and speaks to it. Dostoevsky's reading of Liza Herzen's suicide note seeks to awaken this other voice of suffering, hidden under a mask of "dirt."

54

It is not only in the two essays on Liza Herzen's suicide and "A Meek One" that Dostoevsky shows his special skill at "reading women," but more generally, in the 1876 *Diary* as a whole. A quick overview of this year reveals Dostoevsky's preoccupation with woman. The May issue opens with a discussion of a female would-be murderer, Kairova (*WD*, 470–90). In later installments for May, Dostoevsky discusses a foundling home, and writes about a young woman, Pisareva, who committed suicide. The June issue opens with the death of George Sand, and closes with a discussion of a young woman correspondent, who reminds Dostoevsky of a George Sand heroine. The October issue opens with "A Case That Is Not as Simple as It Seems": a pregnant woman, Kornilova, threw her stepdaughter out a window (*WD*, 640–47). December returns to this case, covers the Liza Herzen suicide, and closes with "A Story from the Lives of Children," a piece about an adolescent girl's experiment with independence and with sexuality (*WD*, 743–48). The girl runs away from her mother for a few days to live on the streets. Dostoevsky comments that "this age (twelve to thirteen) is unusually interesting, in a girl even more than in a boy" (24:58). To be sure, Dostoevsky relies upon stereotypical women's roles in some of these pieces, but for the most part he allows for nuance and complexity.

Dostoevsky's analysis of the Kairova case, like his analysis of Liza Herzen's suicide, goes beyond stereotypes.[30] Kairova had attacked her lover's wife with a razor blade, leaving her victim alive and not seriously injured. The jury acquitted her of the charge of premeditated murder. A correspondent demands to know why the *Diary* is silent about this criminal, for whom nothing was sacred except her own "sexual instincts" (23:5). Dostoevsky comments: "You will say that Kairova's crime was not premeditated, not cerebral, not bookish, but simply 'women's business' [bab'ie delo], not at all complex" (23:9–10). Dostoevsky then proceeds to lay out the complexities, questioning whether Kairova's intention could be deduced from the fact of her unfinished crime. Dostoevsky imagines Kairova now as a timid and unwilling criminal, who would have thrown her weapon away; now as a monster, who would have not only killed her victim, but mutilated the corpse, chopping off her head, nose, and lips. Both outcomes are possible, Dostoevsky argues.

"Women's business" in *A Writer's Diary* goes beyond self-sacrificing love, beyond woman as the bearer of the word. Here, women deliberate, plan, have ideas, and commit crimes, even the unthinkable crimes against children, the kind that Dostoevsky's heroes commit. *A Writer's Diary*, unlike the major fiction, foregrounds the woman protagonist as such, as actor, agent, author, as sexual being, and perhaps especially, as criminal.

What enables Dostoevsky to put pen and sword—or razor blade—into the hand of his madonnas? In order to answer this question, we must consider the configuration of gender roles that producing the *Diary* entails. It is significant that in *The Possessed* the embryonic form of the *Diary* is sketched out by a female character. Liza proposes to Shatov that they publish a year-book of Russian life that would contain "curious incidents, . . . every word and speech . . . with a certain point of view, . . . with an idea that would illuminate the whole" (10:104).[31] Is the ideal diarist a woman? In our analysis of Dostoevsky's responses to Liza Herzen's suicide, we saw that Dostoevsky placed special emphasis on his skill at reading beyond the surface of her text to the suffering that it concealed. Bakhtin uses a masculine coded term, "the penetrative word," to describe this kind of interpretation, which he calls the dialogic address to another's interior voice. I suggest, in contrast, that Dostoevsky as reader of Liza Herzen, and as diarist in general, is playing a role that he himself has coded as feminine in his fiction.

If Dostoevsky may be said to have cast Liza Herzen in the role of one of his underground heroes, then he casts himself, to some extent, in the role of Liza the prostitute, who understands that the underground hero is suffering. He plays Sonia Marmeladova to Raskolnikov. Sonia is the incarnation of "insatiable compassion" (6:243). Dostoevsky uses the same language to characterize Raskolnikov and Liza Herzen. In *Crime and Punishment* Raskolnikov is told that he needs "some air" (6:351); in his first essay on Liza Herzen, Dostoevsky comments that "it became stifling, as if there were not enough air" (23:146). To use another example, Dostoevsky is to Liza Herzen as Prince Myshkin is to Nastasia Filippovna in *The Idiot*. As Bakhtin argues, Prince Myshkin stops Nastasia Filippovna "when she is desperately playing out the role of 'fallen woman'" in front of the Ivolgin family (242). Nastasia Filippovna confesses that she is not what she makes herself out to be, and that the Prince has figured her out.[32] Prince Myshkin, as we have already seen, is a feminized hero.

In our analysis of Dostoevsky's account of Liza Herzen's suicide we have come full circle. We began with the image of the hero-narrator of "A Meek One," who renders and represents the heroine as a dead body. We saw how the Dostoevskian madonna escapes finalization in the hero's discourse by her association with a transcendent discourse. In this final example, we have seen how Dostoevsky trades gender roles with his fictitious heroines, and feminized heroes, who read beyond the surface of another's words to the voice within.[33]

The prototype for woman reading in Dostoevsky, the significance of reading as a feminine activity—at least in its benign sense—may be found in the Gospels. I have already discussed the scene at Christ's empty tomb, but more details can be added now. The women who got to the tomb are Mary Magdalene and Mary the mother of James. An angel tells them the significance of their discovery and instructs them to inform the disciples that Christ has risen. Marin, whom we quoted earlier, argues that the angel's discourse is essentially a reading lesson: "it teaches them [the women] to *read* the facts and events, like a text, where the spaces, absences, or blanks signify—forever—some fillings or presences" (emphasis in original).[34] The women come for the body, but receive instead the word, in multiple senses of the term.

Reading the blank spaces and then bearing a message of salvation is very much a part of Dostoevsky's project in *A Writer's Diary*. The "text" is not the life of Jesus, but the life of Russia. Dostoevsky assigns to himself the Mariological role of bearing the new word of Russia's resurrection. In what is either a blurring of gender roles, or yet another appropriation of feminine power, Dostoevsky takes on the "women's work" of reading with a messianic fervor. In taking on the reader's role for himself in the *Diary*, Dostoevsky permits his real life female protagonists to author themselves, at least to some extent, because he will be their best reader.

Gary Saul Morson

Sonya's Wisdom

> It is natural for a man who does not understand the work-
> ings of a machine to imagine that a chip that has fallen into
> it by accident and is tossing about and impeding its action
> is the important part of the mechanism. Anyone who does
> not understand the construction of the machine cannot
> conceive that it is not the chip . . . but that noiselessly
> revolving little transmission gear which is one of the most
> essential parts of the machine.
> —Leo Tolstoy, *War and Peace*

CHEKHOV AND TOLSTOY stand out as the two most
important Russian writers committed to a view of life that might be called
prosaics.[1] They believed that the most important events in life are not the
dramatic ones that play so large a role in narrative art and romantic ideology
but the ordinary ones we usually do not even notice. In their view, life is
made up of the small incidents of daily life, and selves are shaped by the "tiny
alterations" of consciousness that happen at every moment.[2] Real goodness
consists not of great sacrifices accompanied by impressive rhetoric but of
everyday kindness and goodness. By the same token, real love does not
resemble the great passions of romantic novels; it is not mysterious, tragic, or
fated, as in the stories of Tristan and Iseult or Romeo and Juliet. Rather, it
cultivates the closeness and intimacy of a devoted married couple. Wherever the authors of *Anna Karenina* and *Uncle Vanya* saw melodrama, they
detected falsity.[3]

Tolstoy and Chekhov understood wisdom not as the sort of theoretical
knowledge favored by intellectuals but as the kind of practical wisdom that
helps one in ordinary circumstances. That is why both writers were so hostile
to the intelligentsia. At the end of *Anna Karenina*, Levin learns the menda-
cious pride of abstract intellect, "and not merely the pride of intellect, but
the stupidity of intellect. And most of all, the deceitfulness; yes, the deceitfulness of intellect."[4] Chekhov, too, never tired of pointing out that intellectuals tend to undervalue the practical wisdom of decent people, whose lives

58

they find horribly boring or bourgeois. In his plays, lives are redeemed or wasted by unremarkable actions, daily behavior, and prosaic attention to (or neglect of) others. It is not so much our dreams as our habits that make us who we are.

Both writers therefore tended to construct plots in which a grand or romantic character occupies the foreground: he or she provides the story's dramatic interest. But in the background, calling no attention to herself, there is usually a heroine—Dolly in *Anna Karenina*, Pashenka in Tolstoy's "Father Sergius," or the mother and sister in Chekhov's "House with a Mansard"—who offers an image of real goodness. In this way, Chekhov and Tolstoy make strategic use of what might be called "the decoy technique"; a dramatic character appears to be the most important, but, in these works as in life, the really important people are ones we do not especially notice or value. We must learn to reverse our perceptions.

The real hero of *Uncle Vanya* (that is, the character whom the author values most highly) is Sonya, whose kindness makes life tolerable for the others. The "decoy technique" occurs in the very title of the play. The title overtly names Voinitsky as its central character, and he is indeed the hero of the play's dramatic plot. It is only upon reflection that we recognize that the title also silently evokes Sonya, the undervalued heroine. Voinitsky, after all, is *her* uncle. She alone could call him, with all her touching affection, "Uncle Vanya." (In Russian, Vanya is a diminutive: the title might be rendered "Uncle Johnnie.") Although punctuation is omitted, the title is nevertheless a quotation and therefore tacitly indicates its speaker.

The stage directions work much the same way when they state, with an irony that is apparent only retrospectively, that "the action takes place on the Serebryakov's estate" (*v usad'be Serebriakova*), a phrase that gives the estate to the old professor. In fact, as we learn later when Serebryakov makes his proposal to dispossess his daughter and brother-in-law, the estate belongs not to him, nor even to the Serebryakov family, but to Sonya alone, who has inherited it from her mother. She herself seems barely aware that it is hers and hers alone, and certainly does not treat others as guests. As far as Sonya's behavior is concerned, the estate might as well be her father's, as the stage directions say. As if she were a steward, she manages the land and ensures its profitability. The truly important person, who makes the wealth and life of all the others possible, does her daily work while the others—and the audience—direct their attention elsewhere.

One can appreciate Chekhov's radical innovations in the theater from this prosaic perspective. Of all literary art forms, drama tends to be the most, well, *dramatic*, but Chekhov believed that our interest in the dramatic is harmful. It might even be said that the fundamental theme of Chekhov's plays is theatricality itself, our tendency to live our lives "dramatically." Life, as Chekhov understood it, does not generally conform to staged plots, except when people try to endow their existence with spurious meaningfulness by imitating literary characters and plots, as, unfortunately, people often do. They create "scenes," as we say. In Chekhov, traditional plays imitate life only to the extent that people imitate plays.

Chekhov's major characters typically behave in such a false and melo-dramatic way. His plays center on histrionic people who imitate theatrical performances and model themselves on other melodramatic genres. They posture, seek grand romance, imagine that a tragic fatalism governs their lives, and indulge in utopian dreams while they neglect the ordinary virtues and ignore the daily processes that truly sustain them. The dramatic—or rather, undramatic—exception is Sonya.

Because histrionics is Chekhov's central theme, his plays rely on metatheatrical devices, which show us why the world is *not* a stage and why we should be suspicious whenever it seems to resemble a play. In most plays, people behave "dramatically" in a world where such behavior is appropriate. The audience, which lives in the undramatic world we all know, participates in the more interesting and exciting world of the stage. That, indeed, is one reason people go to plays. In *Uncle Vanya*, by contrast, the world in which the characters live resembles everyday life, but the characters nevertheless go on behaving "dramatically." Consequently, actions that would be tragic or heroic in other plays here acquire the tonality of comedy, or even farce. Chekhov wanted to satirize histrionic living, which he regarded (like all romanticism) as a particularly loathsome form of lying.

Chekhov's major characters are "generic refugees": they act as if they lived in a world of melodrama and romantic fiction, but they are brought into a prosaic world where their poses are revealed as such. In *Uncle Vanya*, therefore, we sense that the main characters are always "overacting." One reason this play has proved so difficult to stage in the right tonality is that the actors must overact and call attention to their theatrical status, *but without ceasing to play real people who truly suffer*. They must not over-overact. Their performance must allude to, but not shatter, the dramatic frame. When we watch *Uncle Vanya*, we do not see actors playing characters, but characters playing characters. They labor under the delusion that this role playing brings them closer to "true life," but in fact it does the opposite. Or, to put the point differently, the audience contemplates real people—people like themselves—who live *citational lives*; that is, lives shaped by literary role playing, lives consisting not so much of actions as allusions. "They say that Turgenev developed angina pectoris from gout. I am afraid I may have it," declares Serebryakov, who, like other characters, would make his very ill-nesses literary (187). We are asked to consider how much of our own lives is citational.

Voinitsky once believed in his mother and in the professor, but has come to recognize their falsehood and cruelty. His mother is portrayed as a typical member of the intelligentsia, always babbling about "the emancipation of women" while urging everyone blindly to obey the old professor. We constantly see her making notes "on the margins of her pamphlet." This stage direction closes act 1, and the phrase is repeated by a number of characters, so by the time the stage directions repeat it at the very end of the play, we sense how irritating and shallow a person this progressive intellectual is. Voinitsky is surely right when he remarks that his mother's "principles" are "a venomous joke" (180). But it is not so much her vacuity as her small, incessant acts of cruelty to her son that deprive her of the audience's sympathy. As her son regrets his wasted life, she reproaches him in canned phrases for not caring more about the latest intellectual movements. We may imagine that his rage at the professor's proposal to deprive him of the estate is fueled by resentment of his mother, who repeats, as she has evidently done many times before, "Jean, don't contradict Alexander. Believe me, he knows better than we do what is right and wrong" (214). Vanya's mother incarnates the combination of grand principles with petty cruelty and neglect.

Vanya has also become disillusioned with the professor's pretensions. He has lived his life in the belief that in working to support the professor's activities as a literary critic, he has been contributing, however vicariously, to great art. He has now recognized that the professor's work is nothing but a modish tangle of empty jargon. But rather than question his fundamental beliefs, he decides that he chose the wrong professor, or should have become one himself. Filled with impotent rage, he regrets histrionically that he is too old to surpass Serebryakov. Chekhov brilliantly merges despair and slapstick humor when Voinitsky declares: "My life is over! I was talented, intelligent, self-confident. . . . If I had led a normal life, I might have been a Schopenhauer, a Dostoevsky. . . ." (216; ellipsis in original). To put it mildly, the choice of Dostoevsky as an example of someone who loved "a normal life" is an odd one.

Like the doctor Astrov, Elena Andreevna, Serebryakov's young wife, combines prosaic insight with melodramatic blindness. Although these two often fail to live up to their own recommendations, they do glimpse the value of ordinary virtues. They even grasp the danger of melodrama, grand rhetoric, and cited self-pity, even if all three vices infect their own speeches. For this reason, Chekhov can use their words to enunciate the play's central values while illustrating the consequences of not taking those values seriously enough.

Elena comes closest to a Chekhovian sermon when she fends off Voinitsky:

ELENA ANDREEVNA: Ivan Petrovich, you are an educated, intelligent man, and I should think you would understand that the world is being destroyed not by crime and fire, but by . . . all these petty squabbles. . . . Your business should be not to grumble, but to reconcile us to one another.

VOINITSKY: First reconcile me to myself! My darling . . .

(191; ellipsis in original).

Elena is quite right that life is spoiled not by dramatic disappointments but by "petty squabbles." All the more ironic, then, that in praising prosaic virtues she cannot avoid the rhetoric of apocalypse.

Elena understands that (as she understates the point) "there is something very wrong in this house" (190), but she does not grasp what would be right. We first see her in act 1 ignoring, almost to the point of the grotesque, the feelings of Telegin:

TELEGIN: The temperature of the samovar has fallen precipitously.

ELENA ANDREEVNA: Never mind, Ivan Ivanovich, we'll drink it cold.

TELEGIN: I beg your pardon . . . I am not Ivan Ivanovich, but Ilya Ilych . . . Ilya Ilych Telegin, or as some people call me because of my pock-marked face, Waffles. I am Sonichka's godfather; and His Excellency, your husband, knows me quite well. I live here now, on your estate. . . . You may have been so kind as to notice that I have dinner with you every day.

SONYA: Ilya Ilych is our helper, our right hand. [*Tenderly*] Let me give you some more tea, godfather.

(179–80; ellipses in original).

If these lines are performed as I think Chekhov meant them, one will detect no reproach, no irony, in Telegin's voice. He has so little self-esteem that he expects to be overlooked, and so he reminds people of his own existence out of a sincere sense that he is too insignificant for anyone to remember. Chekhov uses Telegin as a touchstone for the basic decency of other characters: Is it worth their while to be kind to someone who is obviously of no use to anyone? In this scene, Elena fails the test and Sonya, who calls him "Godfather," passes it.

Unlike Sonya, Elena does not work but, as Astrov correctly observes, infects everyone with her idleness. The old nurse, another prosaically virtuous character, speaks correctly when she complains that the household's ills derive largely from the visitors' disruption of old habits and schedules related to work. Instead, a purely whimsical relation to time now rules, so that Marina has to get the samovar ready at 1:30 in the morning.

Intellectuals may view habits as numbing, but from the standpoint of prosaics, good or bad habits shape a life more than anything else. That is because attention is a limited resource, and most of what we do, we do by habit. Moreover, habits result from countless earlier decisions, and for Chekhov they can therefore serve as a good index to a person's values and past behavior. Relying on beauty and high ideals, Elena does not appreciate the importance of habits, routine, and work. For her, life becomes meaning-ful at times of high drama, grand sacrifice, or passionate romance—that is, at exceptional moments—which is why she is bored when those moments are over. Sonya tries to suggest to her a different view. She values daily work and unexceptional moments, but Elena cannot understand:

> ELENA ANDREEVNA: . . . [*In misery*] I'm dying of boredom, I don't know what to do.
> SONYA [*shrugging her shoulders*] Isn't there plenty to do? If you only wanted to . . . [ellipsis in original]
> ELENA ANDREEVNA: For instance?
> SONYA: You could help with running the estate, teach, take care of the sick. Isn't that enough? When you and Papa were not here, Uncle Vanya and I used to go to market ourselves to sell the flour.
> ELENA ANDREEVNA: I don't know how to do such things. And it isn't interesting. Only in idealistic novels do people teach and doctor the peasants, and how can I, for no reason whatever, suddenly start teaching and looking after peasants?
> SONYA: I don't see how one can help doing it. Wait a bit, you'll get accustomed to it. [*Embraces her*] Don't be bored, darling.
> (203)

Given Elena's usual ways of thinking, she misunderstands Sonya and trans-lates her recommendations into a speech from "an idealistic novel." That, presumably, is why she ignores the possibility of helping with the estate and singles out doctoring the peasants. She imagines Sonya offers a ridiculous populist idyll.

If that is what Sonya meant, of course Elena's objections would be apt. Elena has in mind work as idealized by intellectuals—work to serve human-ity in the abstract—which she correctly rejects as work "for no reason what-ever." What she cannot understand is the possibility of a different kind of work that could be meaningful: prosaic work. Thinking like an intellectual, she believes that either meaning is grand and transcendent or else that it is absent. Her mistake in marrying the professor has convinced her that tran-scendent meaning is an illusion, and so she, like Voinitsky, can imagine only the opposite, a meaningless world of empty routine. But Sonya's actual rec-ommendation is quite different. She takes care of the estate not to serve humanity, but because it *has to be done*; it is, as Levin says in *Anna Kareni-na*, "incontestably necessary" (823). It pains her to see waste or rotting hay. Chekhov had utter contempt for the intelligentsia's disdain for efficiency, profitability, and the sort of deliberate calculation needed to avoid waste. That is one reason the play ends with the long-delayed recording of prices for agricultural products. And Sonya is not recommending serving humanity in general but being kind to the people around one; for Sonya, such people are not representatives of "the People" but her neighbors in need of help.

When Elena characterizes helping the peasants as a literary pose, Sonya replies that she does not see "how one can help doing it." For Sonya, it is not a pose and serves no ideology, but is part of her general habit of caring for people. High ideals or philosophy have nothing to do with what she is saying, as we see when she responds to Elena not with a counterargument but with a sympathetic embrace. Sonya understands that both work and care require *habits* of working and caring, and such habits can not be picked up "suddenly," as Elena correctly observes. But they can be acquired bit by tiny bit. Elena's problem is that she has the wrong habits. What she does not see is that she needs to begin acquiring new ones, which is what Sonya is trying to tell her.

Least of all does Elena need romance, which is what Astrov offers. Like Elena and Voinitsky, Astrov is obsessed with the vision of a brief, ecstatic affair in a literary setting—love in the poetic autumn, amid "the dilapidated country houses in the style of Turgenev" (225). He wants a citational affair. Indeed, Astrov constantly looks for literary images to explain his life. "What's the use?" he says at the beginning of the play. "In one of Ostrovsky's plays there's a man with a large mustache and small abilities. That's me" (182). These self-pitying allusions make him a good example of the "more intelligent" members of the intelligentsia he complains about:

> ASTROV: . . . it's hard to get along with the intelligentsia. . . . All of them, all our good friends here, think and feel in a small way, they see no farther than the end of their noses . . . And those who are more intelligent and more outstanding, are hysterical, eaten up with analysis and introspection. . . . [ellipsis here in original] They whine. . . . [*He is about to drink*]
>
> SONYA [*stopping him*]: No, please, I beg you, don't drink any more.
> (197)

Of course, this very speech exemplifies the intelligentsia's indulgence in self-pitying self-analysis. Astrov whines about whining, and what's more he knows it. But this knowledge does him no good, as Sonya sees.

Some self-destructive behavior can be modified by an awareness of what one is doing, but not the sort of introspection that Astrov describes. On the contrary, the more one is aware of it, the more that awareness becomes a part of it.[5] As Karl Kraus once quipped, psychoanalysis is the disease it purports to cure. The more Astrov blames himself for whining, and for whining about whining, the more he whines about it. This sort of self-pity feeds on itself; so does alcoholic self-pity, which is why Chekhov has him drink while complaining.

To persuade him not to drink, Sonya reminds Astrov of his own speeches about waste: "You always say people don't create, but merely destroy what

64

has been given them from above. Then why are you destroying yourself?" (197). Sonya refers to Astrov's sermons about what we would today call "the environment." So contemporary do these sermons sound that it is hard to see them in the context of Chekhov's play, where they mean something rather different. For Astrov does not object to any and all destruction of trees: "You will say that . . . the old life must naturally give place to the new. Yes, I understand, and if in place of these devastated forests there were highways, railroads, if there were factories, mills, schools, and the people had become healthier, richer, more intelligent—but, you see, there is nothing of the sort!" (208). The chamber of commerce would concur.

What bothers Astrov, and what bothers Chekhov, is *waste*. And waste results not from the lack of great ideals but from lack of daily care. The forests disappear for the same reason that the hay rots: not because of evil industrialists but because, as Astrov says, "lazy man hasn't sense enough to stoop down and pick up fuel from the ground" (183). What destroys forests is not some great social evil but everyday laziness and bad habits or, more accurately, the lack of good ones. Destruction results from what we do *not* do.

Astrov (and Sonya as she repeats the speeches of the man she loves) also give voice to the prosaic view that the ruin of forests, like all lack of care about our surroundings, is not just a symbol but also a cause of impoverished lives. To paraphrase their thought: the background of our lives imperceptibly shapes them, because what happens constantly at the periphery of our attention, what is so familiar we do not even notice it, modifies the tiny alterations of our thoughts. Literally and figuratively, our surroundings temper the "climate" of our minds. Like good housekeeping and careful estate management, unwasted forests subtly condition the lives unfolding in their midst.

Where Astrov and Sonya go wrong is in their rhetoric, which, like Elena's, rapidly becomes apocalyptic or utopian. They praise undramatic care with rhetorical declamation. Paraphrasing Astrov, Sonya says that forests temper the climate and that where climate is mild, "less energy is wasted in the struggle with nature, so man is softer and more tender; in such countries the people are beautiful, flexible, easily stirred, their speech is elegant, their gestures graceful. Science and art flourish among them, their philosophy is not somber, and their attitude toward women is full of an exquisite courtesy" (183). Astrov, like so many Chekhov characters, imagines the glorious future: by planting trees, he explains, he contributes to the climate, and "if a thousand years from now, mankind is happy, I shall be responsible for that too, in a small way. When I plant a birch tree and then watch it put forth its leaves and sway in the wind, my soul is filled with pride, and I . . . [*seeing the workman who has brought a glass of vodka on a tray*] however . . . [*Drinks*]" (184; ellipses in original).

They ask a lot from trees. Sonya's enthusiasm reflects her love for

Astrov, but what does Astrov's reflect? In his millenarian references, we sense his unprosaic tendency, in spite of all he believes, to think in terms of drama, utopia, and romance—and to drink.

Astrov's failure to take his own ideals seriously leads him to his wasteful view of love. He seeks not a happy marriage with Sonya but a brief, adulterous, romantic affair with Elena. John Styan is correct when he writes that if Astrov "could have loved Sonya, they could have been happy," but he is uncharacteristically mistaken when he adds: "that he cannot love her is an example of the pure arbitrariness of life."[6] To gloss the play this way is to accept the very romantic view of love that Chekhov means to question. It is to view love as *passion*, as something one merely suffers as from a potion, like Tristan and Iseult. And it is to overlook a different kind of love, based on intimacy and friendship, which for Astrov is there for the asking.[7]

Critics have missed what I take to be the key scene in the play. Handled with infinite subtlety by Chekhov, it occurs in act 4, just before Sonya's final speech, which is in fact a response to it. Preparing to leave, Astrov is drawn to Sonya, and seems to reconsider his romantic view of love but then does *not* propose to her. This nonproposal scene evidently echoes the nonproposal of Koznyshev to Varenka in *Anna Karenina* and looks forward to Lopakhin's famous nonproposal scene at the close of *The Cherry Orchard*. The difference is that in those works the action that does not happen is explicitly identified as such because the other characters talk about the proposal they expect. In *Uncle Vanya*, the clues are much subtler and so are easy to miss.

Chekhov appears to be using the decoy technique. To illustrate his theme that the most important events occur right before our eyes although we do not notice them, he places his nonproposal firmly on the margins. Our attention is directed elsewhere. The whole fourth act has been one of departure. The Serebryakovs have left, and we expect Astrov to leave as well. Voinitsky has just said that "Everything will be just as it was" (226), so least of all do we anticipate the possibility of a significant change.

The old professor and his wife are gone; a scene of quiet work begins. Astrov, too, has worked here; it has been his refuge. He has often rewarded himself for a month or so of medical labor by escaping here to work on his map. He presumably knows this room quite well, and regrets its loss. We see him "clearing away his paints from the table and putting them in his suitcase" (227) and we sense his sadness. As he prepares to leave, we may suppose that the thought occurs to him that this temporary home could be permanent, that he could be happy here, and could make someone he cares for happy, if only he did not seek the sort of love represented by Elena, whom he has just kissed. He thinks out loud:

ASTROV: It's quiet. . . . Pens scratching . . . crickets chirping. . . . It's warm and cozy. I don't feel like leaving. [*There is the sound of bells.*] They're bringing my horses

. . . . Now nothing remains but to say good-bye to you, my friends, to say good-bye to my table—and be off! [*He puts his charts into a portfolio.*]
MARINA: Why so restless? You should stay. . . .
(228; ellipses in original).

All have agreed that Astrov should no longer stay at the house unless he means to marry Sonya, so Marina's invitation is rich in unvoiced possibility, as is her attempt to delay him with tea, snacks, and vodka. The table to which Astrov says good-bye is his place for work in a house centered around such work. He does not want to leave, and he gives indirect indications that he is reconsidering. He mentions the table, "pauses," waits around, accepts a glass of vodka; and then two more displaced statements of a longing to stay occur:

ASTROV [*after a pause*]: My trace horse has gone lame for some reason. I noticed it
  yesterday when Petrushka led him out to water.
VOINITSKY: You must reshoe him.
ASTROV: I'll have to stop at the blacksmith's at Rozhdestvennoye. There's no help
  for it. [*Goes to the map of Africa and looks at it.*] Out there in Africa now, I
  expect the heat must be terrific.
VOINITSKY: Yes, very likely.
(229)

A lame horse offers a plausible reason to stay, but Voinitsky (unlike Marina and Sonya) misses the point. The reference to the map of Africa has been misunderstood more than any line in the play. Some have taken it as typical of Chekhov's surrealism, and for the excellent Russian scholar A. P. Chudakov, it exemplifies pure irrelevancy in a wholly contingent universe—explanations that work elsewhere in Chekhov but that miss the mark in this case.[8] Astrov's comment exemplifies not irrelevancy but another Chekhovian device, displacement. In mentioning the map, Astrov refers obliquely to his own map. He evokes the aura of the room in which he has worked with great joy and tacitly suggests the possibility of staying. But the very fact that he speaks with such indirection indicates that, for all his hesitation, he will not change his mind.

An affair with Elena and the other literary gestures valued by Chekhov's characters seem to resonate with meaning for them, as prosaic kindness and work do not. Entranced by dramatic meaninglessness, they try to transform their lives into theater, because even a tragic drama offers them a significant story they recognize as such. But such theatricality draws them ever farther from what real meaning would be. Voinitsky above all is drawn to such histrionics. With no story of his own, he borrows dramatic scenes, which is why his behavior is thoroughly false.

In a sense, what is usually taken as the "climax" of the play is created not

67

by the author but by the internal "playwright" Voinitsky. In this scene, he maintains correctly that the plan to sell the estate, which would leave Sonya and himself homeless, is unconscionable. But he gets carried away—better, he gets himself carried away—when he goes on to denounce the quality of the professor's literary criticism. Would the professor's callousness be justified if he were a better critic? But like the author of a melodrama, Vanya wants to raise all issues at once and force the sort of connections found only in a well-made play. As a result, our sympathy for him becomes tinged with laughter at a grown man's tantrum, which he plays for dramatic effect.

Like a performer interrupted just before his great scene, Voinitsky demands that his audience pay attention to his dramatic speech:

ELENA ANDREEVNA: Ivan Petrovich, I insist that you stop talking! Do you hear?
VOINITSKY: I won't stop talking! [*Barring Serebryakov's way*] Wait, I haven't finished! You have ruined my life! I haven't lived! Thanks to you, I have destroyed, annihilated the best years of my life! You are my worst enemy!
(216)

Real anger shades into theatrical rage here. Voinitsky's behavior is simultaneously sincere and assumed, because he seizes on his real feelings to justify a performance. Appropriately enough, it is at this point that he declares he could have become a Dostoevsky, ironically, the author who above all understood how easy it is to take offense and exaggerate a real affront into a theatrical occasion and then, inspired by one's own performance, pass to real vindictiveness, as Father Zossima remarks in *The Brothers Karamazov*.

"I know myself what I must do! [*To Serebryakov*] You will remember me!" Voinitsky proclaims as he leaves the room (217). It is not clear at this point whether he intends suicide or murder, but he evidently signals *something* portentous in advance. Now, it is one thing for an author to engage in foreshadowing, but quite another for a character to do so. Here Voinitsky behaves as if he were a fictional character whose actions are designed from the outset to lead to a definite result. That behavior is ridiculous, because the prosaic world in which Chekhov sets his play is as undramatic as our real lives. And yet it is also weirdly appropriate because, after all, Voinitsky *is* a fictional character, although he does not know it.

When Voinitsky returns with his gun, Chekhov's metatheatrical attack on theatricality reaches a farcical crescendo:

SEREBRYAKOV [*runs in, staggering with fright*]: Hold him! Hold him! He's gone mad!
[ELENA ANDREEVNA *and* VOINITSKY *struggle in the doorway.*]
ELENA ANDREEVNA [*trying to take the revolver from him*]: Give it to me! Give it to me, I say!

VOINITSKY: Let me go, Hélène! Let me go! [*Freeing himself, runs in and looks around for Serebryakov.*] Where is he? Ah, there he is! [*Shoots at him.*] Bang! [*Pause*] Missed him! Missed again! Oh, damn, damn! [*Throws down the revolver on the floor and sits down exhausted.*]

(218)

If this scene is performed as it is written, we will first hear the sound of the pistol shot, then hear Voinitsky *say* "Bang!" First we hear the sound, then we hear the imitation of a stage sound. (And perhaps, if the director should want to stress the artifice, he might choose a "real" pistol that sounds like the prop it is.) Here the absurdity of theatrical behavior and the brilliance of Chekhov's metatheatrical parody become most apparent.

Voinitsky wants to enact a grand and dramatic crime, but he manages only one more petty squabble. Histrionic from the outset, he is trying not so much to shoot the professor as to perform a desperate role. He commits not attempted murder, but attempted *attempted* murder. It is doubtful whether he succeeds even at that.

Throughout this scene, Voinitsky appears to cite his actions as he goes along. Like a child who simultaneously pretends to be a ballplayer and the announcer broadcasting the play-by-play description, Voinitsky *narrates* the action he performs. That is the grotesque comedy of "Bang!" And yet you really can kill somebody that way. Perhaps most of the petty squabbles that, even without pistols, actually spoil lives are cited as well as said. Chekhov appreciated the danger of playing to an absent audience.

Chekhov recognized that audiences do not just happen to witness theatrical performances, they are essential to them. His characters appreciate this fact, too. They know that drama has an ending, which provides a privileged vantage point for an audience to evaluate actions. And they try to live as if their lives had such an audience and vantage point as well.

That is why Chekhov's characters so often seem to be not addressing each other but making a case that the audience will remember when the play is over. But if the real audience understands the *author's* play, it will recognize that such behavior is necessarily false. Those who live their lives as if the ending were what truly matters fail to act responsibly during the only time we have, present moments shared with other people. To live theatrically means to fabricate a false temporality.

In Chekhov's plays, characters frequently imagine what their lives will seem like when the plot of history is over, thereby making history into a very long drama. Three times in *Uncle Vanya* Astrov evokes the image of judges in a future utopia who, living after all historical struggles have passed, look back on "our lives." Like the audience of a play, or angels at the Last Judgment, the ones Astrov imagines will know the whole story and be in a secure position to evaluate our lives. And what will they say? I have already mentioned his hopes that in a thousand years the contribution of his forestry will be evident. In act 4, Astrov spitefully tells Voinitsky to face "facts": "Those who will come after us, in two or three hundred years . . . will despise us for having lived our lives so stupidly and insipidly" (222). He wonders most ambiguously about the judgment of the future in the play's first scene:

> ASTROV: . . . I sat down, closed my eyes—just like this—and I thought: will those who come after us in a hundred or two hundred years, those for whom we are blazing a trail, will they remember and have a kind word for us? No, they won't, nurse!
> MARINA: People won't remember, but God remembers.
> ASTROV: Thank you for that. That was well said.
> (174–75).

In her own way, Marina cautions Astrov against asking such questions: people judge life dramatically and teleologically, but God sees the fullness of each present moment. The only judgment that counts is not deferred but immanent in our daily lives. Or as Pierre learns in *War and Peace*, "God is here and everywhere."[9]

Anyone who knows Chekhov's plays will recognize how commonly speeches like Astrov's are delivered. Chekhov uses them parodically to indicate his dislike for the intelligentsia's grand historical visions and to suggest by negation the importance of responsibility at each present moment. He suspected visionaries of contempt for daily labor and regarded their sense of temporality as dangerous.

In daily life, no less than in politics, teleological living makes us ethically careless. It leads ultimately to a temporal sense like Voinitsky's: "I have no past . . . and the present is awful in its absurdity" (191); "I'm forty-seven years old; if I live to be sixty, I've still got thirteen years to live through. It's a long time. How am I to get through those thirteen years?" (222). *Finita la commedia*: if one attributes significance to plots with an ending, instead of to each prosaic moment, then time without a story becomes an absurd prolongation of emptiness.

None of us entirely escapes playing to the audience and so, for all his satire, Chekhov also expresses sympathy, if not for theatricality, then at least for the circumstances that drive the best of us to performance. An exquisitely subtle mixture of sympathy with irony, of pathos homeopathically tinged with parody, closes the play. Just before the curtain falls, the most admirable and wisest character, Sonya, reacts characteristically to her own deep disappointment over Astrov's departure by comforting her Uncle Vanya. The title seems to allude above all to this speech:

> SONYA: What's to be done, we must go on living! [*Pause*] We shall go on living, Uncle Vanya. We shall live through a long, long chain of days and endless

evenings . . . and when our time comes, we shall die submissively; and there, beyond the grave, we shall say that we have suffered, that we have wept, and have known bitterness, and God will have pity on us; and you and I, Uncle, dear Uncle, shall behold a life that is bright, beautiful, and fine. We shall rejoice and look back on our present troubles with tenderness, with a smile—and we shall rest. I have faith, Uncle, I have fervent passionate faith. . . . [ellipsis added] We shall rest! We shall hear the angels, and see the heavens all sparkling like jewels; and we shall see all earthly evil, all our sufferings, drowned in a mercy that will fill the whole world, and our life will grow peaceful, gentle, sweet as a caress. I have faith, I have faith . . . [*Wipes away his tears with a handkerchief.*] Poor, poor Uncle Vanya, you're crying . . . [*Through tears*] You have had no joy in your life, but wait Uncle Vanya, wait . . . We shall rest . . . [*Puts her arms around him.*] We shall rest!

(230–31; ellipses in original)

For all Sonya's quiet wisdom, even she cannot resist imagining some position outside of life that would allow a special view of it, that would redeem it. Astrov imagines life judged from a glorious future, Sonya imagines the perspective of heaven.

And yet what is truly wonderful about these lines, and what is heroic about Sonya, is what she is doing in the present. As she speaks, Uncle Vanya's self-absorbed mother still "makes notes on the margins of her pamphlet," but Sonya does all she can to comfort him. We love her not for her faith but for her attentive kindness, which is never forgotten even in her own deepest sadness.

Subtly and implicitly, Sonya's speech, along with the slowly falling curtain, breaks the dramatic frame: for we, the audience, *are* in a position outside of life, and we *can* view it "with tenderness, with a smile." We are the redeemers Sonya promises to Vanya.

And if we follow Chekhov's design, we will realize that even though Sonya's life has an audience, ours does not. We will know that one must live without demanding a witness. Redemption belongs neither to an ending nor to a utopian future, but is immanent in the present. Meaningfulness can be achieved only as the old nurse achieves it throughout the play and as Sonya herself does at this very moment: by daily acts of unremarked and unrewarded kindness.

71

Elizabeth Klosty Beaujour

The Uses of Witches in Fedin and Bulgakov

MODERNIST PROSE forms often present the reader with the paradox of cerebral, structurally complex works that express an irrational or antirational content. These works seek an almost geometric perfection of form while simultaneously rejecting intellect as a totally inadequate means of conceiving contemporary experience. Strikingly often it is a witch of a rather special breed who provides the essential thematic and narrative elements without which the intellectual pattern of the novel could not crystallize out. That *voyantes* and sorceresses should people the prose of Western surrealists such as André Breton is not too surprising, but it is surely a nice problem that two of the most self-consciously modernist Russian novels written during the Soviet period,[1] Fedin's *Cities and Years* and Bulgakov's *Master and Margarita*, should depend for both their compositional and moral energies on witches.

No one would dispute, I think, the structural "modernism" of these novels. Both bridge enormous distances of time and space (both could equally well be entitled *Cities and Years*). They create a new order through the juxtaposition of elements of a disparate nature, whether these be newspaper clippings and other realia, or different levels of discourse, or apparently incommensurable genres and levels of narrative and episodic reality.[2] Both novels use the visible disparity of these elements as their essential constructional principle, emphasizing this incongruity and thereby making the ultimate resolution of the oppositions all the more striking. Last, and not of least importance, the resolutions of both novels involve the geometrical figure of the closed circle and are precipitated by a female character who is a witch. Before we can deal with the witches themselves, we must pause to consider their patron. For behind these witches stands the Devil, with whom they are necessarily in league. The presence of the Devil is compositionally and thematically appropriate, not to say inevitable, in such novels. The montage structure itself calls up the Devil because of its deliberate disruption of sequence, a violation of the Chain of Being that allows chaos to show through the gaps. Furthermore, in novels constructed by the juxtaposition of unlike elements, thesis calls for antithesis, negation, and our eternal friend the Devil. Any ultimate harmony depends on his preparatory participation (*pace* Ivan Karamazov). Life itself depends on him, as Woland impatiently explains to Matthew.[3]

It is therefore not surprising to find the Devil or his surrogate as an actor in such novels. But the curious thing about the Devil's role in them is that he does not appear merely as a metaphor for disruption; he is not just the principle of negation that despite itself furthers the dialectical triad. Quite the contrary. The Devil is the source of the active, positive, moral, and compositional energies of these novels.

Let us not forget that although our bad opinion of the Devil has been inculcated in us by Authority, he has often appeared in Western culture as the image of a paradoxical source of life energy. It is by now a cliché of cultural history that in periods when the dominant culture, self-defined as the good, the positive, the legitimate, has become so narrow-minded, so repressive as to be inadequate to the real needs of life, the signs may change.[4] A reversal of roles and values may occur in popular culture, and the Devil appears both as the lord of the underworld and the prince of *this* world, the active principle of life itself.

Seen in such a context the role of the Devil is not only or even primarily evil. It only seems so to narrow-minded representatives of the dominant culture, like Bulgakov's Matthew the Levite. There is even a solid, if underground, tradition that links Jesus and the Devil. Both are interpreted as contrary to the principle of rigidity and restraint of life. One well-known incarnation of the Devil recognizes a brother in Jesus: "Jesus was all virtue and acted from impulse not rules, thus constantly breaking the ten commandments."[5] We are indeed in the realm of the Argument of "The Marriage of Heaven and Hell": "Without Contraries is no progression. Attraction and Repulsion, Reason and Energy, Love and Hate are necessary to Human existence. From these contraries spring what the religious call Good and Evil. Good is the passive that obeys Reason. Evil is the Active springing from Energy."[6]

As the Devil incarnates the virtue of life energy in Blake, so does he in *The Master and Margarita* and in *Cities and Years*. The identification of the Devil and life with all the chthonian elements inevitably entails a close partnership between the Devil and Woman. But this relationship, too, must be seen in the light of the Change of Signs. We must go behind the libelous image of the wicked, snaggletoothed witch to find the Sorceress, who, although she may first have sought the Devil through despair and a desire for vengeance, becomes in his hands, almost in spite of herself, a comforter and healer, a source of mercy. As Michelet and others have noted, the much-maligned Sorceress was, in fact, originally a dominantly positive figure, primarily beneficent, and the spirit from below who animated her was blessed for her activity.[7]

The point of this long preamble is that the witches who people modernist prose are usually descendants of this beneficent sorceress. They are essentially positive, bearers of a necessarily ambiguous restraint-breaking energy. Both Fedin's Marie Urbach and Bulgakov's Margarita are such sorceresses. They share the broad-mindedness of the principle of energy they serve; in these two novels men are divided not into the good and the bad but into the broad- and narrow-minded.[8] That Margarita is a witch requires, I think, no proof. But Marie Urbach's links to the Devil are less immediately visible, although no less significant. For that reason, as well as for the sake of contrariness, I should like to deal with her first.

Although no one would claim that Michelet's *La Sorcière* is in any way normative, his description of the second generation of witches, the daughters of Satan, fits Marie perfectly.[9] Furthermore, Marie's witchery is obvious if one reads the fourth chapter of *Cities and Years* with a minimum of care. The very first thing that is said about Marie Urbach is that gossip holds her to be a witch: "Ask any peasant—she was known throughout the entire district. She turned up everywhere, and always unexpectedly, like a ghost. It was truly a bad sign if Marie ever ran into someone else's yard. After her appearance some kind of trouble was sure to happen on that farm: a horse would fall sick, or a reaper would break, or—at the very least—the milk would go sour."[10] As the sad history of witch trials has proven, she whom public opinion declares to be a witch is a witch in the same way that, Sartre has argued, he is a Jew whom others so define. But Marie is diabolical in activity as well as reputation. The pranks of her childhood, her goatlike, solitary romps on the mountains, her visit to the Devil in his reputed hangout on the mountain nicely known as the Three Nuns,[11] her spooking of passing peasants, her descent into the tomb of the "Stone Margravine"—all have the same character of blasphemous disrespect for an ancient, hidebound order. The peasants have in fact every right to consider that "it was as though nothing less than a demon had settled in the wench, and she was born in an evil hour" (159).

We cannot go into the early career of this Devil's daughter in any detail, but several brief points must be made. Her natural father, Urbach, a man whose origins and life-style are incomprehensible to the local citizenry, turns out to have been a secret socialist, who financially contributed to the disruption of the status quo, and therefore in the eyes of the peasantry, and of his own wife, is a true disciple of the Master of Deceit. Puberty only increases Marie's evident links to the Devil: "From that time, the rumor spread that from her it was but a short distance to the Devil himself, and that it was better not to cross her path" (168–69). The lengthy chapter dealing with Marie's childhood and adolescence constitutes approximately one-ninth of the novel. It is placed just before the novel's halfway point, immediately before the episodes concerning Marie's meetings with Andrei. Her witchery is therefore both thematically and *compositionally* central. It explains her energy, an energy so uncharacteristic of her milieu and of the town appropriately called Bischofsburg whose thoroughfare, Bismarck Avenue, is divided into three branches, one for horsemen, one for bicycles, and one for pedestrians, and is studded with signs containing reminders such as "Dropping papers or fruit peel forbidden!" "Do not break branches or knock off leaves," and "Do not dig up paths with sticks or umbrellas" (249).

In such a world, energy, which desires to break out of deadening restraints, must have the character of disorder and destructiveness and bear the mark of the Devil. This explains why Marie is drawn to a pariah, who at first seems strong and independent.[12] Andrei turns out, however, to be utterly dependent on her for the energy to maintain his belief in himself and to fulfill his mission and duty. Like Margarita, Marie must be the sole moral support of her man, must attempt to nurse him back to moral health and vigor.[13] It is she who must oblige him to return to Russia, where she will join him as soon as possible. Meanwhile, she bends her energy to overthrowing the old in Germany: fraternizing with the enemy; joining in the storming of the prison castle, which is the very stone image of Urizen, inspiring the soldiers to form a city soviet, setting up an office for them, even providing the soviet with its essential symbol of authority: a rubber stamp, which reads "ex libris Marie Urbach."

It ought to be noted here that Marie is not the only daughter of the Devil active in Bischofsburg. The war has turned many women into witches. As they walk circumspectly several paces ahead of their burgher husbands and fathers, the wives, mothers, and fiancées of Bischofsburg have, in fact, secretly gone over to the Devil. They rejoice in the blooming of the prophetic linden tree that last flowered in 1871. This tree had been planted unnaturally upside-down. Its rooting and flourishing were taken by the man who planted it as testimony to the power of God. But we and the women know whose power it really reveals. The women believe that the war will stop when every last woman in Germany has joined in a spell and wears her hair as they and their friends do: quite flat, with a part in the middle. It is the women who insist on freeing the men and the truth hidden in the citadel. And it is a worthy sister of Marie who leads other women to reveal Bischofsburg's greatest obscenity masked as a charitable institution: the storehouse of mutilated soldiers that hides behind the tidy facade of the house at the head of Bismarck Avenue.

Remembering the legless, armless, sightless, hearingless lump of suffering to which she could not even communicate her presence and which had formerly been her husband, Martha Berman leads a group of black-clad women in mourning to the hospital to "resurrect" these living dead.[14] The women are described descending on the hospital like a coven of witches: "The wind jerked and caught up the wailing and groaning, jerked the long crepe veils, and the women in mourning broke into a run. Behind the group in mourning, whirled into a funnel by the wind, swept other women, alone and in groups, who had flown down from no one knew where like leaves at the height of the fall" (316). They carry the broken veterans out from the wards and parade them through the streets. And it is no accident that the woman who leads this parade of life destroyed in the name of order, of dancing demons with metal arms and legs, should be a black-clad widow who hails from a town called Teufelsmühle (Devil's Mill). All these women who turn against order and propriety and godliness in the name of life and energy have once more turned to their ultimate source of help. Thematically speaking, *Cities and Years* therefore contains not one witch, but many. Marie is only the most important of them all.

The novel does not tell us what finally happens to Marie. After she has fought her way to Petrograd by the most unscrupulous means, and found out that Andrei has betrayed her and himself, Marie disappears. The reader knows only that when last seen she was being carried forward by a band of laughing children "tout droit, tout droit" (straight ahead, straight ahead) to the unknown.[15] Andrei, on the other hand, moves at the end of the novel to join the circle of his destiny, to the death we have already seen in the first pages. The snapping shut of the trap, the falling into place of the last, already inevitable events leading to Andrei's death, is circular and satisfying. But it is a circle of despair cut through by an axis of energy. Marie's compositional function is to be this axis of energy, penetrating the juxtaposed narrative elements of this nonorganic and mechanically constructed novel, giving it what life it does contain. She returns from degradation to break through the closed circle of Andrei's fate. For Marie Urbach is the Devil's daughter, and therefore, ultimately, she is in love with life, not death.

The essential compositional function of the Devil and his Queen in *The Master and Margarita* is so obvious as to require little exposition here. But it should be noted from the outset that the complicity of the Devil and Jesus, which we have seen in Blake, is essential to the resolution of Bulgakov's novel, which might just as well also have been entitled "The Marriage of Heaven and Hell." I shall therefore concentrate on the positive elements of Margarita's witchery, for she functions even more clearly than Marie in *Cities and Years* as the bearer of energy and compassion in the novel and as the compositional element whose activity precipitates the final harmony.

Margarita is immediately identified as a witch by a singular intrusion of the authorial voice: "Gods, my Gods, what did she want, this woman whose eyes always glowed with a strange fire, what did she need, this witch with a slight squint in her eye who bedecks herself in mimosa in the spring?" (632–33). The answer, of course, is life, not empty but comfortable propriety. Her energy needs an object, and it flows into the Master, embraces him, enables, even compels him, to complete his book. When, through illness and fearfulness, he destroys the manuscript, Margarita becomes the healing sorceress: she declares that she will cure him, save him, and enable him to write the book again. When the Master disappears, it is almost inevitable that she will call on the Devil. How else is she to find out if the Master is living or dead? Having no other hope, she declares to Azazello that she is "soglasna idti k chertu na kulichki," even ready to go to the ends of the earth for more news of the Master (644). The composition of Margarita's phrase is important here. It is well known that one can conjure up the Devil by merely using a cliché containing his name, as Margarita has. That is how Woland appears at Patriarchs' Ponds and how Azazello has appeared on the bench beside Margarita. But Margarita has done more. The word *kulichki* contains in it the echo of *kulich*, the Easter cake consecrated at the midnight mass. She has called up both the Devil and the Resurrection in one phrase, and she will literally make the paradoxical journey she is prepared to take. Only it is neither so far nor so unlikely as she at first thinks.

It is important to note that Margarita is also wrong about the price she believes she will have to pay when she visits the "foreign gentleman." She, too, has been brainwashed by traditional concepts of the Devil. For although sexual intercourse with the Devil is traditionally as much a part of the bargain for the woman who is Queen of the Sabbath as is the flying cream, the bath, and the ride through the air, it turns out that Woland does not "want her for that."[16] In fact, all the more horrific or degrading aspects of having commerce with the Devil have disappeared from *The Master and Margarita* along with the traditional designation of the Devil as Evil. To take but one example, the guests at the ball kiss Margarita's knee rather than Satan's ass in a most untraditional display of propriety.

Neither Woland nor Margarita participates in any undignified orgies during the ball.[17] Woland officiates only at the culminating festivity, the blood sacrifice traditionally central to the black mass.[18] But here Woland is carrying out the work of universal justice by punishing the informer Baron Maigel. This is no longer a mockery of the most sacred moment of the Christian mass. The direct challenge to Jesus implied by the drinking of blood in the traditional black mass has no place in a world where Christ and the Devil head clearly defined departments of the same enterprise and work together so that "everything will be as it should be, for that is the way the world is arranged" (797).

If the Devil cannot or will not grant pardon (why should he do the business of another department?), it is important to note that Margarita has not lost the power to do good simply because she has sold herself to the Devil. Like the life-giving sorceress of the Middle Ages, her power to do good as well as evil is immeasurably increased by her alliance with the Prince of This World.

Witch Queen Margarita is in fact a most unorthodox combination of prideful headstrongness, vengefulness, and compassion. Out of pride, she at first refuses to ask Woland for anything. This deadliest sin is of course a diabolical virtue, and Woland therefore freely offers her *one* thing. Although her motives for requesting Freida's release are far from unambiguous, Margarita's decision to free Freida with her one wish means sacrificing her own dearest hope, the reunion with the Master, for which she has sold herself, and the salvation of the Master who is dearer to her than her own soul. This, I am afraid, is charity, and Margarita is in fact the true bearer of Christian charity in the novel. The fact that she is therefore a disciple of Yeshua as well as of the Master[19] becomes even more significant when we consider one of the novel's compositional peculiarities.

Many critics have noted that almost everything in the Master's novel is slightly different from the Gospel accounts of the life of Jesus. Some of these discrepancies may be attributed to the fact that the Gospels with which we are familiar are here presented as the result of Matthew the Levite's unfortunate inability to get things straight. But certain other facts, which do not pass through the testament of Matthew, are also different. Most interesting for our purpose is the disappearance of all the women who are present in the Gospel accounts. Yeshua does not even know who his mother is. So the whole mythic structure of purity and virginity that determines the church's alienating attitude toward women disappears from the Master's novel,[20] as does the relevance of the argument used by the intellectual bureaucrat Berlioz to disprove the existence of Jesus.

The feminine element thus removed from the life of Yeshua and his entourage reemerges in full force through Margarita's role in the novel.[21] She is not only the source of the Master's creative energy, the mediatrix between him and life (for which he is otherwise quite evidently inapt); she also becomes the only feminine figure in the final configuration of timeless characters.[22] In the chapter "Absolution and Eternal Refuge," the change of appearance that reveals the eternal essence of the Devil and his three male demons is seen through the eyes of Margarita. She therefore cannot see herself as they ride. But her essence is revealed too, slightly later. When she sees Pilate in his purgatory and demands his release, the text states: "Her completely calm face was veiled by compassion" (sovershenno spokoinoe ee litso podernulos' dymkoi sostradaniia) (796). The traits of the Virgin here show through the witch. Or rather, not the traits of the Virgin but those of Mary Mother of God, who in a widely known Slavic apocryphal account descends to Hell, is harsh in her judgment of those who betrayed her Son, yet nevertheless intercedes with him and obtains a yearly period of release from torment for the damned.[23]

Although the word that releases Pilate must come from the Master, the world-ordering conclusion has been made possible only by the active energy of Margarita. In both moral and compositional terms, she provides the energy that brings this precariously balanced and complex structure into its final position of harmonious resolution.

The endings of *Cities and Years* and *The Master and Margarita* take the preceding narrative sequences out of suspension and resolve them into final crystallization. In *Cities and Years* this effect is reproduced by the obligatory return to the first chapters. In *The Master and Margarita* the two initial blocks, Moscow and Jerusalem, fuse in the timeless ending of the chapter "Absolution and Eternal Refuge" and in the last words of the epilogue.[24] Thus Fedin and Bulgakov resolve their complex surface patterns in an intellectually satisfying way. But the essential element with which these constructions are built and which they serve is not itself intellectual. It is energy. In both cases the bearer of this energy is an incarnation of the necessarily ambiguous life-bringing sorceress, without whose action the entire construction would have remained an arbitrary juxtaposition of disparate elements without aesthetic life.

To some extent the use of witches by Fedin and Bulgakov and the formal pattern of the closed circle are a direct result of Soviet conditions. In both cases we have praise of rebellion balanced by the need to reassert the value of the idiosyncratic artist as orderer of experience in a context where both sense *and* the recognition of the value of individual creative activity seemed to have disappeared. But these two novels do not represent a parochial or isolated phenomenon. Witches, or a thematic element comparable to them that serves a similar formal function, can be found in many male-authored modernist novels, Western as well as Soviet. To take but one example, a most instructive parallel with Fedin and Bulgakov might be seen in some of the works of André Breton, leader of the French surrealist movement. Although his early *Nadja* (1928) bears a superficial resemblance to the techniques and message of *Cities and Years*, the most interesting book for our purpose is *Arcane 17.*[25]

Arcane 17 was written during the Second World War when Breton was in exile on the Gaspé Peninsula, isolated, watching the European world that he had challenged in his own way destroyed in another way, experiencing deep personal grief, trying to conjure this destruction, to assert through a complex, cross-layered metaphoric text that light and dark are inextricably combined; indeed, that light comes only through the experience of the dark.

The poet is separate, lost, and obtuse. From the first sentence of the text, everything is mediated through a woman, Elisa. She is his link to the ambiguity of life: she has undergone suffering so great and senseless in the loss of her child that she has experienced the *Change of Signs*, and the light in her eyes comes from the dark fire of transmuted rebellion. In *Arcane 17*, this woman is *sorcière, fée, voyante*. She is *Mélusine*, bringer of dynastic energy, who must not be seen as she undergoes her mythic transformation. She is the *verseuse* depicted on the seventeenth arcane of the tarot pack, pouring forth two streams beneath the star of Hope. She is the goddess of that morning star, Isis herself.

As Isis, the woman leads us to the fundamental affirmation of *Arcane 17*: "Osiris is a black god" (154). But even Osiris (cousin of Christ as dying god, cousin of the Devil as shepherd of souls) cannot reassemble his dismembered self. Isis must do it, gather the fragments to bring the black god of initiations back to the light. Separation and anguish can be transmuted into harmony only through the feminine force that has comprehended the revelation that night is the source of life. Only through her are the antinomies resolved.

The image of the reassembled Osiris, the desire to overcome fragmentation through the organization of fragments in such a way that their new order becomes necessary and life-bearing, is the basic mythical and compositional idea of many modern novels. Breton has recourse to myth for the same reasons Bulgakov did: in an effort to increase ambiguity and therefore dissipate the opacity that obstinately holds to conventional opinions and suspect defenses. Breton postulates that the man of desire expresses himself through shreds of myth, and that he is always searching for the richest, most complex myth in whose network his own myths can insert themselves and find their place. All three authors turn to myth as the source of this life-giving ambiguity and find in the myths of darkness and night not the demon of negation but the only accessible source of life.

Arcane 17 illuminates the successes and failures of the two Russian novels in one final way. All three use the figure of the circle as a structuring principle, but with varying artistic success. The secret seems to be that Breton and Bulgakov have allowed their male protagonists to follow their female guides into a mythical complexity that alone validates the geometrical figure. Fedin and his characters refuse to take the leap into mythic opacity. The circle of Andrei's fate closes in such a way as to exclude Marie and her message, creating a life closed on itself in isolation rather than wholeness. In Bulgakov's novel, the circle is to be found on both the strictly constructional plane and on the richest, most ambiguous levels of the mythic network of the novel. It is *only* on this mythic level that *Arcane 17*, with its interlocking myths, its vertiginous passage through analogies, forms a circle where separation is transmuted into harmony. Its mythic circularity constitutes an act of confidence in life, love, and the poetic word.

Fedin uses the figure of the circle to trap a character in isolation; Bulgakov's and Breton's circles are magic circles, charms woven with the aid of a sorceress. And Breton seems to have spoken truly not only about himself but also about Bulgakov and other major writers of the modernist tradition when he observed in *Arcane 17*: "Consciously or not, the process of artistic discovery, even though it remains a stranger to the full scope of its metaphysical ambitions, is nonetheless subject to the form and to the very means of proceeding of High Magic. Everything else is destitution, unbearable platitude, billboards and rhyming games" (153–54).

Sona Stephan Hoisington

The Mismeasure of I-330

NUMEROUS ARTICLES have been written in the West about Yevgeny Zamyatin's anti-utopian fantasy *We*,[1] most of them based on the assumption that the male protagonist, mathematician D-503, merits the reader's attention, that what happens to him, what he thinks and feels is crucial and worthy of investigation and analysis. Consequently, critical literature has tended to focus on D-503 and his "rebellion," whether directed outward against the One State or inward against his entropic self.[2] Little attention has been focused on I-330, *We*'s female protagonist. Her role in the novel has been marginalized. All too often she has been regarded as an appendage of the male protagonist. Some critics have even viewed her as a projection of D-503's unconscious or psyche.[3] Because she is female, she has also been identified with Eve, the archetypal temptress, born of Adam's rib.[4] Attesting to the hold gender stereotypes have on us, *both* female and male critics have drawn this conclusion.

I-330, however, has been "mismeasured."[5] She is, in fact, the central force in Zamyatin's novel.[6] Her role is crucial not only on the level of plot (after all she is the leader of the revolutionary Mephi, whose goal it is, in her words, "to break down . . . all walls [and] let the green wind blow free from end to end—across the earth" [157]) but, as we will see, on other levels as well. Highly unorthodox, like the work she informs,[7] I-330 defies easy categorization. In this sense she is markedly different from the conventional female protagonists in the modern dystopias of George Orwell and Fritz Lang. Julia, the heroine of *1984*, is clearly subordinate to the hero, Winston Smith, and vanishes from the novel just as soon as she and Winston are caught in their hideaway over Mr. Charrington's junk shop. Weakly delineated, Julia is described primarily as a youthful body, "only a rebel from the waist downwards."[8] Maria, the female protagonist of Fritz Lang's expressionist film, *Metropolis* (1926), is easily classified as a combination of Mary and the persecuted female. I-330, on the other hand, transcends gender stereotypes. She takes on attributes and mythic qualities traditionally reserved for

81

male heroes and yet retains her own identity. As distinct from the conventional heroine, she is "woman as hero,"[9] a rebel par excellence and the consummate heretic. While D-503 is the central consciousness of *We* (the work consisting of forty entries, purports to be his journal), I submit that the "hero"—both in the sense of prime mover and the character who best exemplifies the novel's governing values—is I-330 and D-503 a "mock" hero.

At first glance I-330 would appear to be a femme fatale: that beautiful, proud, and willfully evil creature so prominent in both the visual arts and literary works at the turn of the century, who lured men to destruction by means of her overwhelming seductive charms.[10] After all, doesn't I-330 employ her sexual wiles to ensnare the narrator D-503, an obedient citizen of the One State, and bring about his downfall? (In Zamyatin's satiric fantasy, which is set 1000 years in the future, the inhabitants of the One State wear uniforms and have numbers prefixed by letters rather than names.) In the early entries of *We*, Zamyatin's portrayals of her are highly suggestive, tinged with eroticism. Significantly, they bring to mind Russian paintings of the period. For example, the descripton of I-330 in entry 4 is reminiscent of Lev Bakst's 1902 painting *Supper*.[11] In that entry the narrator D-503 attends a lecture and is surprised to see I-330 appear on stage to demonstrate the absurd music of the ancients. He describes her as follows: "She wore the fantastic costume of the ancient epoch: a closely fitting black dress, which sharply emphasized the whiteness of her bare shoulders and breast, with that warm shadow, stirring with her breath, between . . . and the dazzling, almost angry teeth. . . . A smile—a bite—to us, below. Then she sat down and began to play" (17; ellipses in original). If we compare this description to Bakst's painting, which Zamyatin very likely had seen at one of the "World of Art" exhibits while a student in Petersburg at the Polytechnic Institute, we note similarities. Dominating the picture are the sinuous lines of the female figure who sits facing the viewer with an enigmatic smile on her lips. The black of her closely fitting, low-cut dress and undulating hat is in striking contrast with the white of her face, neck, and breast.

The description of I-330 in entry 10 is reminiscent of yet another portrait: Yury Annenkov's provocative 1917 painting of his wife Elena. (Annenkov was a close friend of Zamyatin's, and this was a painting Zamyatin knew and admired.)[12] Here the female figure takes possession of the entire canvas and energizes it. The sinuous lines of the knees and the breast are complemented by dynamic diagonal thrusts to the left and to the right. The figure's gaze is averted; it is her left breast in the center, visible through the filmy material of her dress, that confronts the viewer. And in entry 10 of *We*, after I-330 has registered for D-503 (in this futuristic world sexual arrangements are regulated through registration and the use of pink coupons) and summoned him to her room, we read: "She was in a light, saffron-yellow dress of the ancient model. This was a thousand times more cruel than if she had worn nothing at all. Two pointed tips through the filmy silk, glowing pink—two embers through the ash. Two delicately rounded knees . . ." (54; ellipsis in original).

I-330's sensuality, however, proves to be liberating rather than destructive (the same could be said of the Annenkov portrait where the energy of the female figure is conveyed). Here it should be noted that whereas the traditional femme fatale is associated with downward movement, I-330 is associated with upward movement, with flight. The sexual energy that flows from her transforms D-503 psychologically and spiritually. He becomes an individual: not one of but one; he develops consciousness; he begins to dream; a soul, an imagination forms in him. And here Zamyatin reverses the traditional sex roles.[13] In *We* it is the female, I-330, who is the stimulating, fertilizing force,[14] the pollinator; she is compared to a bee, her scent likened to pollen. The male, D-503, is the receiver; he is compared to a flower that blooms, a fruit that ripens. It is I-330 who, metaphorically speaking, "impregnates" D-503, and not the other way around, as he acknowledges after they make love in entry 13, using a fitting metaphor of liquidity: "how full I am!" (75).[15]

Moreover, I-330's mind is as provocative as her body. She is constantly challenging D-503, tormenting him with her questions and mocking sarcasm. When they first meet in entry 2, D says: "We are all so alike. . . ." She: "Are you sure?" (7; ellipsis in original). And in entry 6, when he is distressed by the chaotic surroundings of the Ancient House to which she has taken him and the provocative ancient costume she has donned and accuses her of trying to be original, she mocks him and his world: "Clearly . . . to be original is to be in some way distinct from others. Hence, to be original is to violate equality. And that which in the language of the ancients was called 'being banal' is with us merely the fulfillment of our duty" (28). Much later in the novel (in entry 35) D-503 overhears I-330 urging her fellow Numbers not to surrender to the Great Operation, which through the removal of the imagination promises to turn them all into machines. Once again her words are sarcastic, mocking: "They'll cure you, they'll stuff you full of rich, fat happiness, and, sated, you will doze off peacefully, snoring in perfect unison. . . . Ridiculous people! They want to free you of every squirming, torturing, nagging question mark. And you are standing here and listening to me. Hurry upstairs, to the Great Operation!" (207).

Here then a fundamental difference is revealed between Zamyatin's outlook and that of the Christian tradition. For the traditional Christian believes that the body is separate from—and inferior to—the intellect, that the former (that is, the body/flesh) is closely linked to the female and the latter (that is, the intellect/spirit) to the male. This traditional view is evident in *1984*, where Winston clearly represents the intellect and Julia the flesh. In Zamyatin's *We*, on the other hand, there is a synthesis of mind and body, the body—the source of consciousness, individuality, and creativity—deemed inseparable from the mind. This is brought out in the novel through the image of the "whip," which is associated with I-330: first with her body (in entry 2), then with her laughter (in entry 6), and much later (in entry 35) with her voice. Now the whip is sexually provocative. At the same time it is associated, metaphorically speaking, with irony, sarcasm, and satire—the weapons wielded so effectively by both I-330 and her creator. As his 1924 essay on Fyodor Sologub reveals, Zamyatin placed great value on whips "woven of words," whips that can make man "stop kneeling down before anything or anyone" (*SH*, 221).

I-330 is also associated with snake imagery: her sharp, white teeth bring to mind the fangs of a snake, the "fiery poison" that flows from her into D-503 (in entry 10) is like snake venom, subsequently (in entry 25) we are told that the "thinnest red serpent of blood" flowed from a wound in her shoulder. At first glance this imagery seems again to suggest the femme fatale, since women were frequently likened to snakes and often pictured with them at the turn of the century as a way of emphasizing the evil and base female nature.[16]

The image of the serpent, however, emerges in another, quite different context in entry 11 of *We*, where it takes on mythic overtones. I am referring to the ironic retelling of the legend of paradise by the poet R-13. Since this passage is central to an understanding of Zamyatin's novel, I shall quote it in full:

> ". . . that ancient legend about paradise. . . . Why, it's about us, about today. Yes! Just think. Those two, in paradise, were given a choice: happiness without freedom, or freedom without happiness. There was no third alternative. Those idiots chose freedom, and what came of it? Of course, for ages afterward they longed for fetters. Fetters—you understand? That's what world sorrow was about. For ages! And only we have found the way of restoring happiness. . . . No, wait, listen further! The ancient God and we—side by side, at the same table. Yes! We have helped God to conquer the devil once and for all—for it was he who tempted men to break the ban and taste pernicious freedom, he, the evil serpent. And we, we've brought down our boot over his little head, and—cr-runch! Now everything is fine—we have paradise again." (61)

Ostensibly written in praise of God (that is, the "we" of the One State through whose efforts "paradise" has been regained), the legend is in fact a radical reinterpretation of the myth of the Fall. Rather than emphasizing human disobedience or Satan's treachery, it points slyly to the latter's heroism, for in Zamyatin's rendition it is Satan who impels people to taste of freedom. A reversal of roles and values occurs, and the Devil appears as the active, energizing principle of life itself. This same heroic image of Satan as the "spirit of life" appears in Zamyatin's essays of this period and also in the

84

works of other writers, such as Bulgakov and Fedin.[17] Significantly, the adjective Zamyatin chooses to describe the Great Serpent—*ekhidnyi*—denotes sharp, biting wit as well as evil and cunning (in the translation I quoted it is rendered simply as "evil"). And so we return to I-330, who I submit is an incarnation of the Great Serpent—not Satan's handmaiden but an embodiment of Satan himself.

When critics have discussed I-330's mythic significance, they have invariably identified her, since she is a female, with Eve, although in the novel it is O-90 who is referred to as Eve by the poet R-13 (62). Critics have identified another relatively minor male character in the novel, S-4711, who is frequently in I-330's company, as Satan.[18] The only exception to this is Owen Ulph, who in his article, "I-330: Reconsiderations on the Sex of Satan," identifies Zamyatin's female protagonist with Satan. However, Ulph does not explore the mythic implications of this identification for the novel. Nor does he distinguish between Satan, femme fatale, vampire, siren; he refers to I-330 by all these names.

It has been pointed out by Nina Auerbach that female demons were widespread in nineteenth-century art.[19] It must be remembered, however, that there is a fundamental difference between a demon, which denotes an evil creature (the femme fatale is such a demon) and Satan, who possesses mythic stature within the context of the Judeo-Christian tradition. (Auerbach suggests that nineteenth-century female demons attain a kind of divinity through their association with pre-Christian myths.)

What in Zamyatin's novel suggests I-330's identity with Satan beside the snake imagery? Both the role she plays and the shapes associated with her: after all it is she who impels D-503 to taste of freedom. She causes him to sense his own individuality, to become a distinct "I" apart from the collective "We." (Like Adam in the legend he longs intermittently to return to paradise.) In Zamyatin's novel, "We" is identified with God and "I" with the Devil (128). I-330's name begins with the Latin letter "I" (in his novel Zamyatin, who knew English and had lived in England during World War I, mixes Latin and Cyrillic letters in naming his characters), which suggests the first-person singular pronoun in English.[20] Unfortunately, the effect of this play with shapes and meaning is lost in translation. Quite often Zamyatin drops the number "330," referring to I-330 simply as "I." I-330 is the leader of the revolutionary group, the Mephi, whose name comes from Mephistopheles, a name for the Devil. Through her sarcasm and mocking questions I-330 sows confusion and doubt. Zamyatin associated skepticism, mocking questions, even the very shape of the question mark with the Devil. In a 1921 essay, entitled "Paradise," he observed: "Doesn't the very curve of the question mark—?—suggest the Great Serpent, tempting the blessed inhabitants of ancient paradise with doubts?" (*SH*, 61).

Like Satan, I-330 lures her victims toward the unknown, and this unknown, in the shape of an X, the mathematical symbol for the unknown quantity, is sharply imprinted on her face. "I saw her eyebrows raised to her temples at a sharp angle, like the pointed horns of an X," observes D-503 in entry 2, describing his first encounter with I-330 (7). The comparison to "horns" here strengthens the link established between the X and Satan. In the Russian text X is rendered, not by the visual X shape as it is here in the translation, but by *iks*, the Russian term for the unknown quantity in mathematics (this is a distinction that defies translation into English). However, the reference to the eyebrows raised to the temples at a sharp angle gives the image a visual quality.

Subsequently (in entry 10), when the X image recurs in reference to I-330's face, it has a very strong visual impact because it is rendered by the X shape (this is true in both the Russian text and the English translation) and formed by two triangles, one inverted on the other:

> When she [I-330] speaks, her face is like a rapid, sparkling wheel—you can not distinguish the individual spokes. But right now the wheel was motionless. And I perceived a strange combination: dark eyebrows raised high at the temples—a mocking, sharp triangle. And yet another, pointing upward—the two deep lines from the corners of her mouth to the nose. And these two triangles somehow contradicted one another, stamped the entire face with an unpleasant, irritating X . . . (52–53)

At the same time the image undergoes a very curious transformation, becoming simultaneously an X and a cross: "And these two triangles somehow contradicted one another, stamped the entire face with an unpleasant, irritating X, like a cross. A face marked with a cross" (53). The transformation that occurs here is based on spatial properties: an X turned 45 degrees becomes a cross. The simultaneous perception of the two shapes (and I submit that they are simultaneously present, which has very interesting ramifications for the novel as we shall see shortly) depends on recognition of the shifting point of view. In other words, to perceive both the X and cross the reader must mentally assume two perspectives, much as the viewer of the Picasso painting *Portrait of Gertrude Stein* (1906) must assume different viewpoints because of the ambiguous perspective. As Louise Gardiner notes, in this portrait "the two sides of the mask-like face do not match up; the near side reads almost as a profile."[21]

The lack of a fixed perspective is a feature of modernism, first associated in painting with cubism.[22] (Picasso's *Portrait of Gertrude Stein* is an important work in early cubism.) Zamyatin found this notion of a shifting perspective very congenial for a number of reasons. First of all, it opened up possibilities for visual play. Here, as we see, Zamyatin deliberately plays on the spatial affinities between the X and the cross. More important, it accords with Zamyatin's outlook, for Zamyatin did not believe in immutable truths or in a "finite, fixed world."[23] Boundaries, he insisted, are continually changing.

I have suggested that the X in *We* is linked with Satan. The cross, on the other hand, gives rise to a very different type and range of mythic associations, centered on the notion of the crucified Christ. The image of the cross reoccurs at key points in the novel in connection with I-330, and invariably it is accompanied by telltale signs of Satan: X's, question marks, snake imagery. In other words, the two clusters of mythic associations coexist, and our understanding of this depends on our recognition of the shifting, ambiguous perspective.

Besides the visual image of the cross, the role I-330 plays links her with the crucified Christ. Again critics have tended to overlook this, stressing instead what they perceive as the Christ-like role of the male protagonist, D-503.[24] Like Christ, I-330 is a rebel, a nonconformist who chooses to remain true to her beliefs, to suffer and to die rather than recant and give in to the authorities. Like the crucified Christ, she is betrayed by one of her disciples, in this case D-503. Even those critics, who have recognized that the cross presages I-330's martyrdom,[25] have been reluctant to identify I-330, as a woman, with Christ. Yet as is evident from his essays—particularly the 1918 essay "Scythians?"—Zamyatin identified heretics, that is, spiritual revolutionaries, with the crucified Christ. Like Christ, their way is the way of the cross; like Christ, they choose to suffer (here I quote from that essay) "martyrdom on the earthly plane—and victory on a higher plane, the plane of ideas" (*SH*, 32).

In *We* the cross image appears when I-330 wrestles with the problem of whether to entrust D-503 with the secret of the Mephi conspiracy (the Mephi plot to take over the *Integral* and fly it off into the unknown, the *Integral* being the spaceship designed by D-503 that the One State intends to use to expand its power into the cosmos [entry 23]). The cross image appears again when I-330 raises her hand to vote against the Benefactor on Unanimity Day (entry 25), and yet again when she recognizes the folly of rebelling against the One State, yet refuses to give up, even if it means death (entry 28).

To this crucified Christ, Zamyatin opposes what he terms "Christ victorious"; that is, the institutionalized Christ of the church, a symbol of established authority. In the essay "Scythians?" it is "the victorious October Revolution" that is identified with this latter philistine version of Christ (*SH*, 23). In the novel *We*, it is the female character U (*iu* in Russian), her gill-like cheeks reminiscent of a fish, who incarnates this version of Christ. (The fish was the sign of Christ in the early church, and the One State of *We* is equated with the church, Unanimity Day likened to the celebration of Easter). It is U who watches over D-503 and works to bring him back into the fold, and it is U who reports the Mephi conspiracy to the authorities, although she does not implicate I-330.

Traditionally Satan and Christ have been regarded as antithetical forces. In Zamyatin's world, however, they have a great deal in common. First of all, there is a visual affinity: the *X*, which is associated in the novel with Satan, is also linked with Christ, since *X* is the first letter in the Russian (as in the Greek) word for Christ. There is also a spiritual likeness between Satan and Christ: both fight against rigidity; both incarnate freedom, courage, and rebellion; both are consummate heretics.[26] For Zamyatin, heretic and hero become synonymous. It is the heretic's lot to suffer martyrdom; similarly, the hero is inextricably linked with both tragedy and death.[27] The fact that I-330 is identified with the crucified Christ *and* with Satan makes her identity fluid: she is elusive, almost impossible to categorize. Her boundless mobility continually challenges us as readers to expand our notions of what is possible. It is precisely this heretical dual mythic identification—so startling, so unexpected—that makes I-330 such a singular and dynamic figure, endowing her with extraordinary energy and the power to transform.

To sum up, in Zamyatin's novel the traditional confines of gender are challenged, violated, and ultimately transcended. Zamyatin's concept of the hero/heretic/revolutionary cannot be said to be bound by gender considerations. Zamyatin is not male-centered or female-centered but individual-centered. He envisioned a world, a tomorrow that would "bring the liberation of the individual—in the name of the human being."[28] It behooves us as readers and critics not to be blinded by gender stereotypes but to recognize, as the modernists did, that "different though the sexes are, they intermix."[29] Only through an openness to the myriad of possibilities are we ourselves freed from the constraints of gender and able to move forward on that endless voyage of discovery Zamyatin felt to constitute the very essence of utopia.

Thea Margaret Durfee

Cement and *How the Steel Was Tempered*: Variations on the New Soviet Woman

FEW PEOPLE TODAY would disagree with the perception that literature in the Soviet period was codified, rigid, and dictated "from above." As young people, members of Soviet society were exhorted to read certain paradigmatic works of socialist realist literature, ostensibly with the goal of aiding them in their personal development to become good Soviet citizens. Such works presented very clear patterns of behavior and characters that young adults were encouraged to emulate in their real lives.

In light of this fact, it is interesting to see what the "party line" was on male and female roles in society. Katerina Clark's important study of the socialist realist novel clearly identifies the canon of correct political behavior for men, exemplified in the *positive hero*.[1] But what did such works offer to their female readership? This is the topic of the present essay, which takes a closer look at two classics in the Soviet literary canon: *Cement* (1925) by Fyodor Gladkov and *How the Steel Was Tempered* (1932, 1934) by Nikolai Ostrovsky. We will see that each work presents to the reader a specific feminine ideal, one that clearly reflects the changing policies and system of values in the first and second decades of the Soviet period, respectively.

The Bolshevik Revolution in Russia proved to be the catalyst for a major reexamination of the plight of all types of oppressed groups, including women. Leaders of the new government looked forward to a new equality for women in the workplace, home, and community. They envisioned a *new Soviet woman*, liberated from the oppressive structures of bourgeois life, who would become a fully contributing member in the political, economic, and social reconstruction of society. In order to facilitate this transformation, the Zhenotdel or Women's Section was created in 1919 as a department of the Party Secretariat devoted specifically to women's issues.[2] Founded by a small group of dedicated Bolshevik women activists—chief among whom was Aleksandra Kollontai[3]—its goal was to reach out to and mobilize the female population of Russia to membership and activity within the Communist Party and to lead the revolution in women's roles, aspirations, and attitudes. Its objectives included the assault on patriarchal family structures, the eradication of illiteracy, and the publication of journals that served to maintain contact between the Zhenotdel and its constituency and to inform them of their new rights and responsibilities. Its journal *Kommunistka* (Woman Communist), edited by Krupskaya, Lenin's wife, was designed to teach communist women about political organizational techniques and the condition of women in Russia. On its pages women could read about the family, marriage law, abortion, and changes in relations between the sexes that were necessary to free women from slavery to men.[4] The Zhenotdel was the driving force behind much of the legislation of the early Soviet government regarding women and civil rights.

The First Congress of Soviet Writers held in 1934 officially endorsed a new kind of literature termed "socialist realism," which would provide readers with didactic socialist fiction and, through its characters who struggled with various contemporary problems, offer role models for readers to emulate in their own daily lives. The understanding was that such a literature would also serve to reinforce political ideology and give voice to officially sanctioned social views.

Though it was not pronounced the "official" literary method until 1932, socialist realist writers were already testing the waters in the mid twenties. Fyodor Gladkov, the son of a poor peasant family who became a dedicated Bolshevik well before the Revolution, published his first short story in 1900. Today, he is remembered for the novel *Cement*. Written in 1922–24 and first published in 1925, the work was revised by Gladkov several times to reflect changes in party policies and values. *Cement* occupies a prominent place in the list of exemplary works of socialist realism, and, according to Clark, its plot and positive heroes were imitated more than any others in Soviet fiction (69).

Typically, critical discussions of *Cement* focus on its generic place as the originator of the production novel and therefore consider it to be centered around the male protagonist, Gleb Chumalov, a demobilized military commissar, who returns home after the civil war to find his old town changed: the cement factory where he had once worked is run down and decrepit, and his wife is no longer the obedient woman he left behind but a strong, aggressive member of the Communist Party. Clark's study, for example, views the novel as centered around Gleb's struggle to get the cement factory back in operation and at the same time deal with the traumas of the new civilian life. However, while Gleb is the central male figure in the novel, the character of his wife Dasha is equally significant, as is the story of her day-to-day toil for the social and political transfiguration of women's life. In order to portray all aspects of life transformed by communism, Gladkov devotes as much of the novel to the heroic figure of the new Soviet woman as to her male counterpart.

In contrast to her traditional peasant predecessor in Maxim Gorky's novel *Mother* (1907), which recounts how a peasant mother is awakened to political consciousness and takes over the revolutionary activities of her son, the new Soviet woman has been revolutionarily remade in all ways including physique, occupation, and roles as wife and mother. In *Cement* most of the new characteristics of the ideal Soviet woman are revealed early on, when Gleb first confronts his wife after his return home (much of the novel is narrated from his perspective). He is shocked by what he perceives as her brusque confrontational manner and her neglect of their home and daughter. "This was another woman . . . her face tired . . . and stern as through she were clenching her teeth. . . . His Dasha was strange and remote."[5] Busy from dawn to dusk with work in the Women's Section and exhausted when she returns home, Dasha no longer spends her time cooking or cleaning. She has placed Nurka, their daughter, in the Krupskaya Children's Home, a communal childrearing facility created to release women from domestic drudgery and enable them to join the socialist work force. Dasha's response to Gleb's complaints about their lost domestic idyll reveals the unenlightened traditionality and "bourgeois" selfishness of his views:

> "Lie down and calm yourself, Gleb. I'm worn out from work. Tomorrow I'm ordered into the country again, to organize the Women's Section, and there are bands of roughs throughout the district. . . . Do you want flowers on the windowsill, Gleb, and a bed overloaded with feather pillows? No, Gleb; I spent the winter in an unheated room (there's a fuel crisis, you know), and I eat dinner in the communal restaurant. You see, I'm a free Soviet citizen." (32, 28)

With this last sentence Dasha announces her liberation. She makes it clear that the rules have changed and that she is no longer required to serve as a slave to her husband and home. Her responsibilities lie in the realm of the community as a whole, and her energy is devoted to the building of socialism.

Dasha's comments and indeed her entire persona are closely linked to the Zhenotdel. The women's reforms initiated by Kollontai, Krupskaya, and others are depicted as directly responsible for her phenomenal new strength and power: "Where had Dasha absorbed this power? . . . This strength had awakened and been forged from the collective spirit of the workers, from years of deadly hardship, from the terrible heavy burden of the newly acquired freedom of women. She crushed him with the audacity of this strength" (31). As a exemplar of didactic socialist prose, *Cement* serves as a model for the radical reconstruction of society envisioned by libertarian Bolshevism. Within this context, Dasha is not only a member of the Zhenotdel in the novel; she is the embodiment of the entire group of reforms fostered by this department of the Communist Party. This is displayed in her involvement in local politics (chapter 4), her struggle to become literate (70),[6] and her role in the administration of child and women's shelters (chapters 2 and 11). Not surprisingly, Dasha is successful in all of her endeavors and during the course of the novel she is elected chairperson of the Workers' Club (Comintern) and assumes the position of leader of the local Zhenotdel (chapter 17).

Another way of indicating Dasha's political maturity is through the use of the scale provided by Clark in her analysis of the male protagonist. Clark shows that the typical socialist realist hero undergoes a progression from an initial, elemental state marked by impulsive, "spontaneous" actions and emotions (*stikhiinost'*), to careful deliberation and consideration of his actions and complete political awareness (*soznatel'nost'*, literally translated as "consciousness") (19–24). The figure who aids the hero along his path of growing *soznatel'nost'* is identified as the elder or mentor and is a person who has already completed this progression. According to Clark, this person should also have been "tested by revolutionary or enemy fire, and, as a token of his preparedness for sacrifice, he should bear such scars as physical wounds or personal loss" (169). Judged by this scale, Dasha has already completed this heroic progression and is fully "conscious" by the time she is introduced to the reader in chapter 1. (The account of her symbolic death and rebirth is given in chapter 10, entitled "Strata of the Soul," where we learn how Dasha bravely suffered torture at the hands of the Whites during Gleb's absence, endured rape, and bestowed sexual favors on partisan soldiers. Her ultimate sacrifice is embodied in Nurka's death.) As a result, by the time they meet, Dasha is already fully prepared to serve as Gleb's mentor. In light of this we find that Clark's view (82) that the hero-mentor relationship is dispensed with in Gladkov's novel must be amended. Instead, we would suggest that Shibis, the Cheka head, serves as Gleb's mentor in his interaction with the party apparatus and struggle to remobilize the cement factory and that Dasha serves as Gleb's mentor in the second, equally important plotline of the novel: Gleb's struggle to understand and accept the social and economic transformations of life and the new Soviet woman herself.

Thus, while sometimes Dasha is a source of consternation and anxiety for the positive hero, her terse statements and personal example expose his traditional unenlightened views and indicate his need for change. Moreover, though they are no longer bound by the ties of traditional marriage, she acts as his adviser in the sexual realm, encouraging him to take advantage of his own sexual liberation and another woman's obvious attraction to him (155). Slowly but surely, Gleb learns to curb his violent outbursts against the frightening and unfamiliar ways in which communism has transformed the social landscape and begins to comprehend and accept the ways in which family and interpersonal life have changed, as explained to him by Dasha. By the

end of the novel he has progressed both politically and socially, and she has
only to provide him with gentle encouragement and hope for the future:
"The old life has perished and will not return. We must build up a new life. . . .
Love will always be love, Gleb, but it requires a new form. Everything will
come through and attain new forms, and then we shall know how to forge
new links" (308). Thus she stresses that, though a transformation of personal
life has occurred, the essences remain the same. The new life is not without
love, but love is governed by new, more equitable rules of human behavior.
At the same time, it seems that Gladkov has left the relationship between
Dasha and Gleb open-ended, allowing the reader to speculate about a new
union of these two ideal Soviet citizens, made possible by Gleb's political and
social maturation.

The inner, political sophistication of the new Soviet woman is accompanied by an outer, physical transformation. As Gleb comments when he first
sees her: "Everything about her . . . was strange, not womanly, something he
had never seen before in her" (4). Like the female figure in propaganda
posters of the time, such as A. I. Strakhov's "8th of March—Day of the Liberation of Women" (*8 marta —den' raskreposhcheniia zhenshchin*, 1926),[7]
Dasha is physically as well as mentally suited for the work of socialist construction. She is sunburnt, has a weathered face, and a "stubborn opinionat-
ed chin. Her face seemed larger under the fiery red kerchief with which her
head was bound" (27). Emphasis is placed on her physical and emotional
strength. For the new Soviet woman fashion and femininity are a luxury and
antithetical to communism's spartan tastes. Like her visual counterpart in
early Soviet posters, Dasha wears a red kerchief, the symbol of the women's
movement in Soviet Russia.[8] Even before the Revolution the color red was
the symbol of the revolutionary movement, and strips of red cloth were carried in demonstrations.[9] The red kerchief then became the symbol of the
Bolshevik women's movement, simultaneously expressing support for the
cause, associations with Mother Russia, and a no-nonsense attitude toward
labor and functionality in clothing. Dasha also has the trademark bobbed
hair of a women's rights activist, wears men's clothes, and appears to Gleb
"stern . . . strange and remote" (27). The lack of traditional femininity and the
accoutrements of sex appeal make the new Soviet woman seem inaccessible
and unattainable. Such inaccessibility confuses Gleb and mirrors Dasha's
refusal to allow him immediate sexual access: "Dasha was silent, cold, near
and . . . a stranger" (32; ellipsis in original), "her heart was shut against him"
(32). However, as Gleb progresses further and further toward political consciousness and comes to regard Dasha as an equal, her new physiognomy
becomes more and more understandable and attractive to him. As a result,
though initially put off by her transformation, by chapter 10 Gleb again takes
notice of her "soft full breasts" (152) and finds her "irresistible" (156).

Indeed this new woman is as alluring as she is unfamiliar (Gleb thinks,

"An enigma: was she tempting him as a man, or was she snapping the last threads that bound them together?" [29]), and the combination of this odd new appearance with her sexual liberation seems irresistible to the new men in Gladkov's novel. A constant theme in the work is Gleb's jealousy and competition for Dasha's affections with Badin, the local party chairman. Though neither man is successful in his attempts to force himself on her, Dasha eventually does have an affair with Badin. However, it is not his persistence, but her desire coupled with the thrill of her heroic escape from the hands of Cossack renegades (combined with the "chance" that they wind up together in a one-bed room) that prompts the affair to take place. Her response to this liaison places emphasis on her initial feelings of attractiveness and her ultimate and long-awaited sexual pleasure (134). (This is not to say that she did not have sexual intercourse during Gleb's absence, but the rape she suffered and the sexual favors that she bestowed on soldiers are viewed as sacrifice and duty rendered to the revolutionary cause.)

As a whole *Cement* reflects the Bolshevik women's interest in sexual liberation and freedom from the male proprietorship of bourgeois marriage, and several characters in the novel engage in unstructured liaisons. For the ideal Soviet woman, however, sex is depicted as a form of pleasure for which she only rarely has the time and the energy. In fact, as a type of sexual interaction, it almost seems as if rape plays a much more prominent role in the novel than does free love. Just as Gleb tries to force Dasha to make love to him out of desperation, Badin tries the same approach in the carriage just before they are ambushed, countering Dasha's protests with the following: "On the contrary, I do dare, and don't see any great shame in it. We're a good virile couple. . . . And what I want to do, I do! In a struggle, I use all means" (124). Though he does not succeed with Dasha, Badin later repeatedly rapes Polia, the leader of the Zhenotdel. Within the novel, Polia provides negative contrast to Dasha, as the sensualist characterized by softness (her last name, Mekhova, comes from the Russian word for fur), femininity, and a weakness for material things. She is the example of a failed transformation (significantly, curls are forever escaping from her red kerchief), of a woman who joins the Revolution but cannot stand the tests of communist life and in the end is purged from the party. Gleb and Dasha refer to her as a "weak child" (151), a "little girl" (151), and a "sentimental young lady" (153). Thus, the rape she suffers at Badin's hands is not depicted so much as inappropriate behavior for a party leader as the consequence of her own political and moral weakness. It is logical then that such an approach does not succeed with the politically correct and disciplined Dasha. As we shall see, this disturbing message resurfaces later in *How the Steel Was Tempered.*

As opposed to sexual, or nonprocreative love discussed above, a certain ambiguity seems to surround Dasha's role as a mother, and her placement of daughter Nurka in the communal children's home (and Nurka's eventual death) is one of the most disturbing points in the novel's plot. Though we are meant to realize the political correctness of this action, and we are shown that it is the best possible alternative for the children in the midst of the starvation and disease resulting from the Civil War, initially, the act seems insensitive and cruel, a perception we are temporarily encouraged to feel by Gleb's comments and the bleak picture of reality with which Gladkov confronts his reader. Gleb's criticisms question Dasha's maternity early on: "And Nurka? I suppose you've thrown her to the pigs too, with the flowers? That's a pretty business!" (28). Later, when he sees the children scratching and clawing greedily through the dirt at the Krupskaya Home he declares, "All these poor wretches will starve to death here, Dasha. You ought all to be shot for this job" (35).

However, at the children's home, Dasha is joyfully received, not only by Nurka, but by all of the children who live there:

> "Aunt Dasha has come! Aunt Dasha has come!" . . . The girls . . . kept stretching their hands towards Dasha, clasping violets. Each wanted to be the first to put the flowers into her hands. . . . And Dasha and the children all burst out laughing; and the sun laughed too in at the open windows as large as doors. (36, 37)

Obviously, the message here is that Dasha has given up her own daughter only to become a mother to all children, even to the cosmos itself. Her embrace is even broad enough to encompass bourgeois children. While overseeing the seizure of the belongings of a wealthy family, Dasha finds a doll to give to their little girl, and then chastises the girl's mother for trying to make her return it (175). As above, where Dasha's individual responsibilities as a housewife are transferred to the community as a whole, any implied neglect of Nurka on Dasha's part is more than canceled out by her new role as communal mother. In any case, the enlightened Soviet reader would understand that such social measures are communism's answer to the destruction of the family resulting from capitalist industrialization. As Kollontai explained in her 1918 speech to the First All-Russian Congress of Women: "Capitalism forced the woman also to seek work outside the family, outside the home. . . . What kind of a family life is that, when the wife and mother works for maybe eight, but with travel and everything else, ten hours! The family is less looked after; the children grow up, not under their mother's eyes, but more on the street, left to themselves and all kinds of dangerous occurrences."[10]

In the end, despite a certain trend toward sexual liberation and the possibility of free love, Dasha remains a procreative figure. Within the novel, Gladkov repeatedly underlines the positive, energizing aspects of Dasha's character through the use of folk imagery and the allegorical identification of Dasha with Mother Russia. This identification is summed up in the symbol of the flaming headscarf in which the color red (not only denoting Russia but also symbolizing blood) and sun imagery (symbolically life-giving) are combined. At one point, Gleb opens his eyes to see that "the sun was blazing through the window. Dasha was standing at the table, adjusting her flaming headscarf. She glanced at him and laughed. An amber light shone in her eyes" (33). The fact that this symbol is somehow both progressive and traditional is summed up by Gleb a few lines later: "You are the same woman as before, and you are a new Dasha also. . . . Even the sun shines differently now." To which Dasha cryptically replies, "Yes, Gleb, the sun and the corn have changed" (33). This procreative symbolism, then, complements and balances out the more threatening aggressive and sexually free aspects of the new Soviet woman of the twenties.

As a whole, *Cement* presents a picture of the new Soviet woman as robust, independent, and assertive. She is a woman who has rejected femininity and sublimated personal desires, including motherhood, for the sake of building a new socialist society. The ideal woman here is portrayed on equal footing with men. Dasha is living out Kollontai's vision of "a comradely and loving union of two free, independent self-supporting equal members of communist society" (87). On a societal level, she is not so much a mother or a daughter as a symbolic "sister" in "the one big, universal working family" (Kollontai, 88).

By the early 1930s things had changed. With Stalin's rise to power and the beginning of the Five-Year Plans, the Soviet government began to focus on stabilization and the development of its infrastructure. Likewise the social and cultural realms experienced a trend toward stabilization of various kinds. Literature no longer sought to depict the dynamic heroes of the twenties but returned to more stable characters. Simultaneously, the state actively sought to strengthen the nuclear family since it was considered a microcosmic auxiliary of the state.[11] This return to conservativism was reflected in the abolition of the Zhenotdel in 1930. Political pronouncements of the time reflected a long-suppressed negative attitude toward sexually assertive behavior in women. As early as 1923, Gorky had declared that the great heroic woman of the Revolution had already disappeared to be replaced by "fillies to whom are attributed an overpowering urge towards an exclusively sexual life and sexual perversion of various kinds."[12] Literature, fulfilling its responsibility to popularize party policy, reflected these changes regarding women. Gladkov's *Cement* provides an interesting case in point. In the 1939–40 version of the novel, published in 1947, Dasha's character changed significantly, particularly regarding the episode with Badin. This revision de-emphasized her sexual fulfillment and amplified the threatening, dominating aspects in her behavior.[13] The result of all of these changes was a shift in the persona of the new Soviet woman away from her aggressive, dynamic features toward a more traditional, stable, and maternal role. This becomes clear when we examine the following work.

How the Steel Was Tempered is perhaps the most famous socialist realist novel. Until as recently as the 1970s it was presented as the most important work of fiction for Soviet young people to read and emulate. A semi-autobiographical work, written in the late twenties by party activist Nikolai Ostrovsky and published in the early thirties, *How the Steel Was Tempered* recounts the life of Pavel Korchagin from a small boy living in Ukraine during the Revolution and the civil war, to a young Bolshevik, and finally to a fully politically conscious and responsible member of the Komsomol. Toward the end of his short and painful life, after suffering from tuberculosis, increasing blindness, and a disease of the central nervous system (among other infirmities), Pavel meets Taia, a young rural worker, and they marry. He helps her along her way in political awareness and growing consciousness and dies at the age of twenty-four, leaving her to continue on the path of enlightenment and trusting that she will grow as a responsible member of the party.

If it seems that the new Soviet woman is not very central to this novel, it is largely true. Politically correct women do not appear until the second half of the book, and the woman who participates most intimately in the life of the hero does not come on the scene until the last thirty pages of the 400-page novel. Obviously something has changed in the relative importance accorded the ideal woman's role in the prototypical socialist realist novel.

Perhaps the most obvious difference between this work and the preceding one lies in the political relationship of the ideal man and woman. In this case, roles played by male and female characters in the hero-mentor dynamic are reversed. Instead of being the politically mature mentor figure like Dasha, Taia is the disciple of her husband. Consequently the ideal Soviet woman has become largely peripheral to the central hero-mentor relationship of the novel, and, although she herself may represent varying stages along the *stikhiinost-soznatel'nost'* scale, the positions of central hero and mentor are exclusively male.

However, although the presence of the positive female role model in the novel is diminished, this does not mean that there is a scarcity of female types. One after another women enter the hero's life, each a negative stereotype of feminine behavior, from sexual promiscuity to "feminine weakness." Nelly, the daughter of a rich family from Pavel's childhood, is the most extreme of these examples. After many years have passed, she and Pavel become reacquainted when he is called to fix a light bulb on the train of a rich Polish diplomat. Though she is totally unrecognizable at first, Pavel finally realizes that the rich, well-dressed whore in the car is his old childhood friend. Nelly plays the role of temptress to Pavel, and, made-up and draped in materialistic finery, she is meant to be a symbol of all the excesses which are symptomatic of capitalism and political corruption.

However, even women who are politically correct in the novel are generally guilty in one way or another of minor infractions. We might take for example, Lida, a Komsomolka who, instead of exposing the sexual harassment she suffers at the hands of a comrade, gives in to his insincere dissembling and apologies. Or Katiusha, who lures Pavel away from his studies to attend a "kissing party," where he is confronted with "disgusting and silly" flirting games and the overtures of Mura. Almost all of these women are guilty of the same type of sexual aggressiveness and freedom that was considered a positive aspect of the new Soviet woman envisioned in *Cement*. Most often, these women touch the hero's arm or try to hold his hand, a gesture that may seem insignificant to the reader but is anxiety-ridden for the prudish party man Pavel. In fact, to return to the issue of rape discussed earlier, in one instance such a desire to cling to the hero leads indirectly to rape by midnight bandits. Ostrovsky describes the scene: "Korchagin jerked his arm but Anna, petrified with fear, clung wildly to it. And by the time he was able to tear it loose, it was too late; his neck was caught in an iron grip. . . . Out of the corner of his eye Korchagin had one brief and stark glimpse of the chalk-white face of Anna whom one of the three dragged into the gaping hole in the wall at that moment."[14] Pavel does succeed in driving the bandits away, but not before the damage to Anna is done. Immediately afterward in Anna's apartment, he reruns the episode in his mind, smoking a cigarette as he reflects that he has "just killed for the fourth time in his life." The effect of the combination of this rape scene, the woman's implied responsibility for its occurrence, and the sexual overtones of Pavel's reflections about the episode is truly strange and disturbing.[15]

In contrast to such negative female types, Taia, the woman Pavel marries, is very clearly defined as an ideal for feminine behavior. She is repeatedly held up as *simpatichnaia* (nice), and, as opposed to Dasha's commanding tone, she has a "quiet voice." She is the epitome of demure submissiveness, also in sharp contrast to Dasha's unyielding will and firm control of both her own feelings and the people around her. This new Soviet woman of the 1930s is notable for her excessive modesty, which even extends to the point that she "does not usually admit members of the male sex to her room" (394). Her modesty is shown in high relief against the background of the sexual aggressiveness of the numerous other women in Pavel's life. Her room is filled with things that emphasize both her femininity and "feminine taste" in general: the chest of drawers is covered with knickknacks, and the lace curtain is tied back by a "pale blue ribbon." Unlike Dasha's home where there were no curtains on the windows and the flowerpots were long empty, Taia has "two flower pots with scarlet geraniums and pale pink asters" (304). Even their private spaces express the fundamental differences between these two ideal Soviet women.

The ideal female in *How the Steel Was Tempered* also possesses a very definite set of physical characteristics, even more pronounced than those of Dasha. "She was no beauty," we are told, but then the author draws attention to her "large brown eyes, lightly drawn mongolian brows, the pretty line of her nose, fresh straight lips" and the outline of her "firm young breasts tight underneath her striped worker's blouse" (394). The reader quickly realizes that Taia is very healthy and wholesome. She could just have stepped out of a socialist realist painting, such as S. Riagina's *Higher, Higher* (*Vse vyshe,* 1934).[16] The attention paid to the physical attractiveness of her body stands out strangely in light of her modesty and the hero's squeamishness about physical love, yet it is entirely appropriate to the Soviet ideals of the thirties, which demanded that Soviet citizens be "robust, athletic, sunburned and well-nourished."[17] It also seems to capture the sexual undercurrent of androgyny in the new Soviet woman, who is familiar yet *different.*

In fact, Taia's "firm young breasts" are probably more indicative of the important place that motherhood and maternal duty were accorded under Stalin.[18] By the thirties, motherhood had become central to the definition of femininity. Thus, in Ostrovsky's novel, getting married and having children replace political consciousness as the ultimate goal of a woman's heroic progression. Immediately before Pavel meets Taia, he is impressed to discover that two female friends from the past (both of whom have not been mentioned in the novel for quite a while and will not be mentioned again) have gotten married and have either borne children already or are pregnant. The thematic completion of these positive female characters serves as an introduction to the hero's own long-awaited romantic affiliation and to the appearance of the new Soviet woman in the novel.

This is not to say that Pavel has overcome his earlier shyness and disapproval of romantic involvements. Pavel's marriage to Taia is portrayed as a philanthropic gesture on his part to aid in liberating her from the oppression of her father. His proposal to her speaks volumes about the novel's attitude toward ideal feminine behavior:

> "I give you my hand, little girl, here it is. . . . We can both give each other a great deal. Now, here is what I have decided: our compact will be in force until you grow up to be a real human being, a true Bolshevik. If I can't help you in that I am not worth a kopek. We must not break our compact until then. But when you grow up you will be freed of all obligations. . . . Remember, you must not consider yourself bound to me in any way." (406)

Her answer to his proposal further underlines the chastity of the two young heroes and their union:

> "I have moved the chest of drawers away from the door leading to your room. If

ever you want to talk to me you can come straight in. You don't need to go through Lola's room."

The blood rushed to Pavel's cheeks. Taia smiled happily. Their compact was sealed. (407)

Eventually, however, they do fall in love. In a letter to a comrade, Pavel describes his relationship with his wife, simultaneously encapsulating the role of the ideal Soviet woman in relationship to her husband:

Then there is Taia's education, . . . and of course love, and the tender caresses of my little wife. Taia and I are the best of friends. . . . The other day she proudly showed me her delegate's credentials issued by the Women's Department. This is not simply a strip of cardboard to her. In her I see the birth of a new woman, and I am doing my best to help in this birth. The time will come when she will work in a big factory, where as part of a large working community she will become politically mature. (410)

Thus, though the ideal union, as depicted in *How the Steel Was Tempered*, is almost entirely chaste, it still manages to be highly procreative, though perhaps not in the way we might expect. We are led to assume that though the couple do eventually develop romantic feelings for one another, Taia could not fulfill her role as a Soviet woman and produce a child for Pavel due to his infirmity and illnesses. However, the use of birthing and nurturing imagery in Pavel's letter quoted above seems to make Taia herself the procreative product of their union, with the glory of motherhood being assumed by Pavel! The placement of the "new woman" herself as the product of their union, then, preserves the procreative potential of the new Soviet man and woman and fulfills the state's demands for the perpetuation of the communist family, while at the same time upholding the chaste purity of their union as an ideal of immaculate conception.

As Ostrovsky's novel demonstrates, by the thirties socialist realist literature reflected the resurgence of traditional values regarding women's roles in the family and responsibilities to the state, in response to the state's effort to shore up the institution of the family and restore stability to a ruptured society.[19] Barbara Clement Evans notes that the liberated sexuality and disregard for the family of the new woman of the twenties "were too great a threat to social order and to deeply cherished beliefs about human nature and sexual identity" (233). And, in fact, as we have seen in *Cement*, the Bolsheviks never really rejected the importance of motherhood. Even Gladkov felt the need to endow his radical female with strong maternal overtones, at the same time that he liberated her from a traditional domestic environment. Aleksandra Kollontai herself seems to have suffered from this contradictory malaise. She simultaneously stressed the importance of motherhood and the necessity to

100

"save women's strength from being wasted on the family in order to employ it more reasonably for the benefit of the collective."[20] These two ideas were reconciled in the image of the worker-mother, who, like Dasha, "would no longer differentiate between her children and other children."[21]

In conclusion, we have seen two different visions of the ideal Soviet woman presented in the socialist realist works examined here. In *Cement*, Gladkov presented the reader with a radical liberated woman who acted out the left-wing Bolshevik deconstruction of the family. She was well aware of her new rights and responsibilities as an enfranchised Soviet citizen and was prepared to take advantage of them. Even though Gladkov's vision remains limited by certain chauvinist ideals of women and beauty, the new roles he envisioned for women in political, social, and economic life reflected his attempt to embrace the most radical and progressive views in the air at the time he was writing. In contrast to this, the fictional woman of the thirties represents a decisive step backward toward traditional ideals of feminine behavior such as submissiveness, chastity, and timidity. Such a definition is relative to and therefore necessarily a function of her male companion.

What these two depictions do have in common, however, is a certain tension, an uneasy resolution of conflicting qualities. Each novel seeks to endorse domestic liberation, yet emphasizes motherhood. Both present a vivid picture of the new feminine physiognomy, yet neither succeeds in addressing female sexuality. In *Cement*, Dasha's liberated views provoke anxiety, claustrophobia, and confusion in the positive hero. *How the Steel Was Tempered* flatly rejects female sexuality as bad, dirty, corrupt, or at least indicative of a basic weakness of resolve. Yet perhaps this inherent contradictoriness is not surprising when we remember that the essence of socialist realism as a literary method is, what Clark has termed, its "modal schizophrenia" (37); that is, its attempt to depict mythic men and women of the utopian future, yet simultaneously portray real people who answer the demands of current Soviet policy. Thus, in both of the works examined in this essay the new Soviet woman emerges as a hybrid, the product of a vision that is at once progressive and reactionary, radical yet traditional, reflecting a conservative definition of liberation.

Helena Goscilo

Mother as Mothra: Totalizing Narrative and Nuture in Petrushevskaia

> I give you the destroying mother. I give you her justice—
> from which we have never removed the eye bandage. I
> give you the angel—and point you to the sword in her
> hand.
> —Philip Wylie, *Generation of Vipers*

> Not to be born is best.
> —Sophocles, *Oedipus Colonus*

THE WOMAN WRITER SPAYED

Ever since the Sovietization of Russia, its domestic cultural commentators have sweepingly invoked the term "woman writer" (*pisatel'nitsa*) as at worst an oxymoron and at best an unwitting sign for creative inferiority. Consequently, female authors in Russia who cherish their "femininity" in all spheres of everyday life have defensively insisted on the genderless or masculine nature of their writing. Their Muse apparently answers an unspoken version of Lady Macbeth's appeal for an "unnatural" transformation ("unsex me here" [act 1, scene 5]) that mysteriously suspends gendered identity during moments of creativity.[1] Belief in spayed inspiration suffered a rude shock at the end of the 1980s, when the post-Stalin generation of women writers (e.g., Larisa Vaneeva, Svetlana Vasilenko, Nina Sadur, and Elena Tarasova) collaborated to produce two anthologies of contemporary women's writing: *The Woman Who Doesn't Remember Evil* (Ne pomniashchaia zla, 1990) and *The New Amazons* (Novye Amazonki, 1990).[2] Vaneeva's straightforward preface to the first collection, like Vasilenko's ironic introduction to the second, unapologetically broke with decades-old tradition, to proclaim the explicit relevance of gender to the contributors' authorship. Affronted traditionalists dubbed the contents of these volumes "the new women's prose" and harangued it accordingly. Yet the substantial (if hapless) attention Russians currently accord women's fiction owes less, perhaps, to the innovations of its thirty-something practitioners than to the works of Tatiana Tolstaia and Liudmila Petrushevskaia—and to the feminist movement in the West.

Tolstaia's meteoric rise to fame after the publication of "Peters" (1986), her frequent contacts with the West (where she now resides), and the sardonic provocation of her journalist and lecture persona have earned her a broad-based Western following. Her deliberately inflammatory interviews, as well as her outspoken reviews and articles in the *New Republic*, the *Atlantic Monthly*, and the *New York Review of Books*, have fueled lively controversies that assure her the kind of limelight she might not have attained exclusively through her superb stories. Indeed, some of her most ardent admirers (and detractors) do not suffer from overfamiliarity with her fiction.[3] If Tolstaia's assertive public self and her vivid, intricate prose have not overturned stale misconceptions about women's creativity (sometimes voiced by Tolstaia herself), they at least have prompted the less impermeable Russian critics either to reassess these clichés or to use them sparingly.

Petrushevskaia's "overnight" post-glasnost recognition, for which she struggled approximately a quarter-century, is less dramatic and smaller in scale. The unremitting bleakness of her vision disquiets both Russian and Western readers, and, together with the difficulty of rendering her deceptively shorn style into English, may explain the comparative neglect she has encountered in the West.[4] Whereas Tolstaia's narratives seduce readers, Petrushevskaia's devastate them. Yet anyone seeking documentation of women's experience in contemporary Russian literature would be foolhardy to bypass Petrushevskaia's quantitatively modest but stylistically complex oeuvre, for Petrushevskaia engages readers' passions partly through her highly rhetorical and psychologically harrowing inscription of womanhood.

HOME AND HEROINE: SOCIAL STIGMA AND
EXISTENTIAL STIGMATA

The most productive examination of womanhood in Liudmila Petrushevskaia's fiction entails an analysis of typologies. Indeed, Petrushevskaia's female protagonists may be classified by a typology of function, inasmuch as their literary identity derives from their family roles: primarily, those of mother, wife, and daughter. Since family traditionally has constituted the minimal social unit, at first glance Petrushevskaia's prose invites a reading that emphasizes the disintegration of Soviet society, especially its intelligentsia. Such a reading, however, fails to account adequately for Petrushevskaia's extensive reliance on antiquity as cultural referent—a reliance to which Petrushevskaia herself draws attention by her self-conscious choice of such names as Pulkheriia and such titles as *The Way of Eros* (Po doroge Boga

Erosa), "Medea" (Medeia), and "The God Poseidon" (Bog Poseidon).[5] Far from merely serving as a vehicle for social commentary, family in Petrushevskaia, as in Greek tragedy, metonymizes the human condition.[6] The exalted tone of tragic doom in Euripides and Sophocles that Aristotle deemed requisite for catharsis, however, undergoes radical debasement in Petrushevskaia's modern world in extremis. What Greek tragedy casts as elevated cosmic drama, she decrowns as shabby everyday prosaics. Substituting low-key horror for noble grandeur, she capitalizes on associations with classic antecedents to convey the full magnitude of experiences that her style, by contrast, ironizes and degrades.

Petrushevskaia's fictional world is both overwhelming and overwhelmingly female. An existentialist whose emphatically gynocentric texts probe the "unbearable heaviness of being,"[7] Petrushevskaia constructs a metaphysical/psychic space of absence: her "heroines" all define themselves not through adherence to, but through deviation from, an implicit norm relegated to the boundaries of her narratives but never instantiated within them. That norm is the paradigmatic family, which operates as an organizing trope for the human bonding that Petrushevskaia's fictional universe conspicuously lacks. To establish the lack of ties that would mitigate individual alienation, Petrushevskaia packs her narratives with perversions of what are conventionally posited as expected and desirable standards of role behavior. Her overriding concern, unlike Tolstoy's, is family *un*happiness.[8] Thus spouses and lovers hate, beat, deceive, and drive each other to suicidal despair ("Father and Mother" [Otets i mat', 1989], "A Raw Leg" [Syraia noga, 1973–78], "A Girl Like That" [Takaia devochka, 1988], "Flu" [Gripp, 1969]); adult offspring neglect and steal from their parents, while simultaneously brutalizing their siblings ("Ali Baba" [1988], "Night Time" [Vremia noch', 1992]); fathers abandon families ("Our Crowd" [Svoi krug, 1979]); mothers humiliate, deprive, and kill their children ("Hygiene" [Gigiena, 1990], "The Land" [Strana, 1988], "Medea" [Medeia, 1990]). Little more than the chance byproduct of sexual appetite, small children serve mainly as pawns in the incessant battle between parents driven by their own psychological and physical priorities. With family members consistently violating and instrumentalizing each other, the traditional ideal of the family home as consoling sanctuary erodes into the dreaded house of psychic horrors.

Presiding over that assaultive environment is the central figure of the mother, a figure equated with the benevolent-natural and sanctified as an institution in both Western and Russian culture.[9] Thus Petrushevskaia achieves her most chilling effects by portraying mothers as "unnaturally" incapacitated despots who wield psychological power for their own complex and largely unacknowledged ends: in that regard, as in others, her world manifestly contravenes "nature."

That "unnatural" world conceives of life as a trial, during which Petrushevskaia's characters, always already condemned, struggle to postpone or elude the inevitable penalties inseparable from the negative judgment rendered at (i.e., synonymous with) their birth. Within this endless cycle of universal victimization, mothers invariably both endure and inflict punishment. Although the quintessential identity for a Petrushevskaian mother is that of a hospitalized patient whose hearsay presence exerts a painful influence on her daughter's or son's life,[10] Petrushevskaia's most intricate and disturbing stories figure mothers chiefly as judges and executioners. Psychologically maiming and suffocating the offspring to whom they have given biological life, they erase those offspring narratively by allowing them no existence or voice independent of the voracious maternal ego. In that sense, the totalitarian Petrushevskaian mother mirrors the totalitarian Soviet state. Revealingly, Petrushevskaia's preface to her own collection of fiction recently published in Russia reads: "The author's selections, offered for the reader's *judgment*. Only prose" (Predlagaetsia na *sud* chitatelia vybrannoe avtorom. Tol'ko proza" [my emphasis]).[11]

MOMMIE DEAREST

Located along a continuum of deviation, Petrushevskaia's mothers verbally simulate the posited hypothetical norm of maternity through rhetoric. The double-voiced narrative typical of Petrushevskaia's stories, which is especially pronounced, paradoxically, in her genre of monologues (*monologi*), repeatedly exposes the pathology of mothers' "underground" selves. Unreliable narrators whose very strategies of concealment and camouflage disclose even more than they endeavor to hide, these all-consuming matriarchs inadvertently betray aspects of their psyches unsuspected even by them.

Thus the reader's task is to read for misrepresentation, so as to hypothesize a counternarrative located "between the lines," patched from elements withheld and distorted by the directly articulated text. Just as Chekhov's plays maximize the effect of silence, so the impact of Petrushevskaia's texts hinges on the primacy of the unsaid. Two of Petrushevskaia's "monologues" that superbly display her sophisticated deployment of first-person narrative to expose the rhetorical intricacies of maternal self-presentation are "Our Crowd"[12] and "Night Time."[13] Revelation of character in both hinges on a meticulously orchestrated manipulation of viewpoint anchored in double-voiced narration, in which eruptions by the subterranean "bad Mother" periodically challenge the more palatable version of reality fashioned by the socially-sanctioned "good Mother."[14]

"Our Crowd" depicts a community of marital and parental failures among Moscow's technical intelligentsia. With apparent dispassionate irony the female narrator recounts the amoral antics of her circle of "friends," which include sexual experimentation and infidelity, child abuse, alcoholism, thievery, incest, prostitution, and regular orgies organized around boozing and sexual games. Framing her narration in an avowal of her own cleverness and discernment ("I'm very smart"/"I'm smart, I understand things" ["ia ochen' umnaia"/"ia umnaia, ia ponimaiu"], 116/130; 3/24), the narrator proceeds to catalogue all of her friends' inequities and weaknesses—vanity, promiscuity, disloyalty, anti-Semitism, self-delusion, and so forth—while asserting her capacity for truth-telling and her ("natural maternal") desire to ensure her son's future happiness at all costs. Diagnosed with a terminal illness, she stages a vicious, melodramatic scene in which she beats her son Alesha until he bleeds, anticipating that hatred for her action and indignant compassion for the boy will prompt her remarried ex-husband Kolia and the rest of "her crowd" to take Alesha under their wing. Since the narrative unfolds exclusively from the narrator's viewpoint, it obviously reflects her outlook on events, which induces credulous readers to accept her self-serving version of herself. Yet anyone attuned to Petrushevskaia's authorial habits instantly descries a counternarrative in the story's aporetic passages.

By having the narrator open her account with an echo from Dostoevsky's *Notes from Underground* ("I'm a hard, harsh person" [Ia chelovek zhestkii, zhestokii]), Petrushevskaia urges the reader to analogize her with the Underground Man and his tactics of aggressive self-justification. And, in fact, reading against the trajectory of the narrator's plot, the reader discovers in the gaps a more compelling counterversion of events: what the narrator elevates to the virtue of truth-telling sooner smacks of a malicious desire to wound and shock, thereby forcibly transferring attention from the universally desired Marisha to her own sexually less appealing self. Dismissing her "friends'" dislike of her as *their* failing, she brushes aside the possibility that her insensitive jibes deservedly provoke their antipathy; while satirizing Marisha's sexual-romantic escapades, she passes over her own motivation for such actions as wearing a swimsuit that becomes transparent when wet during the group's camping trips; while sneering at her husband Kolia's mistreatment of their son, she underplays her own readiness to abandon the child for the pleasures of nocturnal carousing; her mother's hospitalization and death receive mention chiefly as additional trials for *her*. Finally, the question arises of how effectively her "crowd," whose selfishness and inability to sustain a nurturing familial environment she herself amply documents, will raise Alesha.

By endowing the narrator with progressive blindness as a premonitory symptom of her disease, Petrushevskaia metaphorically intimates that her melodramatic solution to the dilemma of Alesha's future semi-orphaned state may be myopic—a failure of perception. Categorically and shortsightedly dissociating herself from the base motives she automatically ascribes to others, the narrator parlays her privileged status as narrator into that of a merciless judge exempt from the moral laws invoked to condemn everyone else. Once doubts arise about the accuracy of the narrator's totalizing scenario, purportedly random and insignificant details scattered throughout the text constellate into the shape of a radically different reality, like the shifting pieces of colored glass within a kaleidoscope. That altered perspective precipitates the narrator's fall from her lofty plateau as subject/solicitous mother to object/egotistical rhetorician.

As a profanation of the "quintessentially natural," however, "Our Crowd" cedes pride of place to Petrushevskaia's most nuanced, chilling investigation of totalitarian maternal pseudonurture: "Night Time," whose title primes the reader for psychic devastation in "the heart of darkness."[15] That heart belongs to Anna Adrianovna, who epitomizes the monster Mother, psychologically eviscerating everyone in her orbit through nurture and narration.

WRONG BY DAY, WRITE BY NIGHT

"Night Time" ostensibly recounts fifty-seven-year-old Anna Adrianovna's laudable endeavors to sustain, morally and economically, her family members: her mother Sima, son Andrei, daughter Alena, and grandson Timochka. True to her habit of condensation, Petrushevskaia distributes among these four generations[16] virtually all of her favorite synecdochic signs of existential horror: Sima, presumably a schizophrenic (though only a fraction more insane than anyone else in the story), has been committed by her daughter to a psychiatric hospital, and when in the course of the narrative Anna Adrianovna has her transferred to a mental asylum, the incontinent old woman with a persecution mania helplessly urinates where she stands, awaiting transportation. Andrei, after serving a term in prison, where he submits to presumably forcible homosexual advances,[17] brings two women off the street to his mother's room, where he proves his manhood, to the rhythm of Anna Adrianovna's discreet tapping on the door. Permanently maimed through leaping out of a second-story window after an argument with his wife, Andrei is an alcoholic who appeases his craving for alcohol with money pilfered from his mother. Alena, who abandoned her older child Timochka to her mother's care, inadvertently leaving behind a notebook graphically detailing her sexual encounters with her ex-husband and her married deputy director, now lives with the baby fathered by the latter and expects a third child.[18] Anna Adrianovna alternates between tears of self-pity and vindictive contempt; Andrei steals and drinks; Alena breeds; and Timochka at six has a nervous tic from all of his psychological traumas. Indigent, close to starvation, torn by hysterical jealousy and loathing for each other, the family corroborates Tolstoy's dictum that "each unhappy family is unhappy in its own way" (kazhdaia neschastlivaia sem'ia neschastliva po-svoemu). Not incidentally, references to *Anna Karenina* thickly intersperse the narrative.

Anna Adrianovna promotes her own image as an extraordinary paragon of martyred largesse, a rock of dependability in a morass of appetite-driven, irresponsible self-indulgence: "When he came back from prison, Andrei devoured my herring, my potatoes, my black bread, drank my tea, and, just as before, devoured my mind and drank my blood, his body sustained by my food" (Andrei el moiu seledky, moiu kartoshku, moi chernyi khleb, pil moi chai, pridia iz kolonii, opiat', kak ran'she, el moi mozg i pil moiu krov', ves' sleplennyi iz moei pishchi, 86). The freighted wording of such passages diminishes the adult Andrei into a fetus living off the maternal body, part of Anna Adrianovna's comprehensive imaging of her physical, emotional, and verbal self as devoured by her offspring's needs and demands. As she relentlessly reminds everyone, while eking out a mere pittance through her poetry readings, Anna Adrianovna nevertheless maintains the household, takes in her self-destructive offspring ("I was the only one to save my son from doom" [ia odna iz vsekh, syna spasla ot gibeli, 106]), cooks, launders, and denies herself even minimal necessities for the sake of her beloved grandson, who accompanies her everywhere ("Always and everywhere it's been just you and me, and that's the way it's going to stay!" [Vsegda i vsiudu ia byla s toboi odna i ostanus'! 21; 70]). In short, the self-fashioned icon of Anna Adrianovna as salvatory cross-climber dominates the "monologue" narrative she controls. "But nothing's that simple in this world!" (No vse ne tak prosto v etom mire! 66), as she herself acknowledges: overconscious self-sacrifice frequently originates in less than admirable drives, or, as Camus's irreverent and skeptical Clamence maintains, people climb crosses so as to be seen long distances.[19]

Indeed, a closer inspection of the text's double-voicing unmasks Anna Adrianovna's vaunted Christian self-abnegation as a mode of unappeasable sadistic control and vampirism—all in the name of love, which she trumpets as the most important thing in life ("samoe glavnoe v zhizni," 67). Beneath her rhetoric we uncover the pre-Oedipal mother, an all-powerful, engulfing figure who theatricalizes the Freudian scenario of the mother/child relationship (Doane, 82–83). Hyperbole and melodrama reduce her comments to verbal gesture: she histrionically refers to her son, who calls her "bitch" (suka) and worse, as "my life's sun" (solntse moei vsei zhizni, 81), to her daughter as "my lovely Alenka, my quiet little nestling, who was a comfort to me" (moia krasivaia Alenka, moe tikhoe gnezdyshko, kotoroe sogrelo menia, 83), and to her grandson as the breathlessly capitalized "He" (On), "the holy child" (sviatoi mladenets, 94), and "my star, my guiding light" (moia zvezda, moia iasochka, 67)—while also calling the child "a frigging pest" (svoloch' neotviaznaia, 67). Much like Dostoevsky's two Katerina Ivanovnas (of *Crime and Punishment* and *The Brothers Karamazov*), she theatricalizes her role of martyr through tears, clasped hands, overstated entreaties, invidious comparisons between self and others,[20] and extorts a psychological price for all of her "kindnesses," prompted by bottomless pride. An authority on all questions (e.g., "I know children's hearts" [Ia znaiu detskie serdtsa, 67]), she deems herself an inspired voice articulating a higher Truth—a function associated with her self-proclaimed role of poet:

> Bringing enlightenment, the light *of the law*, to these benighted folk, these swarming masses! The dark conscience incarnate of the people speaks within me and I'm no longer myself, I'm an oracle, I lay down the law! The children who hear me speak—in schools, in summer camps, in clubs—they all shrink and tremble, but they'll never forget! (103)
>
> And I've saved yet another child! I spend my whole life saving everyone! I'm the only one in the entire neighborhood who stays alert at night, listening to make sure no one's crying out! (102)

> (Nesti prosveshchenie, *iuridicheskoe* prosveshchenie v etu temnuiu gushchu, v etu tolpu! Voploshchennaia chernaia sovest' naroda govorit vo mne, i ia kak by ne sama, ia kak pifiia veshchaiu. Kto by slyshal moi mysli v shkolakh, v lageriakh, v krasnykh ugolkakh, deti szhimaiutsia i drozhat, no oni zapomniat! [95] Opiat' ia spasla rebenka! Ia vse vremia vsekh spasaiu! Ia odna vo vsem gorode v nashem mikroraione slushaiu po nocham, ne zakrichit li kto! [95, my emphasis])

In epistemological terms, Anna Adrianovna tirelessly maximizes the subject/object distinction to her advantage.[21] Attributing purely negative motives to all objects of her implacable subjectivity, she not only exempts herself from like judgment, but packages as estimable all of her own impulses and actions, including those that patently mirror behavior she deplores in others. As oracle and ultimate arbiter of human conduct, she publicly denounces strangers' behavior with children, criticizes her adult offspring's and their spouses' hygiene, sexual habits, and choices of partner (e.g., to Alena: "Pay attention. Your husband's got homosexual tendencies. He's in love with the boy" [Imei v vidu. Tvoi muzh s zadatkami pederasta. On liubit mal'chika (Timochka)], 82). Her narrative testifies to the epistemological and psychological empowerment that automatically accrues to every teller of any tale.[22] The teller's privileged position allows her to manipulate perspective, tone, and emphasis so as to convert any phenomenon into its antipode, if she so desires.

Anna Adrianovna exercises her narrative prerogative by deploying the full panoply of rhetorical forces so as to vindicate her conduct and insinuate her superiority on multiple fronts: beauty and sex appeal ("everyone takes me for younger than my real age" [mne moi vosrast nikto ne daet, 67]; "all wives always perceived me as meaning one thing" [vse zheny menia vsegda vosprinimali odnoznachno, 85]); good taste and regal manner ("I behave like

the Queen of England" [ia-to vedu sebia, kak angliiskaia koroleva, 65]);
moral strength ("I never lost my head in any situation" [ia nikogda sebia ne
teriala ni v odnoi situatsii, 75]); self-abnegating generosity, perceptiveness,
and poetic ability. By pointedly dwelling on the near coincidence of her name
with poet Anna Andreeva Akhmatova's, she implies a commensurability of talent: "we're mystically linked by a near-coincidence of name" (my pochti chto
misticheskie tezki, 67). As mother, however (and possibly as poet also), Anna
Adrianovna sooner resembles another Anna: Anna Karenina, with whose pre-
suicidal inner monologue the narrative mode of "Night Time" resonates. As in
the Anna-centered sections of Tolstoy's novel, narration in "Night Time"
functions primarily as accusatory self-exculpation via defamation.

Incorporating alternate voices into the narration, Petrushevskaia
implants clues to Anna Adrianovna's psychological imbalance that multiply
as the text progresses and, by constructing her as objectionable object,
increasingly undermine her reliability as reporting subject. For instance, the
nature of her talent comes under question when we discover that the audience for her poetry readings is composed of children. Moreover, while her
initial deliberate silence as to *why* she lost her job ("I'm not referring here to
how I got the sack" [ia tut ne govoriu o tom, kak menia uvolili, 66]) hints at
political intrigue, in combination with other revelations it invites conclusions
unflattering to her—conclusions subsequently confirmed when she divulges
that her romance with a married father of three led to her dismissal: "I was a
poetess straight out of teachers' training, dismissed from the newspaper
where I'd worked as a journalist for an affair with a married artist, the father
of three children, whom I was seriously preparing to bring up, fool that I
was!" (ia—poetessa posle pedinstituta i vygnannaia iz gazety so stazhem
zhurnalistskoi raboty za roman s odnim zhenatym khudozhnikom, ottsom
troikh detei, kotorykh ia vser'ez sobiralas' vospitat', dura! 82). However self-
servingly Anna Adrianovna orchestrates retrospective scenarios, in passages
such as these she unwittingly betrays precisely what her defensive stratagems
attempt to mask: her vanity, repressiveness, sexual problems, and, above all,
the generational continuity within her family—here, the congruence
between her own and Alena's amorous misadventures. While proclaiming
her dissimilarity to mother and daughter alike, Anna Adrianovna demonstrates her ineradicable sameness, the family resemblance recalling the
shared familial traits binding Anna and Stiva Oblonsky.[23]

Several scenes, in fact, significantly discredit both Anna Adrianovna's
perspective on events and her vaunted perspicacity and magnanimity: for
example, when her husband leaves her, she considers leaping out of the window to punish him (84), à la Anna Karenina; when Alena visits, Anna Adrianovna physically tries to prevent Timochka from opening the door to his
mother, even when the boy screams in protest; when she voyeuristically
peeps at her daughter through a crack, she likewise resists the child's efforts

to pull her away (69). Finally, how can the reader reconcile Anna Adrianov-na's advertised role as protector of children with her confession of carnal (*plotskaia*) love for her grandson:

> I love him passionately, physically. . . . Parents in general, and grandparents especially, love small children physically, and that love takes the place of everything else for them. It's a sinful love, I tell you, it . . . makes the child callous and self-indulgent, as if he understands that there's something impure in it. (58)

> (Ia plotski liubliu ego, strastno. . . . Roditeli voobshche, a babki s dedami v chast-nosti, liubiat malen'kikh detei plotskoi liubov'iu, zameniaiushchei im vse. Grekhovnaia liubov', dolozhu ia vam, rebenok . . . ot nee cherstveet i raspoiasy-vaetsia, kak budto ponimaet, chto delo nechisto. [81])

Despite the rhetorical stratagem of "naturalizing" her inclinations by translating them into universals, the perverseness of Anna Adrianovna's sentiments emerges unmistakably here and confirms the sexual pathology submerged, yet strongly felt, throughout the narrative. It surfaces in her lyrical comparisons of Timochka's urine with the sharp aroma of camomile, and of his unwashed hair with the scent of phlox (67), as well as in her revelatory generalizations, which thinly disguise warped personal convictions and preferences. For example, her reaction to her daughter's diary entry unfurls a catalogue of repellent physiological phenomena in the midst of which she, anomalously, places "love" between convulsions and violence: "O Nature! The Great Deceiver! Why does she require these sufferings, this horror, blood, stench, sweat, slime, convulsions, love, violence, pain, sleepless nights, hard labor, apparently so that everything will turn out fine!" (O obmanshchivaia priroda! O velikaia! Zachem-to ei nuzhny eti stradaniia, etot uzhas, krov', von', pot, sliz', sudorogi, liubov', nasilie, bol', bessonnye nochi, tiazhelyi trud, vrode chtoby vse bylo khorosho!" 72).[24] A similar pathology emerges in a related apostrophe: "O the hatred of a mother-in-law, you're nothing but jealousy, my mother also wanted to be the object of her daughter's love—that is, mine—wanted me to love just her, . . . she wanted to be my entire family, to take the place of everyone and everything" (O nenavist' teshchi, ty revnost' i nichto drugoe, moia mama sama khotela byt' ob"ektom liubvi svoei docheri, to est' menia, chtoby ia tol'ko ee liubila, . . . eto mat' khotela byt' vsei sem'ei dlia menia, zamenit' soboiu vse, 101). If one recalls that Anna Adrianovna calls herself Timochka's "mama," then this passage leaves little doubt that her narrative displaces and projects *her* illicit desires, insecurities, and resentments especially onto her son-in-law, grandson, children, and mother, but also onto any and every acquaintance (shades of Anna Karenina, once more). A nocturnal creature who feels most at ease in the silent darkness, she yearns to swallow up her children, returning them into the womb that functions as one of multiple images of incarceration proliferating in the text (e.g., prison, barricaded rooms, etc.). Anna Adrianovna's externalization of her inner slime—her suppressed instincts and fantasies, in other words—accounts for much of the darkness she communicates to the reader.

Through double-voicing and sporadic inconsistencies the narrative confirms the extent to which Anna Adrianovna suffers from exactly the vices and frailties that she despises in her mother and her daughter, whom Petrushevskaia presents as essentially shadow figures collectively instancing maternal monstrosity. Destructive rituals, in fact, are one generation's legacy to the next.[25]

What distinguishes Anna Adrianovna from her doubles is her "telling power," which assumes the tyrannical form of censorship over all narrative within the story. Apart from slanting her own reporting of events so as to enhance her image, she ensures that all other discourse gets subsumed under her perspective. Hence when directly quoting extracts from her daughter's private (!) diary, she ridicules and ultimately trivializes its contents through cynical editorial commentary, eliminating the subjective immediacy of Alena's impassioned confessions by interposing her viewpoint between Alena's voice and the reader. When Alena reminisces about her husband Sasha's daily habits ("[he] drank tea"; [on] pil chai), her mother parenthetically adds "belched, peed, picked his nose" (rygal, mochilsia, kovyrial v nosu, 71). Or when Alena draws an eloquent parallel between the trauma of her sexual congress with the married deputy director and her father's permanent departure—"when papa was leaving us for good and I kept clinging to his knees, while mother kept pulling me away in a rage, smiling and saying: 'What's the matter with you, girl, as if he's worth it, and you, get out, don't dare set foot, etc." (kogda papa ukhodil ot nas navsegda i ia tseplialas' za ego koleni, a mat' menia v beshenstve otryvala, ulybaias' i govoria: 'Chto ty, devochka, pered kem ty, a ty ukhodi, chtoby dukhy tvoego' i t.d.')—Anna Adrianovna crushingly remarks, "Some comparison—her own father with this . . . with the father of the bastard Katia" (Nashla kogo s kem sravnivat', rodnogo ottsa s etim . . . s ottsom Kati pribludnoi . . . , 72; ellipses in original). To further distance Alena from a possibly receptive reading, Anna Adrianovna—who from the outset usurps Alena's role as mother to Tima ("his mama [I] and his Alena [his mother]"/ego mama [ia] i ego Alena [mat' ego], 94)—substitutes her voice for Alena's by writing her daughter's memoirs about her, A.A.! (92). That dictatorial act of ultimate mediation culminates in Anna Adrianovna's *reductio ad absurdum* pretension to complete objectivity: "That's the scene I wrote, fully self-critical and completely objective" (Vot takuiu ia stsenku napisala s polnym krititsizmom v svoi adres i s polnoi ob"ektivnost'iu, 92). Whatever her defensive rhetoric, in Bakhtinian terms, she cannot resist finalizing all she recounts. Her voice, in fact, reaches beyond the grave in the manuscript submitted to the publisher by her silenced daughter, who speaks only to find a forum for her mother's voice.

The story's conclusion pushes the analogy between narrative and life to its logical limit by conflating the two. Petrushevskaia literalizes the metaphor of Anna Adrianovna's deletion not only of Alena's, but of all independent voices, by having Anna Adrianovna interpret the silence in "her" apartment as indicative of a mass suicide on her family's part.[26] Their escape, however, is not into death, but into life outside the reach of her totalitarian narrative power. In terms of the story's matrix trope, they elude her control by retreating into a diurnal time zone, away from the darkness in which Anna Adrianovna dwells as maternal queen of the night.

If Petrushevskaia's narrative strategies instantly point to her affinities with Dostoevsky, her representation of mothers reveals the Freudian presuppositions informing her concept of familial relations. Such mechanisms as repression, displacement, projection; the pre-Oedipal and Oedipal phases of individual development; and the ascription of countless psychological traumas to derailed or suppressed sexuality (e.g., hysteria triggered by the conflict between desire and defense against it)—these all constitute the chief elements of her ironized family anti-romances. What Anna Freud called "identification with the aggressor," for instance, perfectly captures the syndrome of generational replication in which Anna Adrianovna is unknowingly trapped.[27] Although Petrushevskaia's irremediably tragic view of existence accords with the current atmosphere of apocalypse and absurdity in Russia, for two decades it ran counter to every optimistic myth about the Home and the Motherland devised by Soviet ideology. Official glorification of the Soviet family—with pedestaled maternity as its centerpiece—reached its apogee in the 1970s, precisely when Petrushevskaia's repeated efforts to place her works met with systematic rejection. During the concerted campaign that exhorted women to greater reproductive feats so as to combat the country's announced demographic crisis, government-sponsored publications were understandably reluctant to print fiction that spotlighted the warts and wounds of family relations. Now that "everything is permitted," Petrushevskaia has succeeded in reaching an audience, but one that reads her fiction and drama in the twinned context of *chernukha* (grime and slime) and *pornukha* (porn)—not of Freud and the existentialists, who after decades of prohibition likewise have suddenly become accessible to the Russian public.[28] Yet Petrushevskaia's "heroines" are the Medeas, Jocastas, and Niobes of contemporary Russian fiction; their tales are told in a base key, but their experience of life, with all its senseless horrors, shocks, and ineluctable torments, is the very stuff of tragedy.

113

Gary Rosenshield

Afterword: The Problems of Gender Criticism; or, What Is to Be Done About Dostoevsky?

RECENTLY WOMEN CRITICS and scholars have felt it necessary to justify writing about women in male-authored texts because the propriety or advisability of doing so has been questioned. This issue was brought to the fore by Elaine Showalter in her "Feminist Criticism in the Wilderness" where she argued that feminist criticism had to go beyond feminist critique, in which women critics uncovered or deconstructed the phallocentric ideology underlying the images of women in the fiction of male writers, and engage in what she called gynocritics, women's supportive "criticism" of female-authored texts.[1] What she was saying, in effect, was that feminist critique was essentially only a form of critical realism, whereas gynocritics was the socialist or "feminist" realism necessary for the times. Moreover, it was gynocritics—in combination with various poststructural approaches that tend to undercut the notion of "literature" in favor of texts—that would open up and expand the canon of female-authored texts for women critics and scholars to examine.

Nineteenth-century English literature with its great women novelists somewhat obscures the consequences of the gynocritical approach. Such an approach to American literature, however, presupposes a very different attitude not only toward women writers but toward writing itself. Critically neglected genres traditionally practiced by women such as travelogues, children's literature, memoirs, reminiscences, and autobiographies become revalorized and gain entry into a revised and significantly different canon. Once these works enter into the canon, the notion of literature itself, or texts, must change with it, as must the notion of what "literary" critics do or should do with these texts. A new literary theory becomes necessary to valorize a new canon just as a new canon calls for a new literary theory.

Critics of Russian literature are not at all wary of having to work in more liminal literary areas.[2] Embracing a criticism of prescription, however, is a

114

very different matter altogether. The history of Russian criticism from the middle of the nineteenth century almost to the present day has often been characterized by a simultaneous demand for a critical and a socialist realism: a critical realism that exposes the ills of the despised social order (whether it be tsarist autocracy or Western capitalism); and a socialist realism that provides positive role models, usually in the form of self-sacrificing heroes and heroines who foster solidarity, raise political consciousness, and prepare the groundwork for the achievement of utopia.

All scholars of Russian literature are acutely aware of how critical realism in literature, like feminist critique, evolved into a prescriptive and positively oriented social realism, like gynocritics. The process probably started in earnest with the great literary critic Belinsky who, having rejected his earlier right-wing Hegelianism, began to see literature more and more in utilitarian and socially progressive terms, specifically as a means of carrying on the political struggle against Russian autocracy. Belinsky lauded Dostoevsky's first novel, *Poor Folk*, not so much because it was a brilliant work of art, but rather because it seemed to be Russia's first real social novel, and that was precisely what Russian literature—and Russia—needed most. His disappointment over Dostoevsky's next novel, *The Double*, was not over aesthetics (Belinsky thought that technically *The Double* was if anything more brilliant than *Poor Folk*), but over subject matter: Belinsky did not see the usefulness of a novel about madness, especially a madness with no obvious social genealogy or political implications.

The radical critics Dobroliubov and Chernyshevsky, who saw themselves as disciples of Belinsky, took the implications of their master's new literary approach to their logical conclusions both in criticism and literature. Dobroliubov wrote article after article in which he turned the works of such contemporary masters as Ostrovsky, Goncharov, Turgenev, among others, into paradigms of critical realism, wherein all the ills of Russian society were exposed with the help of the discerning critic. But Dobroliubov and Chernyshevsky were hardly content with critical realism, the literature of exposé; there was something in their religious background that demanded a more hagiographical approach to the written word. Specifically, Dobroliubov wanted a real Russian hero who could serve as a role model for Russian youth. Realizing that none of the current generation of Russian writers was about to pen such a work, Chernyshevsky took up the task himself, producing what would be later known as the bible of the Russian revolutionaries, the novel *What Is to Be Done?* (1863), a title that Lenin chose for his own most revolutionary work on political organization. Despite its absence of literary merit, Chernyshevsky's work had a far greater influence on Russian life and history, if not world history, than any of the works of the great Russian masters, perhaps even more than all of them combined. One of its most unfortunate consequences, however, was its powerful influence on the criti-

cism and literature of the Soviet period, in which socialist realism super-
seded critical realism and became the officially proclaimed method manda-
tory for all writers. Whereas writers in capitalist countries could still write
critical realism, for Soviet writers only an optimistic, supportive, unifying,
class-conscious writing—and of course a corresponding criticism—was
appropriate. As Dostoevsky said of the Russians, they must take everything
to its logical extreme—in real life.

In order to see more concretely the implications of feminist critique
(critical realism) and gynocritics (socialist realism) for Russian literature I
shall discuss briefly three relatively recent feminist overviews of Russian literature: Joe Andrew's radical feminist critique, *Women in Russian Literature, 1780–1863*; Barbara Heldt's gynocritical *Terrible Perfection: Women
and Russian Literature*; and Carolina de Maegd-Soep's "revisionist" *The
Emancipation of Women in Russian Literature and Society: A Contribution
to the Knowledge of the Russian Society During the 1860's.*[3]

Andrew's book, a maximalist and often exasperating example of radical
feminist critique, aims, it often seems, to outfeminize the feminists. Most
Russian writers of the period Andrew covers are presented as prisoners of
patriarchal sexual constructs, almost fated, as it were, to victimize their
women characters even when, on occasion, they attempt to idealize them.
Andrew's role, then, must be to read "otherwise," to uncover the distortions
that male writers impose on their female subjects; that is, to refuse to assume
the passive role of the male reader presupposed by the ideology of the male
text. But male-authored texts are worse than literary distortions: they are
political acts of suppression and indoctrination. Thus Andrew writes that
"the novel, particularly in the eighteenth and nineteenth centuries, functioned—among other things—as an instrument of education and socializa-
tion and, thereby, helped in the general process of policing women, of per-
suading them to consent to their own subordination" (4). We never learn
how Andrew, as a male, can better escape the imprisoning binary oppositions
he has assimilated on entrance into the symbolic order of patriarchy than the
writers he exposes.[4] Given these political and literary presuppositions it is
hardly surprising that Andrew leaves no icon of Russian literature—including Pushkin, Gogol, Lermontov, and Turgenev—intact. Because of the time-
frame of the book (1780–1863) the later Dostoevsky and Tolstoy were not
treated, but had they been included they would certainly have fared no better than their predecessors.

Since Andrew is willing, however, to make the jump from critical realism
(exposé) to socialist realism (edification), all hope for Russian literature is not
lost. But it is Chernyshevsky who emerges as the great writer and hero of
Andrew's tale, the writer who got it all right. Chernyshevsky's feminist novel
What Is to Be Done? (1863), if not the greatest novel of Russian literature
("literature," to Andrew, is an ideological construct designed to keep certain

116

disruptive texts out of the canon), ranks as the greatest *text* of nineteenth-century Russian culture. Except for Chernyshevsky, however, everywhere Andrew looks, he sees misogyny, pornography, textual subjugation, and victimization. There is no textual sin against women that Russia's great writers have not committed. They have presented female sexuality as dangerous and disruptive, a curse that can be safely contained only by death: "Female sexuality leads to death whether they play the patriarchal game or not" (31). The implication of Russian writers' "necrophilic veneration of the death of the woman" is that "the only good woman is a dead one."[5] For Andrew the unbrainwashed woman critic of Russian literature is faced with only three choices: either she must continue along the same line of exposing the phallocentrism of male-authored texts, or turn to a form of socialist realism and extol ideologically edifying works written by males (of the Chernyshevskian sort), or engage in gynocritics.

In *Terrible Perfection: Women and Russian Literature*, Barbara Heldt has chosen the path of gynocritics—but not before she, like Andrew, subjects Russian literature to a radical feminist critique that provides justification of her choice. Although Heldt lodges against Russian literature many of the same charges as Andrew, such as voyeurism, pornography, objectivization, phallocentric nomination, and misogyny,[6] she seems more aware than Andrew of the problem confronting a feminist in deconstructing a literature in which women characters are so frequently held up as paragons meant to inspire males—and other females—to social action. She argues that though women characters in male-authored texts may be positive characters they exist only for the hero; they are always part of his plot. They have no real plot of their own: their plot has been erased.[7] Furthermore, they are "underdescribed," lack complexity, and are described physically, that is, voyeuristically (16). The power and dignity of women, as conceived by male writers, lies essentially in their submission and silence, the basic forms of their "terrible perfection." Women who express their desire, women who are on the brink of autonomy, will be destroyed or transformed into dead princesses, Snow Whites, Madame Bovarys—and Nastasia Filippovnas. "A heroine's insistence on self-definition is usually violently punished, for whether as objects of desire or as objects of male self-definition, their striving toward self-naming has dire implications for the men who do the naming" (62). Thus, according to Heldt, women's terrible perfection is one of the most insidious forms of victimization that male writers can impose on their female characters; more effectively than any other form, it imprisons women with duplicitous encomiums. If male writers are condemned to oscillate between alternative forms of victimization—misogyny and complementarity—it is to women's writing that Heldt must go to find "autonomous beings rather than heroines in search of a hero. The either/or of perfection or doom is not at issue; rather we see the emergence of a female self who exists independently, who is neither destroyed nor redeemed by love, and whose own words build the reality of her inner and outer worlds" (65). Consequently Heldt devotes the largest part of her study to the female lyric and autobiography, genres, in contrast to the novel, where women could still express their essential selves. Heldt's gynocritics brings to the fore the issue of the canon, which is particularly problematic for Russian literature where there are, as in American literature, many fewer prominent women writers than in English literature of the nineteenth century. What Heldt's gynocritics implies for nineteenth-century Russian literature is an aesthetics of exclusion rather than inclusion, of diminution rather than augmentation. For the admission to respectability of women lyric poets and autobiographers at the expense (that is, the exclusion) of the classic male writers cannot but lead to a significant diminution of the canon for women as well; that is, those areas of Russian literature in which women critics will be "permitted" to ply their trade.

It is particularly instructive to witness the problem that Heldt creates for herself as a gynocritic of Russian literature when she confronts Tolstoy, one of the few male writers who, at least in her view, has gotten it right, who has been able to represent androgynous love (Vronsky and Anna); nurture rather than sexuality (Dolly and Levin); and "sisterly compassion for similar struggles" (Anna and Dolly). But Heldt's argument for Tolstoy constitutes nothing less than a deconstruction of her own gynocritical position: in order to justify perhaps a latent love for Tolstoy, she must transform him into a protofeminist precisely in his seemingly most phallocentric text: *The Kreutzer Sonata*. Tolstoy becomes for Heldt what Chernyshevsky was for Andrew: the exception that proves the rule, the man who got it right. But if Tolstoy, and *The Kreutzer Sonata*, can be "reconstructed," what about the other great nineteenth-century male authors and their works? Are they any less susceptible to reconstruction than Tolstoy? However, any opening that Heldt has allowed is necessarily small; as we have seen, in her view Tolstoy is an exception, and moreover, an exception that has to be justified according to a very specific ideological agenda. In the end women will have to write only about the works of other women for there are necessarily few works so ripe for reconstruction as Tolstoy's *The Kreutzer Sonata*.

Perhaps the most intriguing of the three books I am considering on the representation of women in Russian literature is Dutch feminist Carolina de Maegd-Soep's *The Emancipation of Women in Russian Literature and Society: A Contribution to the Knowledge of the Russian Society During the 1860's*. Maegd-Soep argues that the main inspiration and impetus for women's emancipation in Russia from 1820 through the 1860s was the representation of women not in the works of women themselves but in the works of the most prominent male poets and novelists. When women are presented as victims by male writers, they are invariably sympathetically portrayed, shown to be victimized by their environment (yes, even by patriarchal society); but they are never victimized by their creators. Although Cherny-shevsky is also a hero for Maegd-Soep, he represents for her the culmination, not the abrogation, of a tradition.[8] To Andrew, on the other hand, the novel as a genre is not a reflection of the problem, but a significant part of it, and that is why Chernyshevsky was compelled to write an anti-novel, a work that exposed the novel as complicit in a misogynist ideology of oppression.

Maegd-Soep's purpose, in addition to giving "insight into the various aspects of the Russian women's emancipation," is "to show how literature had a beneficial effect on the development of the character of the Russian woman, who managed to become, in a very short time, the pioneer of a new world" (23). The representation of women in the works of Druzhinin, Nekrasov, Goncharov, Herzen, and Turgenev was, Maegd-Soep argues, not only inspiring for young women but was considerably ahead of its time in pointing women to an independence in love, education, and social responsi-bility for which there were no models in Russia or, in many cases, even in Western Europe. Tolstoy remarked that Turgenev's female types came into existence only after Turgenev himself had portrayed them.[9] Young women inspired by women characters in Russian novels authored by males rejected parental values and abandoned their homes in search of causes to which they could selflessly devote themselves.[10]

Maegd-Soep perused much of the nineteenth-century Russian litera-ture written by women during this time (their works are comparable to those of women in America of the same period) and found none of those portraits of idealistic women struggling to overcome the chains of patriarchy, educate themselves, and do something socially useful such as she found in the work of male writers. Russia did not have, Maegd-Soep writes, "a George Sand nor a George Eliot to voice the demands of the women's movement" (99). This conclusion is comparable to the findings of Nina Baym, who, in her reading of the works of American women writers from 1820 through 1870, was unable to unearth "a forgotten Jane Austen or George Eliot, or hit upon even one novel . . . to set aside *The Scarlet Letter*."[11] Furthermore, according to Maegd-Soep (95–110), there were very few, if any, women writers who sup-ported the women's movement in Russia, a finding again not unlike that of Beverly Voloshin who discovered that many women writers in America made a career of advocating the values of the hearth.[12]

Turgenev's influence, bolstered by his artistic mastery, was especially strong on girls and young women, many of whom ascribed their spiritual and social awakening to the images of his women characters. Perhaps what hap-pened to the Russian Victorians in reality is similar to what Nina Auerbach described in reference to the mythic metamorphosis of the woman in Victo-rian culture, where "love does not tranquilize womanhood into domestic confinement, but fuels her latent powers into political life" (37). In address-ing a group of women considering the medical profession, Turgenev outlined the fate he saw for the Russian woman: "Russia's historical destiny has placed on the Russian woman tremendous responsibilities. In carrying them out, she has shown herself capable of so much self-sacrifice, of so much hard and honest labor, that it would be unwise, even sinful, to set obstacles on her fated path, not to help her in every way possible to realize her calling."[13]

While it may be true, as Rachel M. Brownstein argues, that women tend to model themselves after novelistic heroines more than men do after novelistic heroes, it is hard to make a case that in Russian literature "the literary associations that halo the heroine keep her in a traditional woman's place."[14] Vera Figner, one of the most famous women revolutionaries of the nineteenth century, later recalled "how her own attitude toward life and that of her young, revolutionary-minded friends had been influenced by Natasha and Elena," the heroines of Turgenev's *Rudin* and *On the Eve* (Maegd-Soep, 242). And it must be emphasized that when we speak about Vera Figner and her friends we are not talking about academic theoreticians. Figner took part in several assassination attempts against Tsar Alexander II, led the terrorist "People's Will" several years after the assassination, and after having been apprehended in 1884, spent twenty years (1884–1904) in Shlüsselburg Fortress, Russia's highest security prison.[15]

But if one is looking for female empowerment in male-authored texts one need not confine oneself to socially active and iron-purposed heroines. Nina Auerbach, in her work on the representation of women in the subtexts of Victorian culture, offers a feminist revisionist alternative, one that privileges power over autonomy, and even celebrates, in some instances, the potency of the victim. To Auerbach what is most important is not so much social power, but the subterranean "myth of woman," which "flourishes not in the carefully wrought prescriptions of sages, but in the vibrant half-life of popular literature and art, forms which may distill the essence of a culture though they are rarely granted Culture's weighty imprimatur" (10). Myth does not demean, victimize, marginalize, or objectivize women, but enlarges her, aggrandizes her, endows her with supernatural energy and transformational powers that destroy hero and villain alike. Understood psychoanalytically, where what is repressed is precisely what is most important—absence is always more powerful than presence—the victimization of women becomes a male defense reaction against woman's magic, a testimony to her "self-transforming power" (34), "her transcendental potency" (64). For women to be associated with the demon is for Auerbach not slander but an acknowledgment of her mobile powers. She is not an angel in the shrunken world of the home, but a spirit who knows no real walls, and whose "demonism is inseparable from triumphant power" (101).

Auerbach not only makes little distinction between angel and demon, but sees them as essentially one: woman becoming the demon as the angel in her realizes her powers. If Andrew finds a new dispensation in Vera Pavlovna, Auerbach finds it, contrarily, in that deceptive angel of the hearth: "Woman is not frailer than man is, but stronger and more powerful; her nature is broadly demonic rather than fallibly human; she must lead us out of history toward a new dispensation; in short, woman is 'so much more addicted to the practice of the black art' because by definition, woman is an angel" (108); that is, a demon. Auerbach finds power in all those women traditionally seen as the victims of Victorian society. According to her inversionary ratios, fallen women and spinsters alike become icons "of divine-demonic womanhood, harbinger(s) of a transfigured humanity" (222). The so-called liberated women of the time, the counterparts to Chernyshevsky's Vera Pavlovnas, are, by comparison, essentially powerless and without direction. Female victimization exists, but it is often empowered, and where it is not, it is frequently as much male fantasy as hard reality. Have the gains of the autonomous Vera Pavlovnas come at the expense of their oppressed, but more silently powerful sisters?

Here I think we need to ask a hard question: Are Maegd-Soep and Auerbach to be preferred to Andrew and Heldt because they find empowerment in the images of female characters in the fiction of male writers rather than victimization and the deprivation of autonomy? If the criteria for determining whether women should write about women in male-authored texts is based primarily on the positive—whether it be nurturing or empowering—nature of such characterization, then the differences among Maegd-Soep, Auerbach, Andrew, and Heldt narrow considerably and become differences of individual interpretation rather than critical approach, with Andrew and Heldt rejecting the images of women in male-authored texts on the basis of the same criteria that Maegd-Soep and Auerbach accept them: value and power. If value and power are what we read literature for and what we must write about, then the question has already been answered: whether or not one writes about female characters in fiction authored by males depends on the empowering nature of such images.

In order to confront this issue head-on I bring into the argument one of the most controversial figures in Russian literature with respect to the representation of women: Dostoevsky. Being a maximalist by nature, Dostoevsky perhaps provides the test case for any thesis about female characterization in male-authored Russian texts, especially in his exploration of the dynamics of victimization. The issue of victimization has largely been passed over in discussions of Dostoevsky's women characters because the debate on Dostoevsky and women has been carried on in much the same way that Heldt, Andrew, and Maegd-Soep have handled the issue of the representation of women in general.

The issue of Dostoevsky's women was first given its polemical edge by the Russian theologian and philosopher, Nicholas Berdiaev, who saw Dostoevsky's women primarily as tempters and in the end not only of much less

interest than Dostoevsky's heroes but also of much less interest than the
women characters of other Russian writers. Berdiaev argued that Dostoevsky's women were not autonomous figures, but purely functional. They
were used as means to an end, the end being the male hero:

> Women do not have a place of their own in Dostoevsky's works. Dostoevsky's
> anthropology is exclusively masculine. We shall see that women interest Dosto-
> evsky exclusively as a moment in the fate of the male, in the journey of mankind.
> The soul of mankind is above all the spirit of the male. The feminine principle is
> only a theme in the internal tragedy of the masculine spirit, his inner temptation.
> What images of love has Dostoevsky left us? The love of Myshkin and Rogozhin
> for Nastasia Filippovna, of Mitia Karamazov for Grushenka, of Versilov for Kate-
> rina Nikolaevna, of Stavrogin for many women. Nowhere is there a beautiful rep-
> resentation of love, nowhere a female figure who has anything like an indepen-
> dent significance. It is always man alone who is tormented by tragic fate. Women
> are only the internal expression of masculine tragedy. . . . Women's demonic char-
> acter interests Dostoevsky only as an elemental force arousing masculine passion
> and dividing the masculine personality. . . . Women's nature is dark, unillumined,
> it contains an abyss drawing one into it.[16]

Nathan Rosen attempted to refute Berdiaev's argument, not by disput-
ing women's functionality as a category in Dostoevsky's fiction but by rein-
terpreting their function. Rosen agrees with Berdiaev that Dostoevsky's
women do not exist as characters in their own right, that they are essentially
devices for characterizing the heroes; but he sees them as saviors not
tempters. They figure something like Proppian motifs in "an archetypal
plot"—a masculine plot—for the "archetypal Dostoyevskian hero." As Rosen
concedes, his typology is based not on how the women necessarily see themselves, but how they are "seen by the hero."[17]

But from the perspective of radical feminist critique, there may be little
to choose between in Berdiaev and Rosen: despite these critics' diametrical-
ly opposite views of the roles women play in Dostoevsky's novels, they both
see women in Dostoevsky, not as autonomous human beings, but as literary
devices, as opposite sides of the same functional coin. Is this not, then, a perfect example of the dichotomized and functional representation of women
(reinforced and validated by male critics) invariably presented by male writers as either angels or demons?[18]

Autonomy, however, presents no fewer problems than its absence, especially for gynocritics, which Heldt implies is the only recourse for women
critics of Russian literature. This issue, at least with respect to Dostoevsky,
most clearly manifests itself in another typology of Dostoevsky's women
characters, that of Frank Seeley, who, like Rosen, also takes on Berdiaev's
misprision of women in Dostoevsky's fiction—what he calls Berdiaev's "com-

ical cult of masculinity."[19] Rejecting the functionalism of Rosen as well as Berdiaev, Seeley argues that Dostoevsky's women characters are of equal significance to their male counterparts, that Nastasia Filippovna in *The Idiot* is really "a sister soul to Dostoyevsky's great rebels and heresiarchs—a Kirillov or an Ivan Karamazov" (305) and that Sonia Marmeladova in *Crime and Punishment* is "a sort of feminine counterpart of Dostoyevsky's saints—of a Myshkin or an Alyosha" (308). Seeley categorizes Dostoevsky's women in terms of their "dividedness" or "wholeness," with Nastasia Filippovna representing the "divided" nature at one extreme and Sonia Marmeladova the "whole" nature at the other. This distinction enables Seeley to raise Nastasia Filippovna to the level of importance and complexity of Dostoevsky's divided male characters and Sonia even higher, beyond the wholeness of Dostoevsky's saintly males, such as Myshkin and Alyosha. According to Seeley, Berdiaev was wrong, because he failed to see that Dostoevsky's women characters are just like his male characters, that the heroines' plots are no different from those of the heroes. However, does not Seeley's attempt to establish the autonomy of Dostoevsky's women characters—by showing their similarity to their male counterparts—sacrifice the "difference" (not Otherness) that not only distinguishes them from their male counterparts but also provides them with their autonomy *as women*? Can the measure of the success of a heroine be the extent to which she approximates the characterization, if not the character, of her male counterparts? Morover, how valuable is autonomy as a prescriptive category for the characterization of women in nineteenth-century literature? Are we really carried away by Dostoevsky's characters because of their autonomy or left cold or even indignant because of their lack of autonomy?[20] And is it not somewhat curious that Maegd-Soep, Heldt, and Andrew hardly mention Dostoevsky at all? Andrew's work concludes not only with what he regards as the acme of Russian cultural achievement, *What Is to Be Done?* (1863), but also before Dostoevsky's responses to Chernyshevsky's work in *Notes from Underground* and *Crime and Punishment*. Is Dostoevsky's phallocentrism so obvious that it is not even worth mentioning?

It seems to me that the crucial issue with regard to Dostoevsky's representation of women is that Dostoevsky cannot be neatly categorized: he cannot easily be exposed as a writer who textually victimizes his women characters, or, for that matter, as a writer who empowers them. Dostoevsky is a deconstructionist by nature; there are few if any constructs—including gender—that his novels do not radically problematize. Thus it would seem that we are dealing not so much with a failure of interpretation with respect to Dostoevsky's women characters, but with a failure of critical approach. In order to see this more clearly, let me set out the parameters in which victimization and gender are confronted in Dostoevsky's texts.

Although Dostoevsky sees the will to power or the desire to mastery as a universal in human relationships, the vast majority of the victims in his works, sexual and otherwise, are undoubtedly women. The most egregious crime contemplated or committed by Dostoevsky's *protagonists* is clearly the rape of a young girl, the violation of what for Dostoevsky is the most poignant symbol of defenseless innocence. The young female, "the eternal victim," as Rosen observes, is for Dostoevsky, "the primordial image of pain and injustice" (206).

Perhaps Dostoevsky's most detailed and explicit treatment of the victimization of a young girl occurs not in his fiction but in an 1876 article he wrote and published in *A Writer's Diary* on the famous Kroneberg case, where the father, Kroneberg, was accused of brutally beating (torturing) his seven-year-old daughter. Kroneberg confessed that he had beaten his little girl so hard that he himself almost fainted after inflicting the punishment. A former maid in the Kroneberg household and the wife of a porter who lived nearby were unable to bear the girl's suffering. Overcoming their fear of the authorities, they reported the beating to the police. To Dostoevsky, however, the crime committed against the child by Kroneberg's lawyer, Spasovich—the greatest liberal lawyer of his day—was an even greater crime than that of the father. In defense of Kroneberg, Spasovich attempted to undermine the credibility of the beaten little girl by psychologically and morally humiliating and tormenting her in front of the court. The psychological impressions and scars that the girl took from the courtroom would long outlive the welts and even psychological trauma of her father's beating.

> The secret vices of a tiny child (of this seven-year-old!) were revealed aloud before the whole public by grown-up, serious, and even humane people.—What a monstrosity! Mais il en reste toujours quelque chose, for one's whole life—you must understand that! And this will remain not only in her soul but, perhaps, it will even be reflected in her fate. Something foul and bad has touched her in that courtroom, and its trace has been left forever. And who knows?—Perhaps twenty years later someone will say to her: "Even as a child you appeared in a criminal court."[21]

To Dostoevsky the little girl is essentially an innocent babe, a "little seven-year-old creature, completely defenseless . . . with the face of angel," who is "incomparably purer and more sinless" then anyone else in the courtroom (*PSS*, 22:67). To insult such a babe (*mladenets*) is a sin that God will not forget. But the cruelty of the father is eclipsed by that of the lawyer, the king of the newly introduced legal system. The victimization of the innocent has not been alleviated by the jury trial, a recent import from the godless West; rather, it has been invested with a specious ethical justification and, even worse, institutionalized in the Russian bar: personal and arbitrary victimization has been raised to a cold, formalistic, rationalistic legalism. Dostoevsky insists on the innocence of the seven-year-old child in the Kroneberg case. The phrase "seven-year-old" reverberates throughout the article. She cannot conceivably be held responsible for any behavior that would warrant such abuse.

But most of Dostoevsky's adult heroines are responsible in a way that Kroneberg's daughter, by Dostoevsky's definition, could not be. This does not, however, mean that they are not victims. There are, in fact, few of Dostoevsky's works in which the women, especially young women, it might be argued, are not victimized in some way by men and/or male institutions. This is so often the case that one is certainly tempted—-a temptation to which we should not succumb—to see the young victimized female as a central theme running through Dostoevsky's oeuvre.

Now there are three basic arguments that can be made with regard to the victimization of the female that we see in Dostoevsky's works: (1) that Dostoevsky, as Andrew might argue, is not really condemning female victimization but exploiting it for his own and his readers' titillation; (2) that Dostoevsky sees women in varying degrees as victims, and that all his female characters are variations in kind and degree on the same theme; or (3) that victimization and its relationship to femininity is both asserted and then problematized, opened up for continual exploration and redefinition.

Even what seem to be the most straightforward of Dostoevsky's texts never constitute the statement of a position, but rather the testing of it, and so it is with the portrayal of Varenka Dobroselova in his first work, *Poor Folk*, who would appear to be the simplest representation of "the eternal victims." It does not take long, however, to see that Dostoevsky problematizes in Varenka not only the notion of victimization, but gender as well. In the sentimental novel the protagonist is invariably a heroine, with the hero serving primarily as addressee and sounding board for the expression of sentiment. Dostoevsky, however, casts his hero as the sentimental heroine. In *Poor Folk* the vast majority of the letters are his. Even his name, Devushkin, from the Russian word for young girl or woman (*devushka*), bespeaks innocence and virginity. Varenka, his correspondent, comes from the countryside (where she led a most happy existence) to a hostile Petersburg, where, orphaned, she falls into the hands of a procuress, Anna Fedorovna, who sells her to one of her brutish clients, the crude landowner Bykov (*byk* in Russian means bull). Devushkin, who understands more of Varenka's story than he lets on, attempts to help Varenka keep out of the clutches of Anna Fedorovna—who is still after her—by offering as much financial and emotional support as he can muster. However, due to various indiscretions, Devushkin himself becomes impoverished and for a while it is seventeen-year-old Varenka who must support the forty-seven-year-old Devushkin. Realizing that Devushkin is unreliable, Varenka jumps at the chance to marry Bykov, who has now proposed to the girl he seduced in order to produce heirs (a means, we learn, of disinheriting his nephew). We know as well that Varenka is not the only young female who has suffered this fate. The novel discusses other wards of Anna Fedorovna who have and will follow in Varenka's footsteps. Dostoevsky sketches a similar, but even darker, scenario in *Notes from Underground* and *Crime and Punishment*, with the prostitutes Liza and Sonia, the necessary sacrifices, as Raskolnikov cynically states, of the city and progress.

With the later and literarily more mature heroines, we often see victimage more markedly problematized. These women are able to use their image of themselves as victims as justification for their behavior and even as a means of exerting power over others. Victimization, as Katerina Ivanovna shows in *The Brothers Karamazov*, can be a supremely powerful form of self-glorification; and of course it is not only Dostoevsky's heroines who understand this power. Even the rather sympathetically presented seventeen-year-old Varenka (who plays in some ways the most stereotypical role of the victimized young girl) turns out to be much less naive and innocent than Devushkin thinks she is or than Varenka makes herself out to be. Varenka is the author of her own story and much more consciously so than Devushkin, who fancies himself, at times, an author. She carefully manipulates and cultivates her own image based on her reading of French and Russian literary sentimental models. In her reminiscences, which she sends to Devushkin to read, Varenka casts herself as a sentimental heroine, the victim of unrequited love. Yet, despite continual references to herself as helpless and forlorn, she is much more able to survive in the hostile world of Petersburg than Devushkin. Devushkin starts out as financial protector and supporter, but toward the end it is the helpless Varenka who supports Devushkin when he is down and out.

Furthermore, Varenka is not only much more practical than Devushkin; she is also more successful. In contrast to Devushkin, the seemingly helpless Varenka manages to survive on her own for a long period of time and to a certain extent even to restore her good name, something Devushkin strives for the entire novel but never achieves. She becomes engaged to the man who has deceived her, no mean accomplishment for a helpless orphan, and when necessary she is able to use Devushkin to further her marriage plans with his rival. Her behavior in this regard may strike us as insensitive, if not cruel, especially for a young woman who seems otherwise to have the most refined sensibilities. Devushkin, who will die of a broken heart in the end, turns out to be even more vulnerable and in some senses more innocent than Varenka. As so often happens in his works, Dostoevsky has it both ways: Varenka is, to be sure, a victim of her unfortunate situation, but she is far from a mere victim; indeed, she is quite capable of using the perception of herself as a victim to her own advantage. In the end, she achieves her goal. Bykov is obviously no prize—no soulmate at least—but given Varenka's orphaned state in Petersburg, one cannot easily imagine a better resolution to her situation.[22]

The point is that even in the simplest cases Dostoevsky problematizes the notion of victimization and gender and their interrelationship. To speak of simple victimization or titillation (authorial victimization), even to speak of empowerment, is to diminish a text that not only resists reduction but multiplies possibilities. This is why any prescriptive critical program applied to Dostoevsky's works, whether it be radical feminist critique or a positively oriented "socialist realism," will produce little that is not predictable, little that is not antithetical to the spirit of Dostoevsky's major fiction. The idea of choosing to read Dostoevsky's women on the basis of whether they are means to an end or ends in themselves, toys for the author to titillate his male readers or images of empowerment for female readers, entirely misses the point. For Dostoevsky is always testing stereotypes; he takes few things for granted. For him gender and victimization are not modes of characterization but themes for development and exploration. One need not read Dostoevsky otherwise. To read him otherwise is to finalize that which cannot be finalized.

The argument of course can be made that Dostoevsky is an exception that proves the rule—and perhaps not only for Russian literature. But I purposely have taken one of Dostoevsky's least complex female characters to avoid the issue of exceptionality, to avoid the impression that Bakhtin sometimes gives that Dostoevsky is unique. Pushkin is hardly less open than Dostoevsky (as anyone knows who has tried to understand the relationship between Dunia, Minsky, and Samson Vyrin in "The Stationmaster").[23] Tolstoy is neither so antifeminist as he sometimes appears to be or so pro-feminist as Heldt makes him out to be in *Kreutzer Sonata*. What critics have discovered in the portrayals of women in the works of male writers is amply represented in the critical literature, a distillation of which the reader will find in the present volume. The need to justify such critical study as represented here is an unfortunate state of affairs, but it is a task, given the contemporary situation, that must be undertaken. In the final analysis, the proof is not in prescriptions or programs, not in the gender of the critic, but in the individual criticism itself: in its openness to the text and the openings it creates in the text through such openness. We have only one thing to fear: a criticism that prefers closure to openness.

Notes

SONA STEPHAN HOISINGTON, INTRODUCTION

1.   See, for example, Barbara Heldt, *Terrible Perfection: Women and Russian Literature* (Bloomington: Indiana University Press, 1988); Helena Goscilo, ed., *Fruits of Her Plume: Essays on Contemporary Russian Women's Culture* (New York: M. E. Sharpe, 1993); Jane Costlow, Stephanie Sandler, and Judith Vowles, eds., *Sexuality and the Body in Russian Culture* (Stanford: Stanford University Press, 1993); Marina Ledkovsky, Charlotte Rosenthal, and Mary Zirin, eds., *Dictionary of Russian Women Writers* (Westport, Conn.: Greenwood, 1994); Toby W. Clyman and Diana Greene, eds., *Women Writers in Russian Literature* (Westport, Conn.: Greenwood, 1994).

2.   For a critique of this kind of feminist criticism, which was popular in the early 1970s, see Toril Moi, *Sexual/Textual Politics: Feminist Literary Theory* (reprint, New York: Routledge, 1990), 42–49.

3.   This, of course, is not to deny that stereotyped images of women do occur in literature, as recent feminist criticism attests, but all too often the problem is that we as readers are blinded by these stereotypes. As Virginia Woolf observed, "it is far harder to kill a phantom than a reality."

4.   See, for example, Carolyn Heilbrun, *Towards a Recognition of Androgyny* (New York: Knopf, 1973), 49–51.

5.   Carolyn Heilbrun, *Towards a Recognition of Androgyny*, 49, and Lee R. Edwards, "The Labors of Psyche: Towards a Theory of Female Heroism," *Critical Inquiry* 6 (1979): 33–49. Edwards argues that the use of this term "eliminates the awkward distinction between the heroine as heroic figure and the heroine as conventional woman that has perplexed so much recent literary, especially feminist, analysis" (42).

6.   The terms "feminist critique" and "gynocritics" were coined by Elaine Showalter. For her account of the history of feminist criticism, see "A Criticism of Our Own: Autonomy and Assimilation in Afro-American and Feminist Literary Theory," in *Feminisms: An Anthology of Literary Theory*

and Criticism, ed. Robyn R. Warhol and Diane Price Herndl (New Brunswick, N.J.: Rutgers University Press), 168–88.

7. This point is made by Susan Suleiman in a different context in her essay, "(Re)Writing the Body: The Politics and Poetics of Female Eroticism," in *The Female Body in Western Culture: Contemporary Perspectives*, ed. Susan Rubin Suleiman (Cambridge: Harvard University Press, 1985), 22.

CARYL EMERSON, TATIANA

1. For Belinsky on Tatiana, see V. G. Belinskii, *"Evgenii Onegin" A. S. Pushkina* (Moscow: GosIzdKhudLit, 1957), esp. 59–84 (Stat'ia 9-ia). Dostoevsky proclaimed in his Pushkin Speech (1880): "Perhaps Pushkin would have done better had he called his poem by Tatiana's name and not Onegin's. . . . She utters the truth of the poem." Fyodor Dostoevsky, "Pushkin," in Sona Hoisington, ed. and trans., *Russian Views of Pushkin's "Eugene Onegin"* (Bloomington: Indiana University Press, 1988), 56–67, esp. 59.

2. Interestingly, it is Belinsky in his Eighth Article on Pushkin (1844) who defends Onegin against the incipient Tatiana cult. "[T]he heart has its own laws," Belinsky writes. "Therefore, Onegin had a perfect right, without fearing the stern judgment of the critics, not to fall in love with the girl Tatyana and to fall in love with the woman. In neither case did he act morally or immorally. . . . There is nothing dreamy or fantastic about Onegin. He could be happy or unhappy only in reality and through reality." See Vissarion Belinsky, *"Eugene Onegin*: An Encyclopedia of Russian Life," in Hoisington, ed. and trans., *Russian Views of Pushkin's "Eugene Onegin,"* 34, 40.

3. For a survey of the ebbs and flows in Tatiana's critical image (as of the early 1970s), see Geraldine Kelley, "The Characterization of Tat'jana in Puškin's 'Evgenij Onegin'" (Ph.D. diss., University of Wisconsin–Madison, 1976), esp. part 1.

4. Among those critics who have found unpersuasive the final meeting between the lovestruck Onegin and the Princess Tatiana, three will have special relevance for my reading: Nabokov, Little, and Gregg (see below). I lay aside Viktor Shklovsky's famous claim that the narrator's primary stance toward Tatiana throughout the novel—and in fact his stance toward plot in general—is parodic. Two factors suggest caution: (1) Tatiana (like all Pushkin's heroines after the mid-1820s) is smarter than the plots in which she finds herself and does not need the heavy hand of outside commentary to help her outgrow her setting; and (2) the early polemical Shklovsky tends to see parody everywhere; for him the work often serves to legitimate the device and not the other way around. See Viktor Shklovskij, "Pushkin and Sterne: *Eugene Onegin*" [1923], in *Twentieth-Century Russian Literary Criticism*, ed. Victor Erlich (New Haven: Yale University Press, 1975), 63–80.

Shklovskian corrosive parody has a rich legacy. Consider the statement in a brief essay peevishly marking the 1937 Pushkin Jubilee by the émigré scholar Pyotr Bitsilli who asserts that Tatiana, before and after, never understood Onegin, cast unfair aspersions on him at the end, and in fact *"killed* Onegin, turned him from a living human being into a 'laboratory animal,' a 'type'— and what she did with him, others have done with her" ("Smert' Evgeniia i Tat'iana," *Sovremennye zapiski* 44 [Paris, 1937]: 413–16).

5.   Richard A. Gregg, "Tat'yana's Two Dreams: The Unwanted Spouse and the Demonic Lover," *Slavonic and East European Review* 48 (1970): 492–505, esp. 502.

6.   For a discussion of the evolving status of marriage as the novel progresses—from the site of open ridicule to the site of potential honor—see Leonore Scheffler, *Das erotische Sujet in Puškins Dichtung* (University of Tübingen, 1967), chap. 3, "Tat'jana Larina," 178–200. "Marriage is spoken of pejoratively in the first six chapters," Scheffler notes. "Only after the sixth chapter does the accent change. . . . In the eighth book the subject is silently closed. . . . [There,] Pushkin's initial irony about Tatiana is missing entirely" (194).

7.   J. Douglas Clayton, "Towards a Feminist Reading of *Evgenii Onegin*," *Canadian Slavonic Papers* 29 (1987): 255–65, esp. 261. See also Clayton's *Ice and Flame: Aleksandr Pushkin's "Eugene Onegin"* (Toronto: University of Toronto Press, 1985), chap. 1, "Criticism of *Eugene Onegin*" (7–71, esp. 57), for a sociobiographical Soviet explanation of the mature Tatiana that combines both spousal and aristocratic motifs.

8.   William Mills Todd III, *Fiction and Society in the Age of Pushkin: Ideology, Institutions, and Narrative* (Cambridge: Harvard University Press, 1986), 129 [in chap. 3 on *Eugene Onegin*]; see also chap. 1, "A Russian Ideology."

9.   See J. Thomas Shaw, "The Problem of Unity of Author-Narrator's Stance in Puškin's *Evgenij Onegin*," *Russian Language Journal* 35 (1980): 25–42.

10.   For a discussion of Tatiana's reduced "portraiture" and her patterns of detachment and noninteraction, see Kelley, part 1, "Narrated Characterization," esp. 27–57. Also significant, I believe, is the haunting quasi-representational sketch of a kneeling female figure (front or back? clothed or nude?) on an 1824 rough draft of Tatiana's letter to Onegin (reproduced in Clayton, *Ice and Flame*, 137).

11.   Pushkin is responding here (in unpublished draft) to an 1824 article in *Mnemozina* by his friend Vilgelm Kyukhelbeker, in which the author declared "strength, freedom and inspiration" essential to all true poetry and identified inspiration with ecstasy (*vostorg*). Pushkin disagreed. See Carl R. Proffer, ed. and trans., *The Critical Prose of Alexander Pushkin* (Bloomington: Indiana University Press, 1969), 52.

12.   George Santayana, *The Sense of Beauty* (New York, 1896), 235–36, as cited in William K. Wimsatt and Cleanth Brooks, *Literary Criticism: A Short History* (Chicago: University of Chicago Press, 1957), 2:618–19, in the chapter "I. A. Richards: A Poetics of Tension," an excellent survey and critique of Richards's aesthetic positions.

13.   I. A. Richards, *Principles of Literary Criticism* (New York: Harcourt, Brace and World, 1925), chap. 32, "The Imagination," 239–53, esp. 249–52. Richards's comments on the relative value of emotions (of lesser import) and attitudes (of greater) for any given experience recall Pushkin's distinction between ecstasy and genuine inspiration: "It is not the intensity of the conscious experience, its thrill, its pleasure or its poignancy which gives it value," Richards writes, "but the organization of its impulses for freedom and fullness of life. There are plenty of ecstatic instants which are valueless" (132).

14.   "Imagine," Richards writes in chap. 14, "an energy system of prodigious complexity and extreme delicacy of organization which has an indefinitely large number of stable poises. Imagine it thrown from one poise to another with great facility, each poise being the resultant of all the energies of the system. . . . Such a system would exhibit the phenomenon of memory; but it would keep no records though appearing to do so. The appearance would be due merely to the extreme accuracy and sensitiveness of the system and the delicacy of its balances" (104).

15.   A transverse standing wave develops between two fixed nodes when a direct wave, the result of a shock, pluck, or other impact, comes to be superimposed in one direction upon its reflection going the other way. Within this column, troughs and crests pulsating at regular intervals generate a complex matrix of fundamentals, partials, and harmonics. Curiously productive in the analogy is the degree of inner concentration required to resolve these antagonisms, and the fact that a byproduct of this resolution is an exquisite "radiation" of sound—much more complex than can be appreciated by our hearing apparatus, which distorts and orders the escaping aural energy to serve its own, rather primitive "communicative" purposes. The wave itself, wholly occupied by its internal economy, is indifferent to any mesmerizing effects it might have on the air outside. I thank my father, David Geppert, for this suggestive acoustical analogy with Tatiana's "aesthetics."

16.   See especially Leon Stilman, "Problemy literaturnyx žanrov i tradicij v 'Evgenii Onegine' Puskina," in *American Contributions to the Fourth International Congress of Slavists* (The Hague: Mouton, 1958), 321–67; Michael R. Katz, "Love and Marriage in Pushkin's *Evgeny Onegin,*" in *Oxford Slavonic Papers,* ed. J. L. I. Fennell and I. P. Foote, n.s., 17 (Oxford: Clarendon Press, 1984): 77–89; and Stanley Mitchell, "Tatiana's Reading," *Forum for Modern Language Studies* 4 (1968): 1–21.

17. See Kelley, "Narrated Characterization," 129–30.

18. In Tatiana's defense I cite Richard Gregg, who was generous enough to give this essay a careful and compassionate reading: "One could argue that Onegin is for Tatiana a *kovarnyi iskusitel'* in the same way that a shot of bourbon is for an alcoholic. The liquor is, ethically speaking, innocent. But it treacherously tempts all the same."

19. Along these lines, the kindest and most patient reading I know of Onegin's "rejection" of Tatiana's suit occurs at the end of Ludolf Müller's "Tat'janas Traum": he reads the snowy landscape as Tatiana's lonely, internal pre-love state; the accommodating bear as sexuality (the "dark drive of love" that will release her from loneliness); Onegin himself as the one human figure who can tame the frightening ogres that inhabit the hut of potential erotic life; "but the marriage is not consummated. A lack of interest on Onegin's part is not to blame; we saw that in the depth of his being he indeed loves her, and that a longer, well-intentioned neighborly contact could have awakened this seed of love within him." See Ludolf Müller, "Tat'janas Traum," in *Der Welt der Slaven* 7 (1962): 387–94, esp. 393.

20. John Garrard, "Corresponding Heroines in *Don Juan* and *Yevgeny Onegin*" [1993], unpublished ms. Garrard notes that Amédée Pichot's French prose translation of *Don Juan* softened Byron's sarcasm and helped move the focus of the text to Julia; he also notes that the episode of Julia's letter is one of the very few patches of Byron's text free of corrosive narrative irony (a tone Pushkin disliked, and that his own narrator completely drops in chapter 8).

21. Stephanie Sandler has provided the best reading of chapter 8, and of the entire novel, as a "text of renunciation and a text of continuing attraction"; see her *Distant Pleasures: Alexander Pushkin and the Writing of Exile* (Stanford: Stanford University Press, 1989), esp. 207.

22. L. S. Vygotskii, *Psikhologiia iskusstva* [1925] (Moscow: Iskusstvo, 1968), 282–88; in English, Lev Semenovich Vygotsky, *The Psychology of Art* (Cambridge, Mass.: MIT Press, 1971), 222–28. In chapter 9, "Art as Catharsis," Vygotsky expresses dissatisfaction with most explanations of aesthetic response because they ignore a theory of the imagination and a theory of real-life emotions—two components that always interact in our response to art, which is why artistic effect is so much more than an "illusion." Such theories are difficult to come by, he admits, because critics work at the level of analysis; they have no direct access to primary artistic synthesis.

23. The late Iurii Lotman discusses Pushkin's concept of inspiration precisely in terms of such collisions; see his *Kul'tura i vzryv* (Culture and explosion) (Moscow: Gnozis, 1992), 35–43, and the book's final chapter, "The Phenomenon of Art."

24. See Riccardo Picchio, "Dante and J. Malfilatre as Literary Sources of Tat'jana's Erotic Dream (Notes on the Third Chapter of Puškin's *Evgenij*

Onegin)," in *Alexander Puškin: A Symposium on the 175th Anniversary of his Birth*, ed. Andrej Kodjak and Kiril Taranovsky (New York: New York University Press, 1976), 42–55; and more recently Marina Woronzoff (Yale University), "The Tale of Echo and Narcissus Retold: Puškin's Tatjana and Eugene," paper delivered at AATSEEL Annual Meeting, Toronto, December 1993.

25. Here one must supplement Iurii Lotman's gloss on chapter 8, VII, 1–4, in which he apologizes, as it were, for Tatiana's tolerance of the "structured order and mix of ranks and ages" in the aristocratic salon (in Iu. M. Lotman, *Roman A. S. Pushkina "Evgenii Onegin": Kommentarii* [Leningrad: Prosveshchenie, 1980], 346–49). Lotman assures his readers that such an "affirmative assessment of high society" from a heroine representing Russian national virtues does indeed ring oddly in a novel that contains so much social satire. But if we assume, as Pushkin invites us to do, that Tatiana is the spirit not of Russian virtues but of poetry, then nothing could be more appropriate for this hybrid novel-in-verse than admiration for "structured order and mixed rank."

26. See, for example, T. E. Little: "Onegin's journey through Petersburg has a dreamlike quality about it. . . . [His] entry into Tatyana's house resembles the entry of a fairy tale prince into an enchanted castle. He meets no servants; the house appears to be empty." T. E. Little, "Pushkin's Tatyana and Onegin: A Study in Irony," *New Zealand Slavonic Journal*, no. 1 (1975): 19–28, esp. 21.

27. In his survey of dreams in Pushkin, Michael Katz notes the "proliferation of dreams and dreamers in Eugene Onegin," concluding that Tatyana reconciles herself to the results of her choice and station whereas "Onegin remains a slave to his dreams [*mechty*] and is completely unable to accept the realities of life. Therefore she must reject him." See Michael R. Katz, "Dreams in Pushkin," *California Slavic Studies* 2 (Berkeley and Los Angeles: University of California Press, 1980): 71–103, esp. 92 and 99. In my reading, Tatyana is indeed reconciled to her fate—but it is precisely Onegin's realization of this irreversible fact that triggers in him his ultimate *mechta* or fantasy-dream of their final intimate scene.

28. See, for example, Clayton, *Ice and Flame*, 112.

29. Leslie O'Bell, "Through the Magic Crystal to *Eugene Onegin*," in *Puškin Today*, ed. David M. Bethea (Bloomington: Indiana University Press, 1993), 152–70, esp. 164–65.

30. Aleksandr Pushkin, *Eugene Onegin*, trans. Vladimir Nabokov, vol. 2 [Commentary and Index], part 2 (Princeton: Princeton University Press, 1975): 241.

31. T. E. Little, "Pushkin's Tatyana and Onegin: A Study in Irony," 19–28.

32. See Richard Gregg, "Rhetoric in Tat'jana's Last Speech: The Cam-

ouflage that Reveals," *Slavic and East European Journal* 25 (1981): 1–12, esp. 1 and 6. Although mightily bothered by this speech, Gregg does not draw my radical conclusions; he restricts himself to ascribing Tatiana's indiscretions to rhetorical devices and an emotional loss of control, to asking "to what extent do her remarks square with the facts?" to noting that "sincerity is, after all, no guarantee of veracity," and to asserting that although "Tat'jana cannot lie" (why not? Is Gregg under influence of the cult?), "in one crucial area of her experience she is an exceedingly unreliable witness." Kindly reacting to a draft version of this essay, Gregg responded thus to this note: "EMERSON: 'Is Gregg under the influence of the cult?' GREGG: 'Yup.'"

33. Consider Tsvetaeva's ruminations on Tatiana's glorious and tragic fate in "My Pushkin": "A bench. On the bench, Tatiana. Then Onegin arrives, but he does not sit down; rather she gets up. Both stand. And only he speaks, all the time, for a long time, and she doesn't say a word. And here I understand that . . . this is love. . . . My first love scene was an unlove scene: he didn't love (that I understood), for that reason he did not sit down, she loved, for that reason she stood up, not for a minute were they together, they did nothing together, they did everything in reverse. He spoke, she was silent, he didn't love, she loved, he left, she remained . . . . Tatiana sits on that bench forever." Marina Tsvetaeva, "Moi Pushkin," in her *Izvrannaia proza v dvukh tomakh* (New York: Russica, 1979), 2:249–302, esp. 260–61.

34. See the argument in Yury Lotman, "The Transformation of the Tradition Generated by *Onegin* in the Subsequent History of the Russian Novel" [1975], in Hoisington, ed. and trans., *Russian Views of Pushkin's "Eugene Onegin,"* 169–77.

35. Simon Franklin, "Novels without End: Notes on 'Eugene Onegin' and 'Dead Souls'," *Modern Language Review* 79 (1984): 372–83, esp. 372.

36. See, most famously, Yury Tynyanov, "On the Composition of *Eugene Onegin,"* in Hoisington, ed. and trans., *Russian Views of Pushkin's "Eugene Onegin,"* 71–90.

37. Shaw sees three "phases" in the narrator's stance (youthful perceptivity, disenchantment, mature reenchantment), and locates Onegin in an arrested second phase, ripe for reenchantment—although, of course, Onegin remains no poet. J. Thomas Shaw, "The Problem of Unity of Author-Narrator's Stance in Puškin's *Evgenij Onegin,"* 25–42, esp. 35.

JANE T. COSTLOW, "OH-LÀ-LÀ" AND "NO-NO-NO":
ODINTSOVA AS WOMAN ALONE

1. The song "Turgenev Women" (Turgenevskie zhenshchiny) is written by Vasily Shumov and performed by the rock group "Tsentr"; it appears on their 1988 album "Made in Paris" ("Sdelano v Parizhe") [Melodiia]. Shu-

mov's reference to Turgenev Women in the morning mist (v utrennem tumane) reveals his familiarity with Turgenev's own verse—the lyric "Utro tumannoe, utro sedoe," best known and much beloved in its musical setting. Many thanks to my colleague Dennis Browne for bringing this contemporary piece of Turgeneviana to my attention.

2. I am thinking here of the image of the virtuous woman as an "angel in the house," a pernicious image with which English women writers in particular had to come to terms. Nina Auerbach, in *Woman and the Demon: The Life of a Victorian Myth* (Cambridge: Harvard University Press, 1982), discusses both the myth and its multiple subversions in late nineteenth-century British writing.

3. "The Threshold" ("Porog"), in I. S. Turgenev, *Stikhotvoreniia* (Leningrad: Sovetskii pisatel', 1955), 362–63.

4. In his discussion of *On the Eve* Victor Ripp addresses the paradox and problematics of investing great expectations in women whose virtue derives largely from inexperience: they are perhaps innocent (since relatively isolated from corrupting institutions), but how then are they to act forcefully on precisely those institutions without losing their innocence? *Turgenev's Russia* (Ithaca: Cornell University Press, 1980), 159–86.

5. For a discussion of the novel that gives generous attention to polemic occasioned and addressed by it, see David Lowe, *Turgenev's Fathers and Sons* (Ann Arbor: Ardis, 1983), especially chapter 4. For a discussion of the connections of intimate and political relationships in the novels, see chapter 5 of my *Worlds within Worlds: The Novels of Ivan Turgenev* (Princeton: Princeton University Press, 1990).

6. The standard work in English on the woman question (*zhenskii vopros*) is Richard Stites, *The Woman's Liberation Movement in Russia: Feminism, Nihilism, and Bolshevism, 1860–1930* (Princeton: Princeton University Press, 1978). See also G. A. Tishkin, *Zhenskii vopros v Rossii v 50–60 gg. XIX v.* (Leningrad, 1984). I examine women writers' contributions to the discussion in "Love, Work and the Woman Question in Mid Nineteenth-Century Women's Writing," in *Women Writers in Russian Literature*, ed. Toby Clyman and Diana Greene (Westport, Conn.: Greenwood, 1994), 61–75.

7. Actually there are more faithful English renditions of the title: both Constance Garnett's and Isabel Hapgood's turn-of-the-century translations are entitled *Fathers and Children*, as are Richard Hare's (Collier, 1949) and Avril Pyman's (Dutton, 1968). But most translators have opted for *Fathers and Sons*. Rosemary Edmonds is no exception, even though her widely used translation is introduced by Isaiah Berlin's classic essay, "*Fathers and Children*: Turgenev and the Liberal Predicament." Russians themselves seem to have some awareness of the English speaker's dilemma: a Petersburg entre-

preneur whose company goes by the name "Ottsy i deti" professed some uncertainty as to whether his English business card should read "Fathers and Children" or "Fathers and Sons." He assumed that Americans would recognize the latter, but not the former. Since Americans today know the work largely in the Edmonds translation, I expect his hunch is correct.

8.   In Russian these evocative syllables go like this: "oi-oi-oi." See I. S. Turgenev, *Polnoe sobranie sochinenii i pisem* (Moscow and Leningrad: Izdatel'stvo Akademii nauk, 1964), 8:268; hereafter cited as *PSS*. Rosemary Edmonds appropriately translates these syllables with approving male gallicisms better suited to the drawing room than a machismo grunt. The "no" sequence is actually Kukshina's, when she speaks of her "friend" Odintsova in the following terms: "Vprochem, eto by nichego, no nikakoi svobody vozzreniia, nikakoi shiriny, nichego . . . etogo" (*PSS*, 8:261; ellipsis in original). Edmonds's translation makes the best of the negative challenge: "she has no independence of outlook, no breadth, nothing . . ." (144; ellipsis in original). This repeated negation introduces the "nihilist" of love. All quotations from the novel are taken from Rosemary Edmonds's translation of *Fathers and Sons* (New York: Viking Penguin, 1965) and are cited in the text. In Russian, family names of women normally end in "a," and I have adhered to this practice throughout the essay.

9.   Gary Saul Morson argues this point compellingly in a recent essay on the novel. See "Genre and Hero/*Fathers and Sons*: Intergeneric Dialogues, Generic Refugees, and the Hidden Prosaic," in *Literature, Culture, and Society in the Modern Age: In Honor of Joseph Frank*, Stanford Slavic Studies, ed. Edward J. Brown, Lazar Fleishman, Gregory Freidin, and Richard Schupbach, no. 4 (Stanford: Stanford University Press, 1991), 336–81.

10.   The slight confusion regarding her given name seems to echo parodically the "enigmas" of the Princess R. and Odintsova herself.

11.   Turgenev's association of Kukshina with fire is oddly premonitory of the fires that accompanied political disturbances in St. Petersburg in the summer of 1862, the year after the emancipation of the serfs (and the publication of the novel). See Abbott Gleason, *Young Russia* (Chicago: University of Chicago Press, 1980), 166–76.

12.   There is a hint of symbolism at work in these heroines' names: Varvara (the seductress) is a "barbarian"; Liza (the future nun) takes the way of the biblical "narrow gate," her family name Kalitina echoing the Russian *kalitka*, or gate.

13.   It is assumed that Turgenev drew his portrait of a "femme émancipée" from one woman in particular: Evgeniia Petrovna Kittara, whom he met through Marko Vovchok, a Ukrainian woman writer whose work Turgenev had translated. Kittara emerges in Vovchok's correspondence as a somewhat flighty woman of sudden and diverse enthusiasms. See G. B.

Stepanova, "O prototipe Kukshinoi v romane Turgeneva 'Ottsy i deti'," *Russkaia literatura*, no. 3 (1985): 152–54.

14. Dostoevsky's Pushkin Speech of 1881 articulates clearly the programmatic force of such refusal.

15. Amy Mandelker argues compellingly for reading the novel as a tragedy; her discussion of literary traditions of suicide is also germane to my reading of Odintsova. See her *Framing "Anna Karenina": Tolstoy, the Woman Question, and the Victorian Novel* (Columbus: Ohio State University Press, 1993), 93–98.

16. Robert Bell suggests that Artemis and Athena, as virginal goddesses, are both "less human" as well as "more awesome" than Hera, Aphrodite, or Demeter. See his *Women of Classical Mythology: A Biographical Dictionary* (New York: Oxford University Press, 1993), 72. I am indebted in my imagination of Artemis to Nor Hall, who speaks of the goddess in archetypal terms: "She is a wild mountain woman, woman alone, fighter, hunter, dancer, lover of animals, protectress of all newborn sucking and roving creatures, a sister to men and teacher of women. . . . Artemis knew the ways of woman's animal body without being taught. . . . Artemis brings certain caged aspects of feminine nature out of exile." *The Moon and the Virgin: Reflections on the Archetypal Feminine* (New York: Harper and Row, 1980), 109, 122, 123.

17. Ovid provides one of the better-known versions of the myth of Artemis/Diana and Actaeon; *Metamorphoses*, trans. Rolfe Humphries (Bloomington: Indiana University Press, 1955), 61–64. See my discussion of the myth with more specific regard to Bazarov in *Worlds within Worlds*, 134–35. As I suggest in that essay, there are moments within the text that echo the particularities of the myth: when, for example, the narrator himself "watches" Odintsova in the bath (165).

18. "She had caught sight of herself in the glass; the image of her head thrown back, with a mysterious smile on the half-closed eyes, half-parted lips, told her, it seemed, in a flash something at which she herself felt confused . . ." (183; ellipsis in original).

19. The literature on this topic is extensive. See, among others, John A. Phillips, *Eve: The History of an Idea* (San Francisco: Harper and Row, 1984), and Margaret R. Miles, *Carnal Knowing: Female Nakedness and Religious Meaning in the Christian West* (New York: Vintage, 1989). Russian instances of the problem are addressed in the introduction and many of the essays in Jane T. Costlow, Stephanie Sandler, and Judith Vowles, eds., *Sexuality and the Body in Russian Culture* (Stanford: Stanford University Press, 1993).

AMY MANDELKER, THE JUDGMENT OF *ANNA KARENINA*

This essay is an abridged, slightly revised version of chapter 2 of my book, *Framing "Anna Karenina": Tolstoy, the Woman Question, and the Victorian Novel* (Columbus: Ohio University Press, 1993).

1. David H. Stewart, *"Anna Karenina*: The Dialectic of Prophecy," *PMLA* 79 (1964): 266–74.

2. Richard Gustafson, *Leo Tolstoy: Resident and Stranger; a Study in Fiction and Theology* (Princeton: Princeton University Press, 1986), 131–32.

3. A. V. Stankevich, "Anna Karenina and Levin," *European Courier*, nos. 4–5 (1878); translated in *Tolstoy: The Critical Heritage*, ed. A. V. Knowles (London: Routledge and Kegan Paul, 1978), 296, 304.

4. Mary Evans, *Reflecting on Anna Karenina* (London: Routledge, 1989), 40.

5. Henry Gifford, "Anna, Lawrence and 'The Law'," in *Leo Tolstoy: A Critical Anthology*, ed. Henry Gifford (Harmondsworth, Middlesex: Penguin, 1971), 301.

6. Judith Armstrong, *The Unsaid Anna Karenina* (New York: St. Martin's, 1988), 24.

7. Boris Eikhenbaum, *Tolstoy in the Seventies*, trans. Albert Kaspin (Ann Arbor: Ardis, 1982), 138.

8. R. F. Christian, *Tolstoy: A Critical Introduction* (Cambridge: Cambridge University Press, 1969), 175.

9. Viktor Shklovsky, *Lev Tolstoy* (Moscow: Progress Publishers, 1978), 436.

10. The best and most recent discussion of this problem appears in Robert Louis Jackson, "On the Ambivalent Beginning of *Anna Karenina*," in *The Semantic Analysis of Literary Texts*, ed. E. de Haard, T. Langerak, and W. G. Weststeijn (Amsterdam: Elsevier, 1990), 345–52. Jackson concludes that "for Tolstoj the *ethical* injunction—'do not judge'—is also an *esthetic* injunction—one that must govern the authorial stance of the artist, that is, his relationship to his heroes. . . . Tolstoj does not judge Anna. He understands her" (346).

11. Fyodor Dostoevsky, *"Anna Karenina* as a Fact of Particular Significance" (*Anna Karenina* kak fakt osobogo znacheniia), published in *A Writer's Diary* in 1877. See F. M. Dostoevskii, *Polnoe sobranie sochinenii* (Leningrad: Nauka, 1983), 25:201.

12. Cited in Eikhenbaum, 145. Eikhenbaum shows quite convincingly that originally Tolstoy simply translated Schopenhauer's "Mein ist die Rache" into a nonscriptural Russian version, "Otmshchenie moe" (which persisted through several drafts of the early variants), and only later corrected his Russian text against the church Slavic Scriptures.

13.   For a comprehensive study of all the references to the biblical passage in the novel, see Rebecca S. Hogan, "The Wisdom of Many, the Wit of One: The Narrative Function of the Proverb in Tolstoy's 'Anna Karenina' and Trollope's 'Orley Farm'" (Ph.D. diss., University of Colorado, 1985).

14.   Robert L. Jackson, "Chance and Design in *Anna Karenina*," in *Leo Tolstoy's "Anna Karenina"*, ed. Harold Bloom (New York: Chelsea House, 1987), 34.

15.   Martin Price, "Tolstoy and the Forms of Life: 'Inexorable Law'," in Bloom, *Leo Tolstoy's "Anna Karenina"*, 121.

16.   E. B. Greenwood, *Tolstoy: The Comprehensive Vision* (New York: St. Martin's, 1975), 117–18.

17.   Barbara Hardy, *The Appropriate Form* (London: Athlone, 1967), 43.

18.   Jackson, "Chance and Design in *Anna Karenina*," 34.

19.   Gary Saul Morson, "Prosaics in *Anna Karenina*," *Tolstoy Studies Journal* 1 (1988): 1–12. Morson's contention that Dolly is the actual heroine of the novel is debated at length in what follows.

20.   David A. Sloane, "Pushkin's Legacy in *Anna Karenina*," *Tolstoy Studies Journal* 4 (1991): 1–23.

21.   The terms *heroine-ism* and *heroinism* were apparently introduced into criticism by Diana Trilling in "The Liberated Heroine," *Partisan Review* 45 (1978): 501–22 and by Ellen Moers in her *Literary Women: The Great Writers* (New York: Doubleday, 1976).

22.   Armstrong, *Unsaid Anna Karenina*, 120.

23.   Rachel M. Brownstein, *Becoming a Heroine: Reading about Women in Novels* (New York: Viking, 1982), 82.

24.   Iurii Lotman, "The Origin of Plot in the Light of Typology," *Poetics Today* 1 (1979): 161–84. Teresa de Lauretis, "Desire in Narrative," in her *Alice Doesn't* (Bloomington: Indiana University Press, 1984), 116–21.

25.   Evans, *Reflecting on Anna Karenina*, 83.

26.   Joan Templeton, "*The Doll House* Backlash: Criticism, Feminism, and Ibsen," *PMLA* 104 (1989): 33.

27.   Cited in Elaine Showalter, "The Unmanning of the Mayor of Casterbridge," in *Critical Approaches to the Fiction of Thomas Hardy*, ed. Dale Kramer (London: Macmillan, 1979), 99–115.

28.   Tony Tanner, *Adultery in the Novel: Contract and Transgression* (Baltimore: Johns Hopkins University Press, 1979), 12–13.

29.   Much has been made of the fact that Anna apparently has little maternal love for her daughter, Ani. This, together with her rejection of future childbearing through contraception, is taken as a sign of her depravity and loss of maternal instinct. We ought to remember that Anna almost died in her last childbed and therefore medical counsel probably advised her to avoid future pregnancies. Other critics have suggested that Anna felt an unconscious rivalry with a child of her own sex and could only be gratified by

the adulation of a male child (see Armstrong, *Unsaid Anna Karenina*). How-ever, while there is no question that Anna does not love or mother Ani as she loved Seryozha, this does not necessarily imply an absence of maternal feel-ing. Just as an infertile woman who desperately longs for children of her own may find the presence of other people's children intolerable, so Ani is a con-tinual, painful reminder to Anna that she has lost Seryozha: "[She] went to the nursery. 'Why, this is wrong—this isn't he! Where are his blue eyes, his sweet shy smile?' was her first thought when she saw her chubby, rosy-cheeked little girl with her black, curly hair." From *Anna Karenina*, trans. C. Garnett, rev. ed. by Leonard J. Kent and Nina Berberova (New York: Ran-dom House, Modern Library, 1965), 794; hereafter cited in the text.

30. See Nancy Chodorow, *The Reproduction of Mothering: Psycho-analysis and the Sociology of Gender* (Berkeley and Los Angeles: University of California Press, 1978).

31. Evans, *Reflecting on Anna Karenina*, 86, referring to Mary Belenky, Blythe Clichy, Nancy Goldberger, and Jill Tarule, *Women's Ways of Know-ing* (New York: Basic Books, 1987).

32. Other feminist critics have attacked the "idealization of mother-hood" in both its feminist and antifeminist forms, calling it an attempt to romanticize traditional female spheres of influence as idyllic realms of desex-ualized and powerless femininity. See, for example, Jessica Benjamin, *The Bonds of Love: Psychoanalysis, Feminism, and the Problem of Domination* (New York: Pantheon Books, 1988).

33. Gary Saul Morson, "Prosaics: An Approach to the Humanities," *American Scholar* 57 (1988): 523.

34. Morson, "Prosaics in *Anna Karenina*," 4.

35. I stress the primacy of Victorian literary models for the creation of a Russian myth of idyllic family life and childhood. As Andrew Wachtel has recently demonstrated in *The Battle for Childhood: Creation of a Russian Myth* (Stanford: Stanford University Press, 1990), Tolstoy's own autobio-graphical novel, *Childhood*, served as the basis for the subsequent develop-ment of an idealized vision of family life in Russian literature. Wachtel min-imizes the importance of European, and especially Victorian, literary models for the subsequent development of that myth in Russian literature, since "almost every account of childhood published in Russia after 1852 turned to Tolstoy (and not to Rousseau, Dickens, Topffer, or others) for inspiration" (44). However, Tolstoy's own myth of childhood was clearly built upon, or as A. N. Wilson puts it, "Copperfielded" on the Western model. A. N. Wilson, *Tolstoy* (New York: Norton, 1988), 88–95.

36. Discussed in greater detail in chapter 7 of my book, *Framing "Anna Karenina"*.

37. It is interesting to note that the cultural icon of the Lady with the Lamp echoes the mythological figure of Psyche discussed above and at

greater length, with regard to Anna, in my book. Elizabeth Helsinger, Robin Lauterbach Sheets, and William Veeder, in *The Woman Question: Society and Literature in Britain and America, 1837–1883*, vol. 3, *Literary Issues* (Chicago: University of Chicago Press, 1983), point to three stereotypes of women in Victorian literature: the angel in the house, the fallen woman (demon), and the angel out of the house. The latter category would apply to Varenka, who, we may remember, is frequently referred to as an angel in the course of the novel.

38.   Marianna Torgovnick, *Closure in the Novel* (Princeton: Princeton University Press, 1981), 73.

HARRIET MURAV, READING WOMAN IN DOSTOEVSKY

I thank Bruce Rosenstock for his helpful comments on this essay.

1.   F. M. Dostoevskii, *Polnoe sobranie sochinenii*, 30 vols. (Leningrad: Nauka, 1972–90), 24:5. Hereafter all citations of Dostoevsky will be from this edition and will be given parenthetically in the text by volume and page number. Unless otherwise indicated, all translations are my own. A translation of the entire story is found in Fyodor Dostoevsky, *A Writer's Diary*, trans. and annotated by Kenneth Lantz, intro. Gary Saul Morson (Evanston: Northwestern University Press, 1993), 676–717. Hereafter *A Writer's Diary* is cited in the text as *WD*.

2.   Unlike the English, the Russian title, "Krotkaia," shows gender and clearly indicates that the "meek one" is a woman.

3.   F. M. Dostoevsky, "A Meek One," cited by Mikhail Bakhtin, *Problems in Dostoevsky's Poetics*, ed. and trans. Caryl Emerson (Minneapolis: University of Minnesota Press, 1984), 55.

4.   M. Bakhtin, *Problems in Dostoevsky's Poetics*, 63. Unless otherwise indicated, all further references to Bakhtin are to this translation, hereafter cited in the text. There are various senses of the word "dialogic" both in Bakhtin's work as a whole, and in current critical literature. I emphasize Bakhtin's theory of the new configuration of author and hero as he developed it in the Dostoevsky book published in 1963, and not other uses of the word dialogic. For a discussion of the senses of the word "dialogic" in Bakhtin's work as a whole, see Gary Saul Morson and Caryl Emerson, *Mikhail Bakhtin: Creation of a Prosaics* (Stanford: Stanford University Press, 1990).

5.   For an explanation as to why gender does not concern Bakhtin, see Caryl Emerson, "Bakhtin and Women: A Nontopic with Immense Implications," in *Fruits of Her Plume: Essays on Contemporary Russian Women's Culture*, ed. Helena Goscilo (Armonk, N.Y.: M. E. Sharpe, 1993), 3–20. In notes made near the end of his life, Bakhtin suggested, ever so vaguely, a

characterization of "women's speech." He grouped together several types of discourse under the rubric of "the word removed from life: the word of the idiot, the holy fool, the insane, the child, the dying person, and sometimes women." What is meant by "the word removed from life" is difficult to say, but the speech forms Bakhtin describes here suggest a speaker who is perhaps not engaged in the usual Bakhtinian business of loopholes and sidelong glances, whose "I" is not playing a game of hide-and-seek with his or her interlocutor. We can only guess as to whether Bakhtin means to say that "sometimes" women's speech shows this characteristic. See M. M. Bakhtin, *Speech Genres and Other Late Essays*, trans. Vern W. McGee, ed. Caryl Emerson and Michael Holquist (Austin: University of Texas Press, 1986), 148. This would be consistent with what I suggest is the typical form of speech for Dostoevsky's madonna-heroines. For feminist approaches to Bakhtin, see, for example, Dale M. Bauer and Susan Jaret McKinstry, eds., *Feminism, Bakhtin, and the Dialogic* (Albany: State University of New York Press, 1991). The editors note in their introduction that a feminist dialogics would bring together the public, authoritative voice and the private, internally persuasive voice into dialogue (2).

6. For a very fine discussion of Dostoevsky and the problem of women, see Nina Pelikan Straus, *Dostoevsky and the Woman Question: Re-Readings at the End of a Century* (New York: St. Martin's, 1994). See also A. Gizetti, "Gordye iazychnitsy: k kharakteristike zhenskikh obrazov Dostoevskogo," in *Tvorcheskii put' Dostoevskogo: sbornik statei*, ed. N. L. Brodskii (Leningrad: Seiatel', 1924), 186–96. Gizetti argues that for Dostoevsky the ideal woman is the madonna. Dostoevsky, according to the author, could not tolerate the idea of woman as heroine in the sense of actor, but only woman as "podvizhnitsa" (self-sacrificing). For other general discussions of the female protagonist in Dostoevsky, see Barbara Heldt, *Terrible Perfection: Women and Russian Literature* (Bloomington: Indiana University Press, 1992), 32–37; Joe Andrew, *Women in Russian Literature, 1780–1863* (London: Macmillan, 1988); and Igor Volgin, *Poslednii god Dostoevskogo* (Moscow: Sovetskii pisatel', 1986), 186–94. Volgin discusses "silence as a genre," which I will address in this essay.

7. Laura Mulvey, "Visual Pleasure and Narrative Cinema," *Screen* 16 (1975): 14.

8. Teresa de Laretis, *Alice Doesn't: Feminism, Semiotics, Cinema* (Bloomington: Indiana University Press, 1984), 103.

9. See L. Michael O'Toole, *Structure, Style, and Interpretation in the Russian Short Story* (New Haven: Yale University Press, 1982), 43. While I disagree with O'Toole on this point, he offers a sensitive structuralist interpretation of "A Meek One" in *Structure, Style, and Interpretation*, 37–63.

10. Bakhtin, "Toward a Reworking of the Dostoevsky Book," cited by Robert Louis Jackson, *Dialogues with Dostoevsky: The Overwhelming Questions* (Stanford: Stanford University Press, 1993), 278.

11.   Gary Cox, on the other hand, argues that the female victim ultimately comes to dominate over her aggressor, "who submits to her domination and even identifies with her in the role of passive victim." See Cox, *Tyrant and Victim in Dostoevsky* (Columbus, Ohio: Slavica, 1983), 73.

12.   For another reading of the passage, which emphasizes the narrator's resistance to the laws of nature, see Robert L. Belknap, *The Genesis of "The Brothers Karamazov": The Aesthetics, Ideology, and Psychology of Making a Text* (Evanston: Northwestern University Press, 1990), 35.

13.   For a discussion of resurrection and the law of inertia, see Liza Knapp, "The Force of Inertia in Dostoevsky's 'Krotkaja'" *Dostoevsky Studies* 6 (1985): 133–52.

14.   Louis Marin, "The Women at the Tomb: A Structural Analysis Essay of a Gospel Text," in *The New Testament and Structuralism* (Pittsburgh, Pa.: Pickwick Press, 1976), 82.

15.   For a discussion of the iconography of the resurrection, see Leonid Ouspensky and Vladimir Lossky, *The Meaning of Icons* (Crestwood, N.Y.: St. Vladimir's Seminary Press, 1983), 188–92.

16.   For more on this scene, see my *Holy Foolishness: Dostoevsky's Novels and the Poetics of Cultural Critique* (Stanford: Stanford University Press, 1992), 66–68.

17.   Johanna Hubbs, *Mother Russia: The Feminine Myth in Russian Culture* (Bloomington: Indiana University Press, 1988), 229.

18.   For more on Alyosha's memory, see Diane Oenning Thompson, *"The Brothers Karamazov" and the Poetics of Memory* (Cambridge: Cambridge University Press, 1991), 74–89.

19.   Kristeva's characterization of "maternal discourse" may provide a parallel of sorts. As Mary Jacobus explains it, Kristeva's maternal discourse corresponds to the "rhythms, melodies and bodily movements which precede and prepare the way for the language of signification. . . . The maternal . . . persists in oral and instinctual aspects of language which punctuate, evade, or disrupt the symbolic order—in prosody, intonation, puns, verbal slips, even silences." See Mary Jacobus, *Reading Woman: Essays in Feminist Criticism* (New York: Columbia University Press, 1986), 148.

20.   See, for example, Diana Lewis Burgin, "The Reprieve of Nastasja: A Reading of a Dreamer's Authored Life," *Slavic and East European Journal* 29 (1985): 258–68; and Michael Holquist, *Dostoevsky and the Novel* (Princeton: Princeton University Press, 1977), 112–23. The ethical significance of Nastasia Filippovna's image is discussed by Leslie A. Johnson in "The Face of the Other in *Idiot*," *Slavic Review* 50 (1991): 867–78.

21.   See Olga Matich, *"The Idiot*: A Feminist Reading," in *Dostoevski and the Human Condition After a Century*, ed. Alexej Ugrinsky, Frank S. Lambasa, and Valija K. Ozulis (New York: Greenwood, 1986), 53–60.

22.   We might note Dostoevsky's observation in his *Writer's Diary* for

May 1876 that the "main" flaw of "contemporary woman is her extraordinary dependence on certain masculine ideas" (23:28).

23.   D. P. Slattery similarly remarks: "Dostoevsky's frequent use of . . . iconic figures of the Madonna suggests a mode of poetic expression which may be called iconographic, for he wishes to raise up the icon in the community to counteract the liberal, more secular images of idolatry those who are possessed by their own grand idea wish to promote. Their efforts . . . will eventually end in despair . . . while the iconic signs will preserve hope and the possibility of salvation." See Slattery, "Idols and Icons: Comic Transformation in Dostoevsky's *The Possessed*," *Dostoevsky Studies* 6 (1985): 36.

24.   For another comparison of the two accounts, see Ludmila Koehler, "Five Minutes too late . . . ," *Dostoevsky Studies* 6 (1985): 113–24.

25.   The original note was not published at the time; Dostoevsky relied on a text given him by Konstantin Pobedonostsev. See the commentary provided in *Polnoe sobranie sochinenii*, 23:407.

26.   Letter from Liza Herzen in *Arkhiv N. A. i N. P. Ogarevykh*, comp. and ed. M. Gershenson (Moscow and Leningrad: Gosudarstvennoe izdatel'stvo, 1030), 148.

27.   *Golos: gazeta politicheskaia i literaturnaia*, 3 May 1876, no. 122, 4. Turgenev writes that Liza Herzen killed herself after a quarrel with her mother and "in order to annoy her." See his letter to P. B. Annenkov of 15 December 1875 in I. S. Turgenev, *Pis'ma v trinadtsati tomakh* (Moscow and Leningrad: Nauka, 1966), 11:177–78.

28.   See his letter to Dostoevsky of 3 June 1876 in *Literaturnoe nasledstvo* 15 (Moscow: 1934): 130–31.

29.   For a discussion of suicide as a theme in Dostoevsky, see N. N. Sheidman, *Dostoevsky and Suicide* (Oakville, N.Y.: Mosaic, 1984).

30.   Gary Saul Morson sees in Dostoevsky's discussion of this case a highly complex notion of "evolving" intentionality. See his "Introductory Study," in *A Writer's Diary*, 90–91.

31.   For a discussion of the prehistory of *A Writer's Diary*, see Gary Saul Morson, *The Boundaries of Genre: Dostoevsky's Diary of a Writer and the Traditions of Literary Utopia* (Austin: University of Texas Press, 1981; reprint, Evanston: Northwestern University Press, 1987).

32.   Others, however, have argued that Prince Myshkin "monologizes" Nastasia Filippovna. See, for example, Caryl Emerson, "Problems with Baxtin's Poetics," *Slavic and East European Journal* 43 (1988): 503–25.

33.   To be sure, as in every human interaction in Dostoevsky, reading is a "palka o dvukh kontsakh" (literally, a stick with two ends, meaning that it cuts both ways). Reading is not always benevolent. It does not always constitute the other's inner voice, but may take a far darker form. Sometimes reading is an attack on the other.

34.   Marin, "The Women at the Tomb," 96.

GARY SAUL MORSON, SONYA'S WISDOM

1.   The present essay, revised for publication here, originally appeared (under the title "Prosaic Chekhov: Metadrama, the Intelligentsia, and *Uncle Vanya*") in *TriQuarterly*, a publication of Northwestern University (Winter 1990–91), 118–59. All citations from *Uncle Vanya* are taken from *Chekhov: The Major Plays*, trans. Ann Dunnigan (New York: Signet, 1964) and are given in the text.

I have discussed the concept of prosaics in a number of places, including "Prosaics: An Approach to the Humanities," *American Scholar* 57 (1988): 515–28; "Prosaics and *Anna Karenina*," *Tolstoy Studies Journal* 1 (1988): 1–12; "Prosaics, Criticism, and Ethics," *Formations* 5 (1989): 77–95; "The Potentials and Hazards of Prosaics," *Tolstoy Studies Journal* 2 (1989): 15–40; and "Prosaic Bakhtin: *Landmarks*, Anti-Intelligentsialism, and the Russian Counter-Tradition," *Common Knowledge* 2 (1993): 35–54. The term was first used in my *Hidden in Plain View: Narrative and Creative Potentials in "War and Peace"* (Stanford: Stanford University Press, 1987) and is central to the study of Bakhtin I co-authored with Caryl Emerson, *Mikhail Bakhtin: Creation of a Prosaics* (Stanford: Stanford University Press, 1990). On the relation of prosaics to temporality, see my *Narrative and Freedom: The Shadows of Time* (New Haven: Yale University Press, 1994), and Michael André Bernstein, *Foregone Conclusions: Against Apocalyptic History* (Berkeley and Los Angeles: University of California Press, 1994).

2.   The phrase "tiny alterations" is Tolstoy's. See Leo Tolstoy, "Why Do Men Stupefy Themselves?" *Recollections and Essays*, trans. Aylmer Maude (London: Oxford University Press, 1961), 82.

3.   It might even be said that when Tolstoy, after his conversion, became more dogmatic and rejected his two great novels, Chekhov remained truer than Tolstoy to their Tolstoyan prosaic values.

4.   Leo Tolstoy, *Anna Karenina*, trans. Constance Garnett, rev. ed. by Leonard J. Kent and Nina Berberova (New York: Random House, Modern Library, 1965), 831; further references are to this edition.

5.   On the ways in which self-awareness contributes to the inscape of self-destructive mentality, see Michael André Bernstein, *Bitter Carnival: "Ressentiment" and the Abject Hero* (Princeton: Princeton University Press, 1992).

6.   J. L. Styan, *Chekhov in Performance: A Commentary on the Major Plays* (Cambridge: Cambridge University Press, 1981), 101.

7.   In this respect Chekhov belongs to the same tradition of thought as Denis de Rougement, whose classic study *Love in the Western World* (trans. Montgomery Belgion [New York: Harper, 1974]) insists on the destructiveness of romance.

8.   For Chudakov's excellent remarks on irrelevancy in Chekhov, see

A. P. Chudakov, *Chekhov's Poetics*, trans. Edwina Jannie Cruise and Donald Dragt (Ann Arbor: Ardis, 1983).

9.   Leo Tolstoy, *War and Peace*, trans. Ann Dunnigan (New York: Signet, 1968), 1320.

ELIZABETH KLOSTY BEAUJOUR, THE USES OF WITCHES IN FEDIN AND BULGAKOV

The present essay is reprinted from *Slavic Review: American Quarterly of Soviet and East European Studies* 33 (1974): 695–707. Only minor editorial changes have been made for this volume; in particular, quotations in French have been translated into English. Unless otherwise credited, all translations are mine.

1.   Although *The Master and Margarita* was published long after Bulgakov's death, he had worked on it more or less intensively for the last twelve years of his life. He began the story that ultimately developed into the novel ("The Consultant with the Hoof") in 1928. Thus, in a sense, both novels are in conception novels of the twenties.

2.   It matters little for the purposes of our analysis whether the fragment of printed matter stuck into the collage, and creating a new order there, is from a newspaper or part of a page of *Faust*. What René Micha notes about Bulgakov is equally applicable to Fedin: "For the Formalist School, it isn't the substance of an element that is significant, but rather its function. In Bulgakov's work, this function is always ironic." See "Mikhaël Boulgakov ou la Russie éternelle" [Mikhail Bulgakov or eternal Russia] *Critique* 25 (1969): 16.

Both *Cities and Years* and *The Master and Margarita* display many characteristics of what M. M. Bakhtin has called the Menippean strain in literature. See my article "Some Problems of Construction in Fedin's *Cities and Years*," *Slavic and East European Journal* 16 (1972): 1–18, and Ellendea Proffer, "Bulgakov's *The Master and Margarita*: Genre and Motif," *Canadian Slavic Studies* 3 (1969): 615–28.

3.   Mikhail Bulgakov, *Master i Margarita* (Moscow: Khudozhestvennaia literatura, 1973), 776. All references, unless otherwise identified, are to this edition of *The Master and Margarita*. Translations are substantially those of Michael Glenny, *The Master and Margarita* (New York: Harper and Row, 1967), except where a more literal rendition is necessary to clarify a point.

4.   One can find thorough discussions of this phenomenon in Bakhtin's *Tvorchestvo Fransua Rable i narodnaia kul'tura srednevekov'ia i Renessansa* (Moscow: Khudozhestvennia literatura, 1965), which is most easily accessi-

147

ble in the English translation by Helene Iswolsky, *Rabelais and His World* (1968; reprint, Bloomington: Indiana University Press, 1984), and in Jules Michelet, *La Sorcière* (1862), published in English as *Satanism and Witchcraft: A Study in Medieval Superstition*, trans. A. R. Allenson (1939; reprint, Secaucus, N.J.: Citadel, 1973), and Julio Caro Baroja, *The World of the Witches*, trans. O. N. V. Glendinning (Chicago: University of Chicago Press, 1964).

5. William Blake, "The Marriage of Heaven and Hell," in *The Portable Blake* (New York: Viking, 1967), 264.

6. Ibid., 250.

7. Robert Mandron observes: "The medieval sorceress was not yet the persecuted woman she became in the modern period. For the village, for that always somber, ever threatened peasant life, she was a consolation, a source of daily help. . . . This was the first age of sorcery, which fed on old peasant traditions and Christian lessons turned upside down. Sorcery also fed on the anxiety and the powerlessness of men. . . . Damned as impure by the plurisecular tradition of the Church (and Michelet stresses the ambiguity of the cult of Mary which exalted the Virgin and debased the real woman), the sorceress found her revenge in the magical powers which she acquired: a healer, by means of plants and potions, protectress of the weak, she became the helpful sorceress. And the spirit from below who protected and inspired her was blessed as well." Introduction to Jules Michelet, *La Sorcière* (Paris: Julliard, 1964), 11–13. Or hear Michelet himself: "In those days a woman would never have accepted a male physician, would never have put herself in his hands, never have told him her secrets. The Sorceresses . . . were, particularly for women, the one and only doctor" (110). See also the admittedly polemical "Witches, Midwives and Nurses: A History of Women Healers" (Oyster Bay, N.Y.: Glass Mountain Pamphlets, 1973), which contains a short bibliography on the question.

8. It is a curious fact that although this broad-mindedness and openness to the unexpected allows Marie and Margarita rapid, decisive, liberating action and provides them with a sensitivity to pain beyond their own, the same broad-mindedness produces passivity rather than activity in the men they love. The reasons for this are conventional and compositional as well as psychological. Neither Marie nor Margarita is an intellectual. The whole tradition of Russian literature reserves that role to men. (Can one conceive of a book entitled *The Underground Woman in Russian Literature*? Fallen, yes; infernal, yes; even intelligent—but a "superfluous" intellectual?) It is always the male hero who is too liberal or too sensitive or too aware of ambiguities to act. This in itself provides a compositional reason for the depiction of the complementary woman as *energetic*. Conversely, it would seem that the refusal of the Sonia complex (the woman as victim and sufferer) is a compositional possibility only in a structure where there is a male figure substitut-

ed as sacrificial victim: on the one hand Yeshua, Berlioz, Baron Maigel, the Master; on the other, Karl Ebersocks, the mutilated war victims, and the spiritually dismembered Andrei.

9. For example, the following passage about the daughters of Satan applies quite well to Marie: "This one is at most the devil's daughter. She has inherited two things from him, she is impure, and she enjoys manipulating life. . . . She who is born with this secret in her blood, this instinctive knowledge of evil, she who has seen so far and so deep, will respect nothing, nothing and nobody in this world, and will have little faith. Not even in Satan himself, for he is still but a spirit, and she has a taste only for material things. . . . while still very young, she particularly likes to handle disgusting things. . . . She will be a subtle go-between, dexterous, audacious, empirical. . . . Without being good, she still loves life, healing, and prolonging life" (Michelet, *La Sorcière*, 149–50).

10. Konstantin Fedin, *Goroda i gody*, in *Sobranie sochinenii v desiati tomakh*, 10 vols. (Moscow: Khudozhestvennia literatura, 1969–73), 1:59 (all page references are to this edition). Translations are substantially those of Michael Scammell, in his *Cities and Years* (1962; reprint, Evanston: Northwestern University Press, 1993).

11. On one occasion, Marie does not return, and a search party is sent out. It meets a young peasant who has been spooked by the terrible noise that had enveloped him as he passed the Mountain of the Three Nuns: "It had seemed to the youth that the mountains had moved out of place and an evil spirit had been laughing and howling after him. . . . And behind him there had been a whistling and grinding and laughter and howling. Apparently Beelzebub himself was celebrating his birthday" (162). As soon as Urbach hears this, he leaves the search party and heads for the Three Nuns. "He knew his daughter well indeed," as the narrator observes, "if he decided immediately that she would be nowhere else than visiting the Devil" (163). The terrifying spirit was in fact Marie, banging on a sheet of tin. "It is so terrible there you can't resist it," she says, as she comes obediently down at her father's call.

12. The initial illusion of the beloved's strength is characteristic of both Marie and Margarita.

13. Marie's role as energizer and nurse begins the very first time that she comes to Andrei's room. Her first words are, "What is the matter with you: Are you ill? Then why are you holding your head?" Margarita drives the Master on, and waits impatiently for his book to be completed, saying that the novel is her life (*v etom romane ee zhizn'*) (558). When she discovers that the Master has burned the manuscript in an access of fear and illness, brought on by vituperative and unfounded attacks by critics, Margarita cries, "God how ill you look, Why? Why? but I shall save you. I'll save you . . . I'll make you well . . . you will rewrite it" (564). A minor but interesting point is

that both Marie and Margarita come to their man's room rather than meeting at their own homes or in some neutral spot. This is possible only because of the extreme social isolation of both men.

14.   Can it be an accident that these women who raise the dead bear the names of Mary and Martha, Lazarus's sisters? Many of the names are significant in *Cities and Years*. We have already mentioned Urbach and Bischofsburg, but let us also note in passing the names Kurt *Wahn* and Andrei *Start*sov, as well as the archetypically German town of Erlangen.

Resurrection, or at least the possibility of raising and speaking with the dead, is one of the great boons the Devil granted through the sorceress in the Middle Ages: "It is evident thereby that compassion is from Satan's side. Even the Virgin, the ideal of Grace, has no answer to this heart's need. The Church does not meet the need either. It specifically forbids attempting to contact the dead. While books continued to depict the pig demon of the first ages, or the clawed executioner demon of the second age, Satan's appearance had changed for those who were illiterate. He had come to resemble old Pluto, but his pale majesty, in no way inexorable, allowing the dead to return and the living to see the dead, increasingly harked back to the image of his father or grandfather: Osiris, the shepherd of souls" (Michelet, *La Sorcière*, 97).

15.   This scene is part of a Pied Piper complex that begins with a story told by Kurt Wahn before the war, and ends, at least for Andrei, with rats that he seems to see swarming in waves over his feet.

16.   Woland is evidently not averse to taking a tumble with a fair witch from time to time. (He suspects that his rheumatic knee is the result of an encounter with one on the Harz Mountains in 1571. It is interesting that he prefers to treat the knee with his "Old Grandmother's" remedies, rather than go to an eternal or mortal doctor.) The first Soviet edition of *Master and Margarita*, with inexplicable care not to tarnish the Devil's reputation, cut the entire passage.

On flying cream see A. J. Clark, "Some Notes on 'Flying' Ointments," appendix to Margaret Alice Murray's *The Witch-Cult in Western Europe: A Study in Anthropology* (1921; reprint, Oxford: Clarendon Press, 1963), 279–80.

17.   Even his prankster henchmen participate reluctantly and without real pleasure in the traditional ball, which they regard as an obligation of their jobs but ultimately a nuisance (with the exception, of course, of the cat Behemoth, who cavorts with genuine glee in the brandy fountain). The distance that Margarita's escorts maintain from the ball prevents one from having to equate them or her with the real sinners present. Woland's absence for a great part of the ball and his negligent appearance in his torn and dirty nightshirt (a deshabille more characteristic of the intimate Esbat) make it appear that he, too, regards the ball with some scorn.

18.   See Murray, *Witch-Cult*, 150.

19.   It is, of course, no accident that the disciples of Jesus addressed him as Master and that Margarita's hero goes by the same sobriquet quite without irony.

20.   Freud comments on this attitude toward women, particularly in *Totem and Taboo*, trans. James Strachey (New York: Norton, 1950): "Applied to the treatment of privileged persons the theory of ambivalent feeling would reveal that their veneration, their very deification, is opposed in the unconscious by an intense hostile tendency" (66). Michelet has of course commented on this aspect of the cult of Mary, too. A curious, modern-day parallel is the language of the surrealist idealization of women, which was in its own way quite as alienating as Mariolatry—and used many of the same clichés of imagery! See Xavière Gauthier, *Surréalisme et sexualité* (Surrealism and sexuality) (Paris: Gallimard, 1971), 9–114.

21.   One woman does appear in the Master's novel who is absent from the Gospels. In the novel, Judas does not hang himself from remorse (a fine Matthewesque conceit, that!) but is lured to his death by a woman, who serves as the instrument of Pilate's vengeance.

22.   The witch, Hella, seems to have dropped by the wayside somewhere.

23.   See "The Virgin's Visit to Hell," whose oldest Russian copy dates back to the twelfth century. N. K. Gudzy provides a detailed summary of its contents in his *History of Early Russian Literature*, trans. Susan Wilbur Jones (New York: Macmillan, 1949), 46–50.

24.   The first Soviet edition cuts the following crucial passage off the end of the chapter: "and the Master's memory, his accursed, needling memory, began to fade. Someone had freed the Master, just as he had set free the character he had created. His hero had now vanished irretrievably into the abyss; on the night of Sunday, the day of the Resurrection, pardon had been granted to the astrologer's son, fifth Procurator of Judea, the knight Pontius Pilate." In Bulgakov's book's final sentence, "the *knight* Pontius Pilate" is repeated, thus suddenly locking the Master's book and Bulgakov's together in the final words.

25.   André Breton, *Arcane 17* (New York, 1945; reprint, Paris: Eds 10/18, 1965).

SONA STEPHAN HOISINGTON, THE MISMEASURE
OF I-330

Research for this article was undertaken while I was a fellow in the Institute for the Humanities at the University of Illinois at Chicago.

1.   *We* was written in 1920–21 and was deemed too heretical for publi-

cation in Soviet Russia. Translated into English by Gregory Zilboorg, it first appeared in New York in 1924. It could not be published in the Soviet Union until the period of glasnost (1988). Several translations of *We* are available in English. I use Mirra Ginsburg's *We* (New York: Avon Books, 1972), occasionally slightly altered; hereafter cited in the text.

2. A bibliography of articles on *We* in English can be found in Gary Kern, ed., *Zamyatin's "We": A Collection of Critical Essays* (Ann Arbor: Ardis, 1988), 305–6. See also Leighton Brett Cooke, "Zamyatin's *We*: Annotated Bibliography," (1994), unpublished ms.

3. Margaret Wise Petrochenkov, for example, argues that I-330 is a projection of D-503's castration anxiety; see her "Castration and the 'Other' in Zamyatin's *We*," paper presented at the Conference on the Fantastic in New Critical Theory (Texas A&M University, 1990). Christopher Collins, on the other hand, insists I-330 is a "manifestation of D-503's anima"—that is, the female, irrational aspect of his character. See Christopher Collins, *Evgenij Zamjatin: An Interpretive Study* (The Hague: Mouton, 1973), 71.

Andrew Barratt, recognizing that a reassessment of I-330's role in the novel was long overdue, nevertheless sees her significance largely in negative terms, a view with which I take issue in this essay. See Andrew Barratt, "Revolution as Collusion: The Heretic and the Slave in Zamyatin's *My*," *Slavonic and East European Review* 62 (1984): 344–61.

4. See Gordon Beauchamp, "Of Man's Last Disobedience: Zamyatin's *We* and Orwell's *1984*," *Comparative Literature Studies* 10 (1973): 291; Richard Gregg, "Two Adams and Eve in the Crystal Palace: Dostoevsky, the Bible, and *We*," in Kern, ed., *Zamyatin's "We*," 63; and Efraim Sicher, "By Underground to Crystal Palace: The Dystopian Eden," *Comparative Literature Studies* 22 (1985): 386. See also Kathryn M. Grossmann, "Woman as Temptress: the Way to (Br)otherhood in Science Fiction Dystopias," *Women's Studies* 14 (1987): 135–45.

5. I am indebted to Carol Tavis for this term. See her *The Mismeasure of Woman* (New York: Simon and Schuster, 1992).

6. The only critic who has recognized her dynamism is Owen Ulph. See his "I-330: Reconsiderations on the Sex of Satan," in Kern, ed., *Zamyatin's "We*," 80–91. Yet despite this, Ulph spends much of his article analyzing D-503.

7. Zamyatin's novel has been hailed as the first major dystopia of the twentieth century, yet it is a work that delights in its own nonconformity and is wickedly ironic in tone. Zamyatin draws on the language of early twentieth-century painting as well as that of modern mathematics to create a complex system of arresting images in *We*. Time and again he makes revolutionary use of tradition, attesting to the strong imprint on him of literary modernism. For more on Zamyatin's ties to modernism, see Milton Ehre, "Zamyatin's Aesthetics," in Kern, ed., *Zamyatin's "We*," 130–39; Susan Lay-

ton, "Zamyatin and Literary Modernism," in *Zamyatin's "We,"* 140–48; and Sona Hoisington and Lynn Imbery, "Zamjatin's Modernist Palette: Colors and Their Function in *We,*" *Slavic and East European Journal* 36 (1992): 159–71.

8. George Orwell, *1984* (New York: New American Library, 1983), 129. The marginalization of Julia in Orwell's novel is discussed by Daphne Patai in her study, *The Orwell Mystique: A Study in Male Ideology* (Amherst: University of Massachusetts Press, 1984), 243–48.

9. The term is Carolyn Heilbrun's; see her *Toward a Recognition of Androgyny: Aspects of Male and Female in Literature* (London: Victor Golanez, 1973), 49. It is also used by Lee Edwards in her article, "The Labors of Psyche: Toward a Theory of Female Heroism," *Critical Inquiry* 6 (1979): 33–49.

10. For a discussion of the femme fatale in literature see Mario Praz, *The Romantic Agony,* 2d ed. (New York: Oxford University Press, 1970), chap. 4, "La Belle Dame Sans Merci." The most celebrated femme fatale at the turn of the century was Lulu, the female protagonist in Frank Wedekind's plays, *Earth Spirit* and *Pandora's Box* (1893–94).

11. Better known in the West for his set and costume designs for Diaghilev's Ballet Russe, Bakst was also an accomplished portrait painter. A reproduction of *Supper* is found in Dmitry Sarabianov, *Russian Art: From Neoclassicism to the Avant-garde, 1800–1917* (New York: Abrams, 1990), 226.

12. A color reproduction of the portrait is found in *Soviet Art, 1920s–1930s: Russian Museum, Leningrad* (New York: Abrams, 1988), 18. Zamyatin commented on the portrait in an essay "On Synthetism," which was first published as the introduction to a 1922 album of Annenkov's portraits (Iurii Annenkov, *Portrety* [Petrograd: Petropolis, 1922]) and which in many ways served as Zamyatin's modernist credo. "On Synthetism" is translated in *A Soviet Heretic: Essays by Yevgeny Zamyatin,* trans. Mirra Ginsburg (1970; reprint, Evanston: Northwestern University Press, 1992), 81–91. The comment on the portrait of Annenkov's wife, which Zamyatin praised for its "synthetic economy of line," appears on 87. Hereafter Zamyatin's collection of essays is referred to as *SH* and is cited in the text.

13. It has been pointed out that the reversal of sex roles is characteristic of Russian modernism and was practiced in life and celebrated in literature. On this point see Olga Matich, "Dialectics of Cultural Return: Zinaida Gippius' Personal Myth," in *Cultural Mythologies of Russian Modernism: From the Golden Age to the Silver Age,* ed. Boris Gasparov, Robert P. Hughes, and Irina Paperno (Berkeley and Los Angeles: University of California Press, 1992), 53 and 65.

14. Thus, I-330 can hardly be said to be "infertile," as critics have claimed, dismayed by the fact that she bears no offspring. See, for example, Andrew Barratt, "Revolution as Collusion," 360. In the first chapter of his

study, Collins too faults her for being "childless" and argues that this indicates that "she and her doctrine of eternal revolution are ultimately limited and incomplete in themselves." Collins, *Evgenij Zamjatin*, 25.

15.   For a discussion of images of liquidity in *We*, see S. A. Cowan, "The Crystalline Center in Zamyatin's *We*," *Extrapolation* 29 (1988): 160–78.

16.   Ample documentation is provided in Bram Dijkstra, *Idols of Perversity: Fantasies of Feminine Evil in Fin-de-Siècle Culture* (New York: Oxford University Press, 1986). Lulu is called a snake, when she is introduced in the prologue of Wedekind's *Earth Spirit*.

17.   In this regard see Elizabeth Klosty Beaujour, "The Uses of Witches in Fedin and Bulgakov," in the present volume.

18.   See Gregg, "Two Adams and Eve," 65 and Sicher, "By Underground to Crystal Palace," 386.

19.   Nina Auerbach, *Woman and the Demon: The Life of a Victorian Myth* (Cambridge: Harvard University Press, 1982), 75.

20.   Actually here there is a concurrence: the symbol "I" is used in Russian to denote the Roman numeral I, but it is called "*az*," which is both the name for the letter *A* in Russian and the word for the first person singular pronoun in Church Slavonic.

21.   Louise Gardner, *Art Through the Ages*, revised by Horst de la Croix and Richard G. Tansey, 8th ed. (New York: Harcourt Brace Jovanovich, 1986), 900. Picasso's *Portrait of Gertrude Stein* is reproduced on 899.

22.   See Gardner, *Art Through the Ages*, 900–901.

23.   In his 1923 essay, "On Literature, Revolution, and Entropy," Zamyatin wrote: "The finite, fixed world . . . is a convention, an abstraction, an unreality" (*SH*, 112).

24.   See Gregg, "Two Adams and Eve," 66; Collins, *Evgenij Zamjatin*, 75; and T. R. N. Edwards, *Three Russian Writers and the Irrational: Zamyatin, Pilnyak, and Bulgakov* (New York: Cambridge University Press, 1982), 77. The exception is Barratt who argues that D-503 is in fact a travesty of Christ. See his article, "The X-Factor in Zamjatin's *We*," *Modern Language Review* 80 (1985): 668.

25.   Murl Barker, "Onomastics and Zamjatin's *We*," *Canadian-American Slavic Studies* 11 (1977): 555 and Barratt, "The X-Factor in Zamjatin's *We*," 668.

26.   A discussion of the spiritual affinity between Satan and Christ, termed "the marriage of heaven and hell," can be found in Beaujour's "The Uses of Witches."

27.   Zamyatin made this point in his 1924 essay, "Fyodor Sologub." "The hero," he wrote, "is indissolubly linked with tragedy, with death. Only the philistine is indestructible, deathless" (*SH*, 221).

28.   A quote from Zamyatin's 1919–20 essay, "Tomorrow"; see *SH*, 52. Here I have modified Ginzburg's translation.

29. Virginia Woolf, *Orlando, a Biography* (New York: Harcourt Brace Jovanovich, 1928), 189.

THEA MARGARET DURFEE, *CEMENT* AND *HOW THE STEEL WAS TEMPERED*: VARIATIONS ON THE NEW SOVIET WOMAN

1. Katerina Clark, *The Soviet Novel: History as Ritual.* (Chicago: University of Chicago Press, 1981) See, for example, chap. 2, esp. 46–48; hereafter cited in the text.

2. For a discussion of the Bolshevik women's movement in the decade after the Revolution, see Barbara Clement Evans, "The Birth of the New Soviet Woman," in Abbott Gleason, Peter Kenez, and Richard Stites, eds., *Bolshevik Culture* (Bloomington: Indiana University Press, 1985), 220–37; Gail Warshofsky Lapidus, *Women in Soviet Society: Equality, Development, and Social Change* (Berkeley and Los Angeles: University of California Press, 1978), 54–94, and Richard Stites, *The Women's Liberation Movement in Russia: Feminism, Nihilism, and Bolshevism, 1860–1930* (Princeton: Princeton University Press, 1978), 317–45.

3. Kollontai was most noted as being the only woman commissar in the Bolshevik government, but she was truly multifaceted. In addition to her activities on behalf of the women's movement in Russia, she also wrote stories that painted "a radiant vision of the new heroine, self-supporting, living alone, doing social or political work, and 'wresting from life small earthly joys of physical love.'" Aleksandra Kollontai, *The New Morality and the Working Class* (Moscow, 1919), 7; cited in Xenia Gasiorowska, "Dasha Chumalova and Her Successors," *Slavic and Eastern European Journal* 15 (1957): 262.

4. Evans, "The Birth of the New Soviet Woman," 226.

5. Fyodor Gladkov, *Cement*, trans. A. S. Arthur and C. Ashleigh (1929; reprint, Evanston: Northwestern University Press, 1994), 27. All further quotations are taken from this translation of the 1925 version of the novel and are cited in the text.

6. She is depicted laboring to read August Bebel's *Woman and Socialism*: "She murmured, gulped, struggled with difficult words and raced over the easy parts. Then she stumbled again, looked away for a moment, thinking and scratching her eyebrows, then began reading again" (70).

7. A reproduction of this poster is found in Stephen White, *The Bolshevik Poster* (New Haven: Yale University Press, 1988), 120. It also appears as the cover illustration of the Northwestern University Press reprint of *Cement*.

8. In her study of the female form in political iconography, Elizabeth Waters notes the visual importance of the red kerchief: "The kerchief, tied at

the nape of the neck and the color red became [the working woman's] chief iconographical attributes. . . . The development of female icons was a matter of necessity, and the Zhenotdel and a whole host of other party, government, and public organizations moved to fill this gap, producing illustrated materi-al that addressed a female audience. The red-kerchiefed *proletarka* circulat-ed first and foremost in this new political space designated exclusively for the eyes of women." Elizabeth Waters, "The Female Form in Soviet Political Iconography: 1917-32," in Barbara Evans Clements, Barbara Alpern Engel, and Christine D. Worobec, eds., *Russia's Women: Accommodation, Resis-tance, Transformation* (Berkeley and Los Angeles: University of California Press, 1991), 234, 235. In addition to Waters, other scholars who have specif-ically focused on this issue of the new female body in Soviet visual iconogra-phy include Victoria E. Bonnell, "The Representation of Women in Early Soviet Political Art," *Russian Review* 50 (1991): 267-88 and Nicoletta Misler, "1937: Designing the New, Socialist Body," unpublished ms.

9. Waters, "The Female Form," 229.

10. A. Kollontai, "The Family and the Communist State," in *Bolshevik Visions: First Phase of the Cultural Revolution in Soviet Russia*, ed. William G. Rosenberg (Ann Arbor: Ardis, 1984), 81; hereafter cited in the text.

11. See Clark, *The Soviet Novel*, 114-15. In an article published in 1937 in the journal *Krasnaia Nov'*, educator Anton Makarenko wrote, "The fami-ly is the primary cell of society, and its duties in child-rearing derive from its obligations to produce good citizens." "Kniga dlia roditelei," *Krasnaia Nov'*, no. 7 (1937): 15; cited in Clark, *The Soviet Novel*, 115.

12. Maxim Gorky, "The Disintegration of Personality," in *On Literature* (Seattle: University of Washington Press, 1973), 128.

13. The 1947 version of the episode ends as follows: "Dasha found it somehow amusing: she felt that Badin had been emptied, that his strength had been poured into her, into Dasha. All she had to do was to give Badin an order and he, like a dog, would do whatever she desired." Cited in Edward Vavra, afterword to *Cement*, enl. ed. (New York: Ungar, 1980), 323.

14. Nikolai Ostrovsky, *How the Steel Was Tempered*, trans. R. Prokofie-va (Moscow: Progress Publishers, n.d.), 304. Hereafter this translation is cited in the text.

15. We should also note that the cowardly Anna is completely the oppo-site of Dasha, who saves Badin's life when they are ambushed and then acts so courageously that she is released by her Cossack captors.

16. For an illustration of this painting, see *Russian and Soviet Painting*, exh. cat. (New York: Metropolitan Museum of Art, 1977), 118.

17. Misler, "1937: Designing the New, Socialist Body."

18. See Lapidus, *Women in Soviet Society*, 113–15.

19. See Evans, "The Birth of the New Soviet Woman," 232-33.

20. This is a quotation from Kollontai's 1923 book, *The Labour of*

Women in the Evolution of the Economy; cited in Lapidus, 61.

21. Louise E. Luke, "Marxian Woman: Soviet Variants," in *Through the Glass of Soviet Literature: Views of Russian Society*, ed. Ernest J. Simmons (New York: Columbia University Press, 1953), 35. In her 1918 speech Kollontai stated: "Instead of the narrow love of a mother for her child alone, a mother's love must grow to include all children of the great working family" (88).

HELENA GOSCILO, MOTHER AS MOTHRA: TOTALIZING NARRATIVE AND NURTURE IN PETRUSHEVSKAIA

My thanks to Barbara Heldt for noting the parallels between Philip Wylie's concept of "Mommism" and the bloodcurdling maternal image in Petrushevskaia's work, and to Josie Woll for responding with her characteristic blend of generosity and keenness to an earlier version of this essay.

1. For an analysis of why Russian women disavow gender as a pertinent component in their work, see Helena Goscilo, ed., *Skirted Issues: The Discreteness and Indiscretions of Russian Women's Prose* (Armonk, N.Y.: M. E. Sharpe, 1992), 3–17.

2. Until recently, Slavists duplicated the Soviet habit of ignoring Russian women's literary works, omitting mention of them in literary surveys and largely excluding them from anthologies of stories and novellas. For English translations of recent Russian women's prose, see *Balancing Acts: Contemporary Stories by Russian Women* (Bloomington: Indiana University Press, 1989; New York: Dell, 1991); *Soviet Women Writing: Fifteen Short Stories* (New York: Abbeville Press, 1990); *Lives in Transit: A Collection of Recent Russian Women's Writing* (Ann Arbor: Ardis, 1994). For an analysis of that prose, see Helena Goscilo, "Coming a Long Way, Baby: A Quarter-Century of Russian Women's Fiction," *Harriman Institute Forum* 6 (1992): 1–17; the introduction to *Sexuality and the Body in Russian Culture*, ed. Jane Costlow, Stephanie Sandler, and Judith Vowles (Stanford: Stanford University Press, 1993), 27–38; Helena Goscilo, ed., *Fruits of Her Plume: Essays on Contemporary Russian Women's Culture* (Armonk, N. Y.: M. E. Sharpe, 1993); Susan Hardy Aiken, Adele Marie Barker, Maya Koreneva, and Ekaterina Stetsenko, eds., *Dialogues/Dialogi* (Durham: Duke University Press, 1994), passim; the introduction to Goscilo, *Lives in Transit*.

3. With the exception of one story, "Plot" (Siuzhet), all of that fiction is available in English translation: *On the Golden Porch*, trans. Antonina W. Bouis (New York: Knopf, 1989); *Sleepwalker in a Fog*, trans. Jamey Gambrell (New York: Knopf, 1991).

4. Translations of Petrushevskaia's fiction may be found in the collec-

tions mentioned above, as well as in volumes listed in Marina Ledkovsky, Charlotte Rosenthal, and Mary Zirin, eds., *A Dictionary of Russian Women Writers* (Westport, Conn.: Greenwood, 1994), 506.

5. Petrushevskaia's invocation of myths and texts from Greek antiquity constitutes only one of her many links with Dostoevsky. On those links, see Helena Goscilo, "Petrushevskaia's Vision: No Ray of Light in the Kingdom of Darkness," paper presented at the AAASS conference in Miami Beach, Florida, 1992.

Her prose and drama are thoroughly literary, replete with wide-ranging intertexts on the level of echoes, verbatim quotes, ironizing of characters, revision of genres, etc. The most obvious examples include *Three Girls in Blue* (Tri devushki v golubom), "Elegy" (Elegiia), "The Lady with the Dogs" (Dama s sobachkami), "The New Robinson Crusoes" (Novye Robinzony), "The Story of Clarissa" (Istoriia Klarissy), "The New Gulliver" (Novyi Gulliver), "Songs of the Eastern Slavs" (Pesni vostochnykh slavian), and "Ali-Baba."

6. Not coincidentally, in "Night Time" Petrushevskaia's narrator through suggestive negation ironically analogizes the story's events with those of Greek tragedy and alludes to ancient Greek divinities.

7. On the existentialist element in Petrushevskaia, see Natal'ia Ivanova, "Bakhtin's Concept of the Grotesque and the Art of Petrushevskaia and Tolstaia," and Helena Goscilo, "Speaking Bodies: Erotic Zones Rhetoricized," in Goscilo, ed., *Fruits of Her Plume*, 27–30 and 142–46, respectively. For an introduction to Petrushevskaia's work, see Helena Goscilo, "Petrushevskaia's Vision." For an astute commentary on "Night Time," see Josephine Woll, "The Minotaur in the Maze: On Lyudmila Petrushevskaya," *World Literature Today* (Winter 1993): 125–30.

8. The centrality of the family in Petrushevskaia's oeuvre is signaled by such titles as "Uncle Grisha" (Diadia Grisha, 1987), "The Case of the Virgin Mary" (Sluchai bogoroditsy, 1988), "Kseniia's Daughter" (Doch' Kseni, 1989), "Father and Mother" (Otets i mat', 1989), "A Mother's Greetings" (Materinskii privet, 1990), "Wife" (Zhena, 1990), "Orphan" (Sirota, 1990), and "Fairy Tales for the Whole Family" (Skazki dlia vsei sem'i, 1993).

9. As Mary Ann Doane argues, association of the maternal with the natural has its counterpart in the equation between the paternal and the social, the latter carrying with it issues of identity, legality, and inheritance. Because Petrushevskaia's concern is with primal, not social configurations, she investigates maternal modes. See Mary Ann Doane, "The Moving Image: Pathos and the Maternal," in *The Desire to Desire* (Bloomington: Indiana University Press, 1987), 70–95; hereafter cited in the text.

For a discussion of maternity's role in Russian culture, see Helena Goscilo, "The Gendered Trinity of Russian Cultural Rhetoric Today: or the Glyph of the H[i]eroine," in Nancy Condee, ed., *Soviet Hieroglyphics*

(Bloomington: Indiana University Press, 1994), 70–95.

10. In accord with the "unnatural" principles structuring Petrushevskaia's fictional universe, hospitalized mothers require instead of providing care; homes prove prisons instead of havens; mothers spend money not on their children's needs, but on their own alcohol (e.g., "The Land"); offspring resent parents instead of respecting them, etc.

11. Liudmila Petrushevskaia, *The Way of Eros* (Po doroge boga Erosa) (Moscow: Olimp-PPP, 1993).

12. Written in 1979 and published in *Novyi mir*, no. 1 (1988): 116–30; translated in *Glasnost: An Anthology of Russian Literature under Gorbachev*, ed. Helena Goscilo and Byron Lindsey (Ann Arbor: Ardis, 1990), 3–24. Cited passages will be identified throughout by two sets of page numbers in parentheses, referring first to the Russian original and then to the translation.

13. First published in *Novyi mir*, no. 2 (1992): 65–110; translated as Ludmilla Petrushevskaya, *The Time: Night* (London: Virago, 1994). Despite the accuracy of Sally Laird's translation, the literal rendition of the title yields an awkward English for which I have substituted the more natural-sounding *Night Time*. Where quoted passages are identified by two sets of page numbers, the first refers to Laird's translation, occasionally slightly altered, and the second to the Russian original. Wherever only one page reference is given, it is to the Russian original, and the translation is mine.

14. According to Freud's disciple Melanie Klein, one of the major rites of passage negotiated by children en route to psychic stability as they mature is their ability to synthesize the "bad Mother" who thwarts their desires and the idealized "good Mother" who nurtures them. Curiously, Petrushevskaia displaces that opposition onto the mothers, who exaggerate to themselves (or their readers) their role of "good Mother" so as to deny their behavior as "bad Mother." See Eli Sagan, *Freud, Women, and Morality* (New York: Basic Books, 1988), 188–90.

15. *Night Time* is reprinted in Petrushevskaia, *The Way of Eros*.

16. Characteristic of Petrushevskaia's hyperbolism here is the situation of Anna Adrianovna's "friend" Nadenka, whose sick mother is not only hospitalized but also legless (67–68).

17. Petrushevskaia's treatment of the homosexual motif evidences her mastery of allusion and hint. Alena's handsome husband Sasha avoids army service out of fear that his looks will cause homosexuals to single him out for attention (75). Upon his release from jail, Andrei, who sardonically calls his cap "kepka-pediraska" (74), comments on Sasha's good looks with a "strange laugh" (82). When combined, these two details suffice to convey Andrei's involvement in homosexual activities during his incarceration.

18. The scenario of Alena's life recalls Dostoevsky's "accidental families" on the edge of existence.

19. "Après tout, vivre, au-dessus reste encore la seule manière d'être vu

et salué par le plus grand nombre." Albert Camus, *La Chute* (Paris: Editions Gallimard, 1956; New Jersey: Prentice-Hall, 1965), 32.

20.   For instance, she admits that Timochka imitates her posture of supplicant in clasping his hands and practically genuflecting when he wants his own way: "Timochka . . . folds his hands in prayer and virtually falls on his knees, imitating me, alas" (Timochka . . . skladyvaet ruki i chut' li ne na koleni stanovitsia, eto on kopiruet menia, uvy, 66).

21.   One of her chief means of inscribing a tyrannical subjectivity is through iterated use of the possessive: even when she refers to her children and grandson by name, she calls them "my Andrei," "my Alena," etc. In her eyes, they exist solely as extensions of her, which explains her statement: "At night, only at night did I experience the happiness of motherhood" (Nochami, tol'ko nochami ia ispytyvala schast'e materinstva, 84). Like Dostoevsky's Stavrogin, Anna Adrianovna is a nocturnal creature, the darkness figuring her destructive, chaotic impulses.

22.   Perhaps no work exploits this potential more dramatically and cleverly than Agatha Christie's *Murder of Roger Ackroyd*, which capitalizes on the trust automatically invested in the narrator, only to reveal finally that he is the murderer.

23.   Particularly noticeable in sexual matters, that sameness is stressed through Petrushevskaia's use of time-sanctioned animal imagery for male potency. Anna Adrianovna refers to Alena's sexual partners as male dogs (*kobeli*), while her own unacknowledged susceptibility to male advances is linked with horses, e.g., in the episode describing her purchase (which she can ill afford) of a narcotic medicine for a stranger ("The friend, . . . middle-aged, handsome, mournful" [Drug, . . . skorbnyi, krasivyi, nemolodoi, 69]) who "puts his hands on her" ("the weight of a man's hands" [tiazhest' muzhskoi dlani]), begging her to save his ailing horse, even as the text makes clear what Anna Adrianovna cannot or refuses to see—that he and his companion are drug addicts or alcoholics ("right there they . . . started wolfing down the tablets from the paper container" [oni tut zhe . . . nachali vykusyvat' tabletki iz bumazhki, 69]).

How daughters cope with their mothers' negative examples is a major concern in Petrushevskaia's prose. In "Father and Mother," for example, the long-suffering Tania finds salvation and ultimate escape through rejection of everything that is synonymous with the maternal. "Kseniia's Daughter," by contrast, shows the ways of the affectionate prostitute mother inherited by the prostitute daughter. See *The Way of Eros*, 78–81, 53–57.

24.   Here and elsewhere Anna Adrianovna's deep-rooted revulsion for "lack of cleanliness" suggests a sense of obsessive guilt or unfocused repression. She nags both of her children for not washing enough, expatiates on her own impeccable hygiene, and seems uncontrollably preoccupied with what Bakhtin called the bodily lower stratum—returning again and again to its

grosser manifestations, such as excrement, urine, malodor, and the like.

25.   Both Sima and Anna Adrianovna engage in shouting matches with their daughters, whom they suspect of usurpation (101); both lock themselves in their rooms when they feel threatened (102); both make life unendurable for their sons-in-law, whom they denigrate as "parasite" (*darmoed*) and "bloodsucker" (*krovopiets*), unfit to shoulder obligations as head of the family (100–101); both terrorize everyone in their vicinity so as to assert their rightness (99), and so forth. Unlike Simone de Beauvoir's "dutiful daughter," Petrushevskaia's launches into psychological warfare with her mother, only to replicate, in her turn, the strangling pressures that pass for parenting in Petrushevskaia's chilly world.

On rote repetition among generations of woman as symptomatic of Russia's recent "feminization of history," see Goscilo, "The Gendered Trinity of Russian Cultural Rhetoric Today."

26.   The speed with which Anna Adrianovna tellingly concludes that silence means death implies a scenario of wish fulfillment. Earlier in the story she assumes that her mother has planned to hang herself because of the furniture rearranged in Sima's room, where she barricades herself.

The story's ending is redolent not only of the Matrena sequence in Dostoevsky's *Possessed*, but also of Thomas Hardy's *Jude the Obscure*.

27.   Although the term was coined by Freud's sister Anna Freud (see *The Ego and the Mechanisms of Defense* [1936]), earlier in his essay on female sexuality Sigmund Freud defined the mechanism in unusually simple terms as the conversion of passivity into aggression when a specific experience is replayed, but with roles reversed: "[The child] tries to do itself what has just been done to it." See *Freud on Women: A Reader*, ed. Elisabeth Young Bruehl (New York: Norton, 1990), 333.

28.   An exception to what strikes me as the reductive tendency among Petrushevskaia's Russian detractors and admirers alike is Mark Lipovetskii, who shares my view of Petrushevskaia as a modern reincarnation of ancient Greek tragedians. See his review of *The Way of Eros*: "Tragediia i malo li chto eshche," unpublished ms. It is no coincidence, of course, that both Albert Camus and Jean-Paul Sartre in their essays and drama also turned to ancient myths for inspiration *cum* validation of sorts.

GARY ROSENSHIELD, AFTERWORD: THE PROBLEMS OF GENDER CRITICISM; OR, WHAT IS TO BE DONE ABOUT DOSTOEVSKY?

1.   Elaine Showalter, "Feminist Criticism in the Wilderness," in *The New Feminist Criticism*, ed. Elaine Showalter (New York: Pantheon, 1985), 243–70.

2.   For a discussion of nineteenth-century Russian literature as a liminal literature that did not fit well into the Western European canon, see Gary Saul Morson, "Introductory Study: Dostoevsky's Great Experiment," in *A Writer's Diary*, by Fyodor Dostoevsky, trans. and annotated by Kenneth Lantz (Evanston: Northwestern University Press, 1993), 1:1–8.

3.   Joe Andrew, *Women in Russian Literature, 1780–1863* (London: Macmillan, 1988); Barbara Heldt, *Terrible Perfection: Women and Russian Literature* (Bloomington: Indiana University Press, 1987); Carolina de Maegd-Soep, *The Emancipation of Women in Russian Literature and Society: A Contribution to the Knowledge of the Russian Society During the 1860's* (Ghent: Ghent State University, 1978). All subsequent references to these works are given in the text.

4.   For one of the more extreme statements of this position, see Teresa de Lauretis, "The Violence of Rhetoric: Considerations on Representation and Gender," in *The Violence of Representation: Literature and the History of Violence*, ed. Nancy Armstrong and Leonard Tennenhouse (New York: Routledge, 1989), 239–58. De Lauretis argues that the notion of violence is "inseparable from the notion of gender" (240). Nancy Armstrong goes even further and insists that all representation, irrespective of point of view, is a form of political violence; indeed, that all representation is violence. See Nancy Armstrong, "Introduction: Representing Violence, or 'How the West Was Won,'" in *The Violence of Representation*, 10. "By virtue of being academics, we are therefore directly involved in the violence of representation. . . . There is no position of non-power from which we can write and teach. The question is rather how to become politically self-conscious" (25–26).

5.   This is Judith Fetterly's formulation. See her book, *The Resisting Reader: A Feminist Approach to American Fiction* (Bloomington: Indiana University Press, 1978), 71. Nina Auerbach, on the other hand, has argued more interestingly and imaginatively that "the very rigidity of the categories [in Victorian fiction] of victim and queen, domestic angel and demonic outcast, old maid and fallen woman, concentrates itself into a myth of transfiguration that glorified the women it seemed to suppress." See Nina Auerbach, *Woman and the Demon: The Life of a Victorian Myth* (Cambridge: Harvard University Press, 1982), 9; hereafter cited in the text.

6.   For Heldt, as we shall see, with the possible exception of the late Tolstoy, male writers really cannot get women right: in fact, a male author creating a female character is a paradox and "necessarily an act of voyeurism" (*Terrible Perfection*, 62).

7.   This position is elaborated by de Lauretis, who insists that female autonomy is impossible in masculine narrative. Quoting Lotman's structural theory of plot typology (Iurii Lotman, "The Origin of Plot in the Light of Typology," *Poetics Today* 1 [1979]: 161–84), de Lauretis writes: "In the mythical text, then, the hero must be male regardless of the gender of the

character, because the obstacle, whatever its personification (sphinx or drag-on, sorceress, or villain), is morphologically female—and, indeed, simply the womb, the earth, the space of his movement. As he crosses the boundary and 'penetrates' the other space, the mythical subject is constructed as a human being and as male; he is the active principle of culture, the establisher of dis-tinction, the creator of differences. Female is what is not susceptible to transformation, to life or death, she (it) is an element of plot-space, a topos, a resistance, matrix, and matter" (de Lauretis, "The Violence of Rhetoric," 251).

8.   Maegd-Soep is as much an admirer of Chernyshevsky as Andrew, and she offers a revisionist interpretation of Chernyshevsky's wife, who she claims has been maligned (*Emancipation of Women*, 312–20).

9.   Maegd-Soep, *Emancipation of Women*, 242; and I. S. Turgenev, *Polnoe sobranie sochinenii i pisem*, 28 vols. (Moscow and Leningrad: Izda-tel'stvo Akademii nauk, 1960–68), 8:522; hereafter cited as *PSSiP*.

10.   As Maegd-Soep points out, many of these women were also helped along their way by their revolutionary brothers (*Emancipation of Women*, 89).

11.   Nina Baym, *Women's Fiction* (Ithaca: Cornell University Press, 1978), 14.

12.   Beverly Voloshin, "A Historical Note on Women's Fiction," *Critical Inquiry* 2 (1976): 820.

13.   Turgenev, *PSSiP*; *Pis'ma*, vol. 13, part 2:112–13.

14.   Rachel Brownstein, *Becoming a Heroine: Reading About Women in Novels* (New York: Viking, 1982), 295. In her review of Brownstein's book, Patricia Meyer Spacks casts doubt on the distinction between female and male readers of fiction. See her "Character Lessons," *New Republic* (28 Feb-ruary 1983): 36. Albert Thibaudet, however, based much of his—some now might say phallocentric—theory of the novel on different female and male responses to the representation of love. *Don Quixote* and *Madame Bovary* are, according to Thibaudet, anti-romances directed against "la liseuse." See his *Réflexions sur le roman*, 6th ed. (Paris: Gallimard, 1938).

15.   If we accept Oscar Wilde's famous view regarding life imitating art, then the greater number of negative views of women in the literature of the time should have had a deleterious rather than a positive influence on women's maturation and assumption of social responsibility. Either way, this is a dangerous road to take. Do we really want to ascribe to Turgenev and other male creators of positive female role models the responsibility for the terroristic activities of the revolutionaries who swore they received their inspiration from Russian literature? In "The Decay of Lying" Wilde observed, "The Nihilist, that strange martyr who has no faith, who goes to the stake without enthusiasm, and dies for what he does not believe in, is purely a lit-erary product. He was invented by Tourgenieff and Dostoieffski." "The

Decay of Lying," in *De Profundis and Other Writings* (London: Penguin, 1954), 75.

16.   Nikolai Berdiaev, *Mirosozertsanie Dostoevskogo* (Prague: YMCA Press, 1923), 113–18.

17.   Nathan Rosen, "Chaos and Dostoyevsky's Women," *Kenyon Review* 20 (1958): 264; hereafter cited in the text.

18.   "Thus, Thackeray implies, every angel in the house—'proper, agreeable, and decorous,' coaxing and cajoling hapless man—is really, perhaps, a monster 'diabolically hideous and slimy.'" See Sandra M. Gilbert and Susan Gubar, *The Madwoman in the Attic* (New Haven: Yale University Press, 1979), 29.

19.   Frank Friedeberg Seeley, "Dostoyevsky's Women," *Slavonic and East European Review* 39 (1961): 302; hereafter cited in the text. To be sure, Berdiaev was far from setting Dostoevsky up as an ideal in terms of the creation of women characters. Although Berdiaev argues that romantic love is a foreign plant on Russian soil, in his view Pushkin and Tolstoy, in contrast to Dostoevsky, were nevertheless capable of creating truly independent female figures (Berdiaev, *Mirosozertsanie Dostoevskogo*, 113–15).

20.   Here is not the place to examine the notion of autonomy. Probably what is generally meant by autonomy is not so much "three-dimensional characters" as what Bakhtin has called independent voices, voices that are in dialogue with that of the author or author-narrator.

21.   F. M. Dostoevskii, *Polnoe sobranie sochinenii*, 30 vols. (Leningrad: Nauka, 1972-90), 22:51; hereafter cited in the text as *PSS*.

22.   The alacrity with which Varenka accepts Bykov's proposal may even point to something more than making the best of a bad situation. Perhaps the real relationship between Varenka and Bykov has been from the very beginning far more complex than has been previously assumed.

23.   In *Poor Folk*, Dostoevsky clearly utilizes the relationships in "The Stationmaster" as a foil for the relationship between Devushkin, Varenka, and Bykov (Varenka and Devushkin even discuss "The Stationmaster" in their letters to each other). But, more important, Dostoevsky follows Pushkin by boldly inverting and subverting the literary genre and gender stereotypes of his time.